THE DRUM PROGRAMMING HANDBOOK

8249-5836-5963-9088

THE DRUM PROGRAMMING HANDBOOK

THE COMPLETE GUIDE TO CREATING GREAT RHYTHM TRACKS

JUSTIN PATERSON

THE DRUM PROGRAMMING HANDBOOK
THE COMPLETE GUIDE TO CREATING GREAT RHYTHM TRACKS
JUSTIN PATERSON

A BACKBEAT BOOK
First edition 2015
Published by Backbeat Books
An Imprint of Hal Leonard Corporation
7777 West Bluemound Road,
Milwaukee, WI 53213
www.backbeatbooks.com

Devised and produced for Backbeat Books by
Outline Press Ltd
3.1D Union Court, 20-22 Union Road,
London SW4 6JP, England
www.jawbonepress.com

ISBN: 978-1-4803-9287-8

DESIGN: Paul Cooper Design
EDITOR: John Morrish

Printed by Everbest Printing Co. Ltd, China

15 16 17 18 19 5 4 3 2 1

CONTENTS

CONTENTS

INTRODUCTION

Drum programming

has long been a hugely important part of music production. It is employed regularly, if not exclusively in every popular genre. Many people will realise that a human does not play acoustic drums in electronic dance music, but the art of drum programming extends far beyond. Whilst sometimes it is obvious that programming has taken place, there are many instances when it is not obvious, and when done really well, not even to the trained ear. Everyone has heard programming, regardless of their musical tastes. It is a part of the daily soundtrack to our lives, from smooth jazz during the TV show credits to all the various commercials in between, from the techno pounding out from the passing car to the latest video game, and from metal on the radio to movie music at the cinema.

In today's computer-dominated era of music making, many people engage in programming their own drum parts. For some, it comes quite naturally, but for others it remains a dark art. Even highly evolved composers and musicians who play pitched instruments often encounter difficulties when it comes to drum programming. Whereas an understanding of melody and harmony can translate easily between pitched instruments that might be programmed, there is just something about drum parts that can prove elusive. Of course, there is the old joke... What is the difference between a drummer and a drum machine? You only have to punch the rhythm into the drum machine once. Yes, Mr Guitar Player, but you also have to get it right!

Drummers can often develop sophisticated technique on an acoustic instrument, but still face difficulties when required to translate this into programming a part that remotely resembles a human. The computer environment is different, and taking long-practised technique and real-time performance and converting it to a programming mind set is a very particular skill – a skill that must be specifically learnt.

Programming drums, or indeed programming any musical part is a skill that can be developed just like playing an instrument. If you are a beginner, then you need to learn some basic moves and before long you will be able to create something more satisfying. As you develop your skills, you will wish for something more challenging. Even once you are experienced, there will always be things that you do not know. With practice, you can get better and the music that you make will get better. People will respond more favourably to your music in whatever context they are listening. Fellow musicians will be inspired and casual listeners will be more likely to tap their foot or want to dance. Studying any musical

INTRODUCTION

instrument is a journey of lifelong learning – the more you practice, the better you get. Period. Drum programming is just the same.

Many computer musicians already create gratifying drum parts by using high technology tools, but these parts are often more to do with the software developer than the user. Surely as musicians we all owe it to ourselves to strive for integrity and truly control all aspects of our music. High-tech painting by numbers can take you so far, but there comes a time when you want to reach further. That might mean listening to music that you admire, but cannot yet make, or it might mean crossing into an unfamiliar genre.

This book is designed to first establish an understanding of the necessary theory for more sophisticated programming, and then apply some basic programming concepts mixed in with some tips that should give even the experienced programmer some fresh ideas. The book will then work through a number of different approaches to programming drums and take on numerous musical styles on the way. It does not matter what music you are into personally, since the examples are only vehicles for useful technique, and you can apply it to your own music in your own way. The book will also consider related topics such as music production in relation to drum parts, using a synthesizer to create unique drum sounds and even how to rattle around in your kitchen and build a sophisticated drum part from your utensils.

If you are new to drum programming, then this book will take you on a structured and satisfying journey to a comprehensive understanding of the art. If you are more experienced, then you will still find that there is plenty of material to inform and inspire you, and it is likely that you will become a much more sophisticated musician by jumping into this book part way through and then following its course. Regardless of your starting point, the book becomes more complex and starts to mix different techniques and approaches together.

Sometimes you will have to reread sections several times and often you will need to refer to your software manual. You will have to practise, and practice takes time. Make sure that you give it sufficient time. It should be fun though. As you work through the book you will develop, and your perspective will change and it could even be worth revisiting earlier chapters with that fresh perspective. After a very short period of time using this book you should find that your music is developing and your approach is becoming more sophisticated. Increasingly, you will get your own ideas and develop your own sound when programming just like any fine musician. Welcome to the art of drum programming.

Where you see this symbol, the drum pattern or track is available to download from halleonard.com/mylibrary. Enter your 16-digit access code, found at the front of the book, and you will be taken to the book's webpage. Pattern numbers in the book correspond to file numbers on the mylibrary site.

A SHORT HISTORY OF DRUM PROGRAMMING

CHAPTER 1

A SHORT HISTORY OF DRUM PROGRAMMING

Because programming is such an integral part of everyday studio practice, and centred around the computer, many people assume that it is a recent phenomenon. In fact, programmed music has been around much longer than computers and has changed immeasurably within the digital era. In order to understand how we got to where we are today, how the art form has evolved, and perhaps where we might go in the future, it is useful to consider the history of drum programming.

THE PRECURSORS

We should first define what we mean by programmed music. Normal human performance of music will generally involve the performer making some sort of gesture to interact with an instrument so it produces a sound, preferably a sound of the performer's choosing, at a time that they intended. If, on the other hand, we set up an instrument in advance so that it can play a desired sound without further direct human interaction, then we could describe this instrument as having been programmed. We would only need to tell this instrument when to start doing what it does.

A 19th century orchestrion. A pinned barrel triggers drums, cymbals and other instruments.

Wind chimes date back to Roman times. The physical dimensions and construction of each chime determines its sound; we can choose these, and you could think of the act of hanging the chimes in a windy place as starting the music. Of course, we have no control over when a given chime sounds, but we could think of this as an early form of programming.

In the eighth century, a Buddhist monk developed a water-driven system that would strike a bell on every hour and a drum on every quarter hour. Of course, this device was a clock, but not only could he choose the sounds, he could choose when they played. The 'music' created by the bell and drum was controlled with the same basic parameters that we use today. Drum programming had arrived.

The complexity of chimes in striking clocks in clock-towers has evolved over the past 900 years or so. In 1598 the first musical clock was constructed; it played a different piece of music every quarter of an hour. The leading technology that developed for these devices was the pinned barrel. This involved a rotating cylinder. The cylinder had a number of pins sticking out of it at specific places. As the cylinder turned, each pin could be made to push a lever at a precise point in the cylinder's rotation, and the lever would trigger a chime.

It is said that the first music box was built in Byzantium in the ninth century: a sculpture of birds that appeared to sing. Over time, pinned barrels

CHAPTER 1

Captain Scott took a player piano, or pianola, to the base camp for his ill-fated expedition to the South Pole in 1912. Dog handler Cecil Meares is powering the music by pedalling.

became the principal technology for music boxes, too, and later the device known as a barrel organ. The barrel organ typically featured a number of organ pipes through which air was blown, but only when triggered by the pin layout. Many incarnations of barrel organs were developed, powered by anything from a water-driven system to a human operator.

Sometimes, barrel organs also sported curious sculpted figures. These were made to move by strings attached to levers that were also triggered by the pins. Such a system actually demonstrated a form of the audio-visual synchronisation that is crucial to every movie and video game today. In the middle of the 19th century an instrument known as the 'orchestrion' was developed. This machine was controlled by a pinned-barrel and had a number of organ pipes, drums, and percussion instruments that were played with mechanical levers. This was the first time that multiple drums were sequenced.

In the beginning of the 19th century, the weaving industry developed perforated paper cards that were linked together to form a long control reel for automated looms, with the perforations

A SHORT HISTORY OF DRUM PROGRAMMING

taking the role of the barrel pins. Towards the end of that century this approach found its way into the piano, creating what was called the 'player piano'. The player piano had a roll of punched paper inside it. This roll served just like a pinned barrel to control playback, and these instruments were often powered by a pair of human feet. It is interesting that we still often refer to the MIDI note editor in a Digital Audio Workstation (DAW) as the piano roll editor; you can now see the origins of this name.

Paper rolls were also used to program electronic sound generators in 1948, when composer Percy Grainger invented The Free Music Machine. This device used multiple rolls in order to control pitch, volume, and timbre. A few years later saw a device called the Electronium emerge. Only one was built, but for the first time notes could be both programmed and played back electronically – the future was about to begin. So far, we have paid little attention to electronic drums simply because very few existed, but read on.

THE DRUM MACHINE

The Rhythmate machine was also released in 1948, invented by Harry Chamberlin in the US. At that time, electric organs were popular in the home and there was an appetite for something to play along with in the absence of other musicians. The Rhythmate used recordings of a real drummer that were on a loop of tape. The loop length was such that, as it played round and round, the beat repeated seamlessly. The machine featured a number of different styles of rhythm, and some basic control over playback speed (tied to pitch). Functionally, what it did was very similar to what many people do with samplers and loops today.

The Wurlitzer company primarily manufactured organs, but it produced its own drum machine (again as an accompanist) in 1959: the Side Man. This device actually created its sounds using tube technology and sequenced them in predefined patterns, in a number of different styles of the day. The sequencer was constructed from a disk with a number of electrical contact points positioned around it in several concentric circles, each of which represented a different drum. An arm with matched protruding contacts rotated

David Byrne and Brian Eno experimented with programmed rhythm, sampling, and loops on albums such as My Life In The Bush Of Ghosts.

CHAPTER 1

The EKO Computerhythm and the punchcards used to create its rhythms.

over this disk triggering different drum sounds, and this arrangement worked rather like the pins on a barrel. The wheel could rotate faster or slower thus changing tempo, but unlike the Rhythmate, the sounds themselves did not change with tempo. The Side Man also featured a number of buttons that the user could use to trigger individual sounds – perhaps to add their own break beats.

In 1972, the first user-programmable drum machine was released – the EKO Computerhythm. It is said that only about 20 were ever manufactured, in Italy, and it was hugely expensive. The machine could be loaded with preset rhythms using punchcards – cards with a pattern of holes punched in them, rather akin to a piano roll. More importantly, however, there was a matrix of pushbuttons, in which each row corresponded to a given drum. Each row had 16 buttons and so they represented a time grid that corresponded to 16th-notes (semiquavers). This interface has defined drum programming to the present day, and many contemporary software systems still use it in principle. Musicians of the day found incredible freedom in being able to create their own patterns at last. Electronic music pioneer Jean Michel Jarre used the Computerhythm on his album *Oxygène*. This was the first time most of the public had ever heard drum programming.

Analogue-synthesizer sequencers existed throughout most of the 1970s, but these were limited to 8 or 16 individual steps (single notes). The digital Roland MC-8 MicroComposer was released in 1977, and it initially offered up to 1,100 notes as well as playing more than one simultaneously. It could also repeat sections of programming in a very basic way. Using this device with analogue sound sources, it was now possible to program extended musical arrangements, and sequenced phrasing became more musical for it.

A SHORT HISTORY OF DRUM PROGRAMMING

Sly and The Family Stone (above) made extensive use of a Maestro Rhythm King drum machine on their 1971 album There's A Riot Going On. *The Fairlight Computer Musical Instrument (below) introduced the world to sampling and software-based graphical sequencing.*

One major problem with the Computerhythm was that if you wanted to change rhythm or needed to switch the machine off, for instance to transport it, the rhythm information was lost. It was in 1978 that the Roland Corporation produced the CompuRhythm CR-78, which offered four user-programmable memories in which you could store four different beats that you had created. The step programming method was a precursor to the classic Roland TR-808 that was yet to come, but you had to buy an additional box – the write switch (WS-1) – which only had two buttons, for stepping through the pattern and entering a drum hit. Many people will recognise the sound of this machine from the introduction of the classic Phil Collins song, 'In The Air Tonight', the bit before the famous drum fill.

Only a year later came a quantum leap in technology with the launch of the first Fairlight Computer Music Instrument (CMI), for the price of a house. Through its various incarnations over the next couple of years, the CMI introduced sampling and, in its second version, software-based graphical sequencing, not to mention a host of other radical features. It had a computer frame, a music

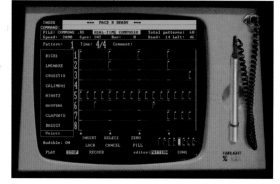

Jean-Michel Jarre used the EKO Computerhythm on his album Oxygène. *You can see it at the top right of the picture.*

■ **CHECK OUT**

Frank Zappa's *Jazz From Hell* album. Zappa was known as a fine composer and influential guitarist, but on this album he also demonstrates some incredible and innovative Synclavier programming.

keyboard, a QWERTY keyboard, floppy disk drives, and a screen that the user could interact with using a 'light pen' attached to a wire.

The CMI had a number of screen pages with different functions, and it was Page R where pattern sequencing was done. This page was the precursor to most drum programming interfaces today. The CMI was used by pop royalty of the day and can be heard on tracks by Peter Gabriel, U2 and Kate Bush amongst many more.

The Linn LM-1 Drum Computer came out in early 1980 for around $5,000, which, although a very large amount of money in those days, was very much less than the cost of a Fairlight CMI. The LM-1 was a programmable hardware box that could play samples of real drums, although because computer memory was so expensive it did not feature any 'long sounds' like cymbals. It did however have the first swing facility that allowed the creation of what were referred to as shuffle grooves. It also had the first quantisation facility, called 'timing correct'. Another first was that the LM-1 offered the ability to construct a song from a pool of patterns, something that became standard for many subsequent drum machines and still holds relevance to many programming workflows today. The use of samples and subtly-swung grooves rapidly expanded through popular

CHAPTER 1

A SHORT HISTORY OF DRUM PROGRAMMING

music. If you are wondering what a Linn machine sounded like, just listen to Michael Jackson's track, 'Thriller'.

The Roland TR-808 Rhythm Composer is another hardware box that appeared a few months later in the same year. Rather than using samples, this machine synthesized its sounds in real time. The synthetic nature of its sounds received some criticism in the wake of the LM-1, although it was roughly one fifth of the price. Its second-hand value fell as further, more sophisticated machines superseded it, and this made it affordable for musicians in the emerging house and hip-hop genres. Its sound subsequently became synonymous with urban genres, and has remained hugely popular ever since.

Just one interesting feature of this machine is that the sounds could be changed via their edit knobs without disrupting the pattern playback, something that more modern drum machines took a long time to implement. The 808 was undoubtedly ahead of its time and needed music to catch up to fully show what it could do. It has featured on more hit records than any other drum machine. To hear it, you could listen to a classic oldie like Marvin Gaye's 'Sexual Healing', or a more contemporary hip hop track by Dr. Dre. The popularity of the 808 was such that Roland released a digital version of it in 2014, the TR-8.

Kraftwerk were said to have modified a Vox Percussion King drum machine to allow it to be played with home-made trigger pads.

CHAPTER 1

One problem that musicians had long experienced was that of trying to make various machines that they owned talk to each other and play in time as a unit. It was not until the MIDI (Musical Instrument Digital Interface) protocol was formalised in 1983 that this really started to become possible. Regardless of manufacturer, any device that used the MIDI standard would understand any other, and they could both connect with the same sort of cable. It was now possible to have a single sequencer that could connect to numerous synthesizers and a drum machine and drive them all simultaneously. People also started to program drum parts from their MIDI-piano keyboards. The Roland TR-909 was one now-classic drum machine that offered MIDI compatibility in 1984, and is still very popular (also integrated into the TR-8, above).

With the enhanced connectivity offered by MIDI, the hardware sequencer started to develop rapidly and became increasingly sophisticated, even becoming the hub of many studio setups. Audio such as vocals and guitars still needed to be recorded on tape, but a special synchronisation signal – time code – could also be recorded that slaved the playback of the sequence to that of the

Ultravox used a Roland CR-78 drum machine on 'Vienna', their biggest hit.

CHAPTER 1

A SHORT HISTORY OF DRUM PROGRAMMING

tape, allowing simultaneous operation. FSK (Frequency Shift Keying) was one such time code, but it had the disadvantage that for synchronisation, the tape had to be played from the beginning every time. SMPTE (Society of Motion Picture and Television Engineers) time code was more sophisticated, and allowed synchronisation when starting playback at any point in a song. Due to the generally superior interfaces and features, programming drums still typically happened in a drum machine rather than a sequencer.

Before synchronisation, for human musicians to play along with programmed drum parts, the programmed part had to first be finalised and recorded to tape, and then the human part recorded as well. Synchronisation allowed human musicians to be recorded alongside programmed parts yet leave the programmed part open to change since it was still running 'live' from the drum machine. Such an approach also allowed better production.

Yellow Magic Orchestra were among the first bands to make use of a programmer, Hideki Matsutake, in the studio and live.

THE COMPUTER ERA

As with so many things, computers changed everything. Alongside numerous developments of hardware, a number of manufacturers produced software MIDI sequencers. The Synclavier and Fairlight CMI apart, the interfaces used for programming up until this point had typically been physical buttons and knobs, with at best an LCD screen of a few centimetres in dimension. It now

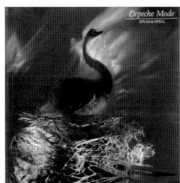

CHAPTER 1

*Afrika Bambaataa's
smash-hit hip hop track
'Planet Rock' featured the
Roland TR-808.*

became possible for software developers to offer a programming interface the size of a computer monitor: much smaller than those of today, but still an order of magnitude larger than an LCD screen of the time. In addition, it was clear that processing power and storage capacity were increasing rapidly. It was about to become preferable – and much more powerful – to program drums directly from the sequencer.

The Steinberg company released Multitrack Recorder for the Commodore 64 computer (then, the only type that was really used for music applications) in 1984. This was a 16-track MIDI sequencer that allowed 16 different synthesizers or indeed drum machines to be controlled simultaneously. Multitrack Recorder developed into a package called Pro-16 – the first incarnation of what was to become both Cubase and Nuendo. In the same year, the Ensoniq Mirage sampler emerged. Whereas sampling had been the domain of the professional studio, the affordability of the Mirage quickly found a mass-market and a new sonic vocabulary was born as 'everyone sampled everything'.

A SHORT HISTORY OF DRUM PROGRAMMING

Intended for gaming, the Atari ST computer came out in 1985 with 0.5 MB of memory and a processor that ran at 8MHz. Crucially, it sported built-in MIDI ports. The timing accuracy of these ports quickly became revered, and the Atari ST became the platform of choice for many. Also that year, MOTU released a sequencer called Performer, but that was for the rival Macintosh platform; it is called Digital Performer today. A year later saw both the Opcode MIDIMAC sequencer, and Steinberg Pro-24 for Atari. The following two years would first see Cakewalk, a sequencer for DOS on PC (even though an early form of Windows existed), and C-Lab Creator for Atari. Creator was the forefather of Apple Logic Pro, and Cakewalk that of Sonar.

So it went on – you get an idea of the familiar computer and software race that has existed ever since. For many musicians, programming drums was now something that they did with a computer; but remember that the computer only controlled MIDI notes, and all the sounds still came from hardware units.

Electronic drums – pads designed to be played with sticks, existed throughout the 1970s, but it was in 1986 that the Simmons company released the SDS-1000 kit with an add-on box called the TMI (Trigger to MIDI Interface). This kit came with a hardware box called a 'brain' which had sounds within it; drum pads could be plugged into it and played like an acoustic kit. The important thing about the SDS-1000 was that it could be connected to the TMI, which had MIDI connectivity and therefore provided the first opportunity that drummers had to use their hand and foot performance technique to program a sequencer. Physical triggers that clipped onto acoustic drums and generated MIDI notes were soon to follow.

The Akai MPC range was born in 1988 with the release of the MPC60, a combined hardware sequencer and sampler with many features of Linn machines. This device also had velocity-sensitive rubber pads on its front panel designed for finger-tapping beats in real time and recording them into the sequencer. This format has proved most enduring, and after many incarnations, the MPC is still produced and remains very popular with urban music producers. The matrix of square rubber pads has also been borrowed by many manufacturers and can be seen on numerous contemporary devices.

The Akai S1000 sampler was also released that year, as part of the company's professional sampler series. The S1000

Phil Oakey of The Human League, who made early use of the Linn LM-1 drum machine on their breakthrough album Dare.

New Order's 'Blue Monday' made use of an Oberheim DMX.

allowed two samples to be joined together in the fashion of sound design, and its visualisation of an audio waveform helped more accurate editing. UK producer Martyn Phillips was the first person to cut up and re-sequence a sampled loop when he applied this technique to the famous 'Funky Drummer' drum-loop derived from James Brown's 1970 track of the same name. This technique went on to become the backbone of jungle drum programming in the 90s. The S1000 also offered the first time-stretch function that could change the speed of the sample without altering the pitch.

CHAPTER 1

A SHORT HISTORY OF DRUM PROGRAMMING

This technology was a significant development in the application of drum-loops. The S1000 had many notable users including Moby and Nine Inch Nails.

1990 was notable for the first release of Cubase for Atari computers. Although it was MIDI only, the now familiar interface with the regions residing in channels on a timeline was first seen here. 1990 also heralded Audio Vision for Macintosh by Opcode. Soon renamed Studio Vision, this was the first piece of software that could sequence both MIDI and audio, and importantly the user could see these side by side, which was a great breakthrough when programming. One year later, Digidesign Pro Tools emerged, which on top of MIDI, allowed four tracks of digital audio to be played simultaneously with the aid of additional hardware. Although it might have been considered luxurious to apply these to drums, modern multitrack editing was first facilitated here. The DAW (Digital Audio Workstation) was now born, and numerous manufacturers developed these

Artists such as The Beastie Boys sampled beats from classic rock tracks like Led Zeppelin's 'When The Levee Breaks' and used them alongside drum machines.

CHAPTER 1

throughout the remainder of the decade, providing sophisticated editors for programming MIDI drums that played from external hardware, not to mention the numerous other features such as automation.

It is perhaps worth noting that at the same time as the DAW was developing, hardware was still very much alive. Increasingly popular were modules. These were effectively synthesizers without keyboards, designed to be mounted in a rack and capable of producing large numbers of exotic sounds. From 1991, examples such as the Emu Proteus World offered world-percussion sounds amongst its pitched content, and the specialist drum-sound module, the Alesis D4, offered a huge palette of choice. The D4 was also notable for its 12 trigger inputs that, in response to suitable audio events, could both trigger internal sounds and create MIDI notes for transmission to other sound sources. One synthesizer that offered interesting possibilities for drum programming was the Korg Wavestation. The 1990-94 Wavestation was able to play a sequence of sampled sounds in response to a single key being held down, and moving a joystick would provide variations and switches in the pattern.

Hardware workstations also continued to evolve. A workstation was a device that had a keyboard, a synthesizer, a sequencer, effects, and possibly a sampler all in one self-contained unit. They were designed to allow the creation of complete backing tracks, although they were limited in their handling of audio, often relying on sampling capability. By the end of the 90s, a device such as the Korg Triton offered powerful facilities for programming drums as just a small part of what it actually did.

THE RISE OF SOFTWARE

Opcode released the software language Max in 1990. This was a visual programming language where the user could design musical tools and instruments by connecting a number of visual objects together and setting their parameters. Max allowed people to construct unique musical instruments that transmitted MIDI information to hardware sound sources. For drum programming, it became possible to create algorithmic pattern generators that constantly modified the beat according to a rule set, and much more. Max developed to include MSP in 1997. MSP allowed users to manipulate digital audio, and so it then became possible to create novel samplers and sound-mangling devices. Jamie Lidell and Radiohead's Jonny Greenwood are notable examples of Max/MSP users.

A panacea that programmers and producers have long craved, and found (often time-consuming) workarounds to emulate, was audio quantisation. Although software sample editors had been around for a while, the release of Propellerhead ReCycle and is associated REX file format in 1994 was significant. This system used transient detection and beat-slicing to facilitate changing the tempo of a loop without changing its pitch. ReCycle exported individual notes from the loop as audio files, and produced a MIDI file that drove a compatible sampler which played

back all these slices just as if the loop had not been cut up; the MIDI notes could then be quantised or have their timing adjusted in other ways, for instance to make a straight groove swing. This also allowed re-sequencing of the slices to be done much more easily. ReCycle exists in an almost unchanged form today, and many pieces of contemporary software are still REX-compatible. The workflow and approach defined by ReCycle also carries through to numerous current devices.

Of course, computers were becoming increasingly capable, and software exploited this. In 1996, Steinberg released the Cubase VST (Virtual Studio Technology) DAW. VST was a protocol that other manufacturers were invited to follow, which specified how software effects – plug-ins – should be designed and should operate, thus setting a new standard of compatibility. This was followed in 1999 by VST 2.0, which extended the protocol to include MIDI-controlled software

Orbital's 'Halcyon' was based around a TR-808 beat.

*Norman Cook, better
known as Fatboy Slim,
mastered the art of
layering sampled drum
loops to create infectious
dance music.*

instruments. Drum machines were obvious candidates for design in this format. Other manufacturers also developed their own formats such as the Microsoft DirectX and the Apple AU (Audio Units).

Audio quantisation also emerged in the DAWs of the late 90s, for example, time stretching to M-points in Cubase VST, or stripping silence and snapping regions to the grid in Logic. These techniques were profound in that human performances could be recorded, and their timing adjusted according to the desire of the programmer. These early processes were laborious and often created sonic artefacts, which might be tolerated as the price of such control; but in 2001 the Beat Detective function of Pro Tools HD became the preferred tool for audio quantisation of drums. It featured both transient detection and time correction and could be used on many types of material with minimal artefacts.

Drum replacement involves the detection of the transients in a drum recording and the automated substitution of a sampled sound for a particular drum. It is often employed if the recorded sound is less than ideal or simply needs to be changed during the production process. Although this technique has its roots in production, it might be regarded as a form of programming. Drumagog, a piece of software designed to perform this process was released in 1999. Numerous plug-ins can now perform replacement, and it is increasingly becoming a native function in DAWs.

1998 saw the launch of Sony ACID, which offered automatic time-stretching of loops to the project tempo. This facility was radical and made it very easy to layer loops of different tempi on

A SHORT HISTORY OF DRUM PROGRAMMING

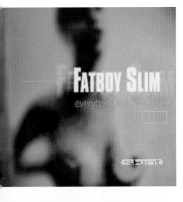

*Guitarist Pat Metheny
commissioned his own
orchestrion, using
software to trigger a range
of mechanical instruments
in response to his playing.*

CHAPTER 1

top of each other. Ableton Live offered 'warping' in 2001. Not only could this automatically match to tempo, but it had advanced transient detection and efficient audio quantisation. In its earliest incarnation it did not support MIDI, and it was a few years until it became a full-featured DAW. In 2003, Live also introduced a feature called Legato, which allowed switching between loops at any point in the bar, whereby the next loop would continue playing from that same point. This was significant in that it was not necessary to retrigger a loop from its first beat, something that had previously taken considerable editing.

In the new millennium, the DAW became ever more sophisticated and ubiquitous at the expense of hardware. All the principal DAW manufacturers leapfrogged each other with feature sets, although all did roughly the same thing. Editing audio regions became the preferred way of working for many people who had previously run loops from samplers, and software samplers themselves drove most hardware examples into extinction. The much larger amounts of memory available in modern computers, the larger interface, and native disk storage and organisation all contributed to this evolution. Cubase SX 2.0 offered 'Timewarp' functionality in 2003: this also allowed audio quantisation via time-stretching. Other manufacturers followed, with 'Audiosnap' in Sonar 6 in 2006, 'Elastic Audio' in Pro Tools 7.4 in 2007, and 'Flextime' in Logic Pro 9 in 2009.

In tandem with the DAWs, plug-ins, both native and third party, rapidly became more sophisticated. And a plethora of soft drum-machines emerged, often as sound sources driven by the DAW sequencer, but often with inbuilt sequencing functions as well. The Rompler emerged. This was a sample-playback plug-in that could not actually sample, and the audio content that shipped with these became increasingly large, running into gigabytes.

Native Instruments released the first version of Battery in 2001. This was a sample-playback plug-in that offered numerous velocity layers for enhanced realism with acoustic instruments, and through its various incarnations offered detailed performance articulation such as flams and drags. FXpansion BFD came out in 2003 and set a new standard in intensity through its velocity layers, round robin and extensive articulations. Both of these instruments offered multiple output channels into the DAW, although they were not the first to do this.

The step-sequencing of early drum machines also migrated to software. On this platform, it was often accompanied by pattern-based automation that could modify parameters in time with the sequence. Filter cut-off frequency, panning, effect sends and the sound-generation parameters could all be set on a note-by-note basis. Native Instruments' Reaktor has evolved from the late 1990s to the present day. This system was modular and shipped with many different types of instrument, from synthesizers to sequencers. It offered a number of step sequencers that were capable of intricate programming with both samples and synthesized sounds.

Reaktor's modularity allowed users to modify the instruments and create custom versions, and in addition to its stand-alone mode, it could also be used as a plug-in. Tim Exile designed a number of unique instruments for Reaktor that he uses in improvised live performance with a

A SHORT HISTORY OF DRUM PROGRAMMING

Skrillex, the American dubstep artist, is known for his stuttering effects with audio and samples. He won a Grammy for his album Bangarang.

number of hardware controllers. Propellerhead Reason, first released in 2000, offered numerous step-sequencing options and innovative control of automation. Reason did not record audio and so could not be regarded as a DAW until its version six in 2011.

Spectrasonics Stylus RMX came out in 2004. Based on their earlier Stylus plug-in, Stylus RMX was a loop player that featured a REX-like system called Groove Control that allowed a wide range of tempi to be played. Building layers of loops that locked together was automatic, but perhaps the most radical innovation were the algorithmic variations that could be applied to the loops. Using these could provide constant variation, almost as if a human was improvising around the basic theme of the loop. The loops could either be triggered by MIDI keys or dragged on to a track in the DAW as a MIDI sequence. Recent versions have included the Time Designer module, which allows easy manipulation and transfer of groove timing between the different loops in the plug-in and the DAW.

A number of plug-ins offered pattern-based virtual drummers featuring internal sequencing with patterns controlled by key switching. In 2013 Logic Pro X was launched with a feature called Drummer, which was the first native algorithmic drummer. The user had to do very little to make it

CHAPTER 1

Metal band Meshuggah are famous for their live shows but nonetheless programmed the drums for their album Catch Thirtythree.

work, and its style was controlled through selection of a number of personas; kit pieces could be mixed and matched, and the complexity of the patterns it played could be controlled. It offered an interesting approach in offering fills at specific points in the sequence.

In 2014, iZotope launched BreakTweaker. This plug-in has a six-track step sequencer, but interestingly, any note event can be set to 'MicroEdit'. In a manner sonically reminiscent of the company's earlier Stutter Edit plug-in, here individual notes could be made to stutter, and various parameters associated with the stuttering could be changed to give a vast array of intricate sounding rolls. Before iZotope, these had to be painstakingly programmed by hand. There is also considerable sound-design potential through the novel approach to contouring raw audio.

CONTROLLERS

Some interesting developments in programming have come via hardware. The 2008 Monome controller is a box with a matrix of backlit buttons. The Monome makes no sound and functions purely as a controller. It needs bespoke software in order to then communicate with other musical devices via MIDI (or another protocol called OSC). Although this device is slightly obscure, it gave rise to other button-matrix controllers such as the Novation Launchpad, a year later. The Launchpad is primarily designed to work with Ableton Live, and it features clever visual feedback via its button backlights, and a number of modes of operation. The pads are multi-function, and change what they do depending on context. Although both of these devices seem a little abstract at first glance they represent a new mode of programming and live performance.

Also in 2009, Native Instruments' Maschine drew from the Akai MPC range in both look and broad approach, but it included a software interface that dovetailed into the hardware. Maschine offered sequencing, sampling, and beat-slicing, but with a focus on an integrated workflow. Users include top remixer MK. Ableton Push offered bespoke hardware for Live in 2013, again with a focus on integration and centred around a matrix of pads.

CHAPTER 1

A SHORT HISTORY OF DRUM PROGRAMMING

2010 was the year that Apple released the iPad. There are many musical apps for the iPad and indeed other tablets, and there are many interesting and innovative ways to employ multi-touch, not least for drum programming. The available apps are broadly in two categories, either offering virtual drum pads on the screen that can be tapped to create sound, or some sort of control interface that can manipulate parameters either on a native app, or a DAW on a host computer. Working only in the audio domain at present, BeepStreet Impaktor is an innovative app that allows the user to tap fingers on any surface while the app triggers internal percussion sounds in response.

Musically-relevant connectivity, both iPad to the outside world and inter-app, has slowed the adoption of this platform to a degree. The Audiobus system allows audio to be transmitted between apps, but MIDI is still to fully come of age. Many developers have created musical control surfaces, and some have offered modular systems that allow users to build their own custom

The xx employ a programmer, Jamie xx, rather than a conventional drummer.

CHAPTER 1

interfaces, such as the Liine Lemur and Cycling '74 Mira (for Max/MSP). Some people now use software of their own design along with mechanical hardware interfaces to control acoustic sound generators, basically replacing the pinned barrel with software. Examples of this include Pat Metheny, on his album *Orchestrion*, and sound-installation artist Felix Thorn. Metheny's incredible robot responded to his own improvisation on the guitar, and Thorn builds sequencer-driven robots. Robotic musicians have arrived!

CONCLUSION

So, that was a crash course in the history of drum programming. It is interesting to note how the concept of programming can be taken back so far in history, yet certain periods in recent times are intense in their contribution to the evolution of the tools. This chapter only highlights a number of innovative technological developments that advanced the art of drum programming; many further important and interesting devices have contributed along the way. In the next chapter, we will define the terminology and technical terms that we need when programming, and also explain how you can use this book to the best effect in your own study of the art of drum programming.

Most hip hop is built around programmed drums. Top producer Alex da Kid (left) studied his craft at the University of West London.

USING THIS BOOK

CHAPTER 2

This book is all about drum programming, but before we start we need to consider how you can get the most out of the book. This chapter will offer some thoughts and concepts, cover some essential background theory and terminology, and help you to understand how to relate the beats and information we present here to your own system. Of course, if you are an experienced programmer already, you can skip this chapter and start programming in Chapter Three if you want; but there could be elements and language that are not entirely clear if you don't read this one first. Even if you skip forward now, do come back and read this chapter at some point.

LEARNING YOUR TOOLS

When you are learning a piece of software, everyone enjoys diving in to see what can be done with a few clicks. While this is important, it should not replace reading the manual. When you are exploring the software, there will be functions that seem obscure, and possibly others that do not seem to do anything. You may or may not discover why the obscure functions are provided; or you may realise that those that do not do much are probably being used in the wrong context.

The software's manual will give you the bigger picture. Only by reading the manual will you understand the range of your software's capabilities. This knowledge is essential for fully releasing your musical expression. Top producer Brian Eno once said that the studio is a musical instrument – learn to play it.

A popular way of learning software today is to look at tutorials on the Internet. There are many excellent written examples published by magazines, and many more published by professionals and enthusiasts. It is a good idea to glance over the entire article before studying it. A given tutorial might look relevant but end up going in a direction that doesn't meet your needs. Video tutorials can also be excellent, but sadly, there are as many bad ones as good out there. Anyone with screen capture software can post anything in the hope of presenting themselves as an of expert, and they frequently do so.

It is also quite possible that you might encounter a good tutorial that addresses the subject at too high (or low) a level for your current needs. It is always worth watching more than one video on a subject to assess the quality of a given presenter and to fill in any gaps. Internet tutorials must not completely replace reading your manual.

It is a good idea to use browser bookmarks to catalogue the tutorials that you read or watch (think of an organised naming system for them); particular functions might not seem relevant at the time, but you may need to find them again later.

Forums can also be excellent and can put you in touch with helpful experts. It is a very good idea to join at least one forum that specialises in each piece of software that you own. You will

CHAPTER 2

typically have to register, but they are almost always free. Spend some time learning how to search the most appropriate area of the forums, since if you post a question that has already been asked many times, the response you get might be a little hostile. People who respond on forums do wish to help, but they do not like it if you don't bother to look first; part of the point of a forum is to form a searchable archive of problems and solutions.

Also, remember that some of the people who post on online forums do not always have relevant experience, context, or expertise; sometimes they offer opinions rather than facts. Sometimes people respond too concisely to understand, or sometimes ambiguously. You must learn to see past all this. A golden rule is to be polite and to use correct grammar and accurate spelling; you will be much better received if you do.

If you are posting a problem, take the time to explain it as precisely as you can in the most detailed context, and be sure always to include the specification of hardware, and version numbers of OS and software that you are using. The better you explain, the better chance you have of getting an accurate solution to your problem without having to answer another six questions whilst your problem is narrowed down and other readers lose interest.

Lastly, practise with your software. Modern software tools are fantastically expressive musical instruments. Everyone understands that it is impossible to make a nice noise with a violin without practising long and hard. Unfortunately, much of the instant gratification that is built into modern software (and its marketing) gives the impression that fulfilling results can be obtained without effort. Many users take this route, and consequently, all their music sounds the same. The only way to release your own creativity, the creativity that drew you towards this world in the first place, is to master your tools. Practice, backed up with informed reading, will help you move towards your personal goals more quickly and to a better end result.

BEATS, TEMPO, AND NOTE VALUES

To program fluently, it is essential to understand the way music is divided up along its time line. What follows is not intended as a comprehensive explanation; it simply highlights the most important concepts. Many additional resources are available, and you might wish to study these in detail until you are fully comfortable.

'Beat' can be a confusing word. When you listen to a piece of music and tap your foot, the pulse that you are responding to is referred to as the beat of the music. Although this pulse might be very obvious in a piece of dance music, via the kick drum, it exists in almost all forms of music. That is true even in slow orchestral tunes, where no instrument is obviously stating it; that is part of the reason orchestras need a conductor. Regardless of genre, the beat is the golden thread and reference point to which all the musicians constantly refer.

Next, the word 'beat' can be used as a measure of time for a short section of music. When you are tapping your foot as above, the time from one tap to another might be referred to as being one beat. Similarly, three taps could be called a duration of three beats. As a location in the music, the second tap might be referred to as a beat 2. Lastly, there is of course the drumbeat, which can be shortened just to 'beat'. This is commonly understood as the musical parts that the drums play in a tune: "that drummer played a funky beat", etc.

Music is typically divided up into repeating clusters of beats, typically in fours or sometimes in threes. One of these groups is referred to as a bar, and the beats might be counted, "one, two, three, four" repeatedly. This concept introduces the 'time signature'. When we are counting to four we might say that we are playing in four, or in 'four-four time', written in text as 4/4. 4/4 is an example of a time signature.

Alternatively we could count only to three – "one, two, three" repeating with a constant pulse. We might then say that we were playing in three, or (confusingly) in 'three-four time', written in text as 3/4, which is a different time signature. It is only the first number that matters when counting. Other groupings of beats do exist, but this book is only concerned with playing in four.

Like beat, the term 'groove' also has multiple meanings. It can be a rhythmic passage played by any instrument, and when referring to drums it becomes synonymous with drumbeat. Groove will be used in this way in this book. Groove can also refer to the particular feeling and sound given by a human performance. Lastly, groove can also refer to minute timing adjustments that might be applied when programming. Although this might appear confusing at first, once you understand the various concepts, the context in which the word is used will not be ambiguous.

When dealing with drums, something that can appear confusing is the notion of note length. When you hit a drum, it only lasts for a very short time. This is true, of course, but in the programming environment, the system that we must use applies to all instruments. If you imagine blowing a trumpet, you could start blowing at the same place in the bar (say beat 1), but hold the note for a longer or shorter amount of time. If, when playing in four, you held the note for four beats – the entire bar – this note would be referred to as a whole note (also known as a semibreve).

If you held the trumpet note for only two beats then it would be referred to as a half-note (minim). This note would finish by the end of beat 2, and you could play another half-note starting on beat 3, thus fitting two of them into a single bar. If you played these half-notes on a drum, you would simply hear two short hits: the first on beat 1 and the second on beat 3. Back on the trumpet, if you blew a series of smooth notes, one on each beat, each of these notes would have a duration of one beat and each would be referred to as a quarter-note (crotchet). You could play quarter-notes on a drum on each of these beats, but you would hear gaps between each hit due to the shortness of the drum sound.

You might see the pattern now… the note name gives an indication of how a bar of four is divided up into fractions. You could count each of these quarter-notes as "one, two, three, four" and you might have heard someone in a band saying this before the start of the song. This is referred to as the count-in, or count-off, and it indicates to all members of the band how fast the

CHAPTER 2

song is and when to expect the next number one. That is likely where they all start playing, hopefully at the same speed.

The speed of these beats is referred to as the tempo (plural: tempos or tempi) of a tune and is typically measured in beats per minute (bpm), so if you were counting once every second, you would be playing at 60bpm. If you were counting twice every second, you would be playing twice as fast, or at double the tempo and be at 120bpm. Traditionally, you could set a metronome to click at a specific bpm to help you keep time whilst playing. Sometimes in the world of computer music this sound is referred to as the click or the click-track.

A typical rock song might be at 120bpm; a drum & bass song might be at 170bpm; a dubstep tune might be at 140bpm. It is important to understand that this system only gives an indication of how fast the quarter-notes are moving and has nothing at all to do with the density of the musical arrangement, or the genre of the music, although it is quite common for DJs to associate tempo with specific club music styles.

Let us return to considering the whole note, half-note, and quarter-note. In another naming system, your computer will typically refer to these as 1, 2, and 4 respectively – the denominator of the fraction. Regardless of the naming system, each of these three is said to be a different 'note value'; but there are other note values too. If you spoke the word 'and' (often written as a plus-sign or an ampersand) in between each beat without changing tempo, you would have a total of eight

AMERICAN NAMES		BRITISH NAMES
Whole note		Semibreve
Half-notes		Minims
Quarter-notes		Crotchets
Eighth-notes		Quavers
16th-notes		Semiquavers
32nd-notes		Demisemiquavers

> **TIP**
>
> A great tip is to practise counting all the note values out loud along with music; the out loud bit is important. This is an immensely powerful aid to understanding where particular musical events are happening in the bar, and it will really help you to translate these to your own programming.

The relationship between various note values.

CHAPTER 2

sounds in the bar, and would be speaking a note value of eighth-notes (quavers), or 8 in computer-speak. We could refer to a particular note's location in a bar as being '2&', meaning that the notes starts on the eighth-note after beat 2. You can also add -e and -a between the eighth-notes (1e&a2e&a3e&a4e&a) and then you are speaking 16th-notes (semiquavers); your computer will refer to these as 16.

Twice as fast as 16th-notes would be 32nd-notes (demisemiquavers), but there are no commonly used syllables for counting these.

You will notice in the illustration on page 37 that each time we generated a faster note, we divided by two. This is not always the case, and sometimes the quarter-notes are instead divided by three. This has a distinctly different musical feel. These note values are often referred to as eighth-note triplets (quaver triplets) or even just triplets, and your computer will likely label them as 8T or 12 (12 being the number of these note values that fit in a bar of 4/4). When people count them out loud, they often say: 1tt2tt3tt4tt, making sure that the speed of every syllable is even. Of course, the quarter notes are still falling in exactly the same place; we are simply dividing each beat differently.

In most contemporary styles of music, tunes typically either use a mixture of eighth-notes and 16th-notes, or use only triplets. There is no reason why they cannot be mixed together, but in terms of the rhythm section of a band, they tend not to be. Melodies are different, however, and frequently combine them. Another common note-value is the 16th-note triplet (triplet semiquaver), which takes each eighth-note and divides it by three; computers usually refer to these as 16T or 24. These notes are often mixed with eighth-note triplets, but are just as comfortable when mixed together with eighth-notes and 16th-notes – it is all about clusters of them having a note that lands on the &s, something that they share with eighth-notes and 16th-notes.

Do read the manual for your preferred software and it will likely expand on this concept. Remember, do not skip over any of this if you do not understand how it works, since not only is this the language that we will use in this book and in other things that you might read, it is the shared language of musicians.

WHAT IS A DAW?

We will use the term DAW to represent Digital Audio Workstation. This is a category of software that offers an environment and tools for contemporary music making in your computer. Many manufacturers offer DAWs of broadly similar functionality. These include: Ableton Live, Apple GarageBand & Logic Pro, Avid Pro Tools, Bitwig Studio, Cakewalk Sonar, Cockos Reaper, Image-Line FL Studio, MOTU Digital Performer, PreSonus Studio One, Propellerhead Reason and Steinberg Cubase & Nuendo.

CHAPTER 2

UNDERSTANDING THE GRID

Note values are typically mapped out graphically in the editor(s) of your DAW, with time flowing from left to right. You will be able to align the notes that you input with particular positions on the grid. The grid displays time positions relative to the bars and beats, and will typically display different pitches or drums on its vertical axis. The grid's resolution might vary depending on how closely you zoom into it. Some systems allow the display of different resolutions on different visual lanes, each associated with a particular drum.

It is well worth the effort to find out if you can manipulate the grid with key commands rather than with the mouse, since this will allow a much faster way of working once you are comfortable with using the commands from memory. If your DAW has them, you should also learn the key

A typical piano-roll editor.

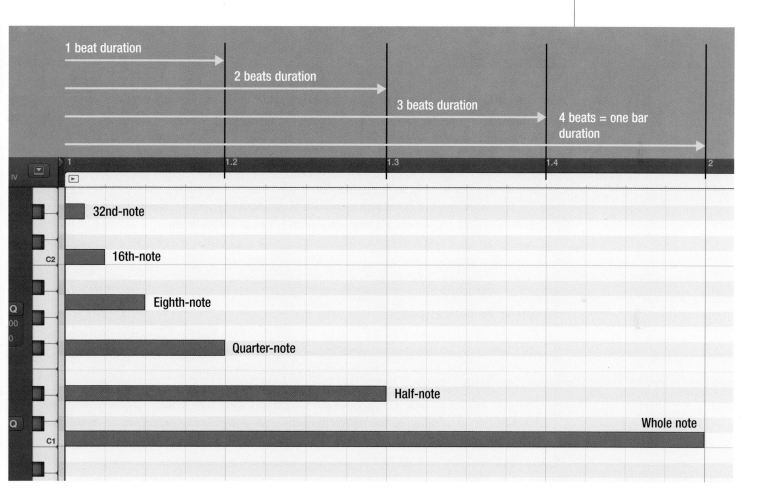

commands for scrolling both horizontally and vertically, zooming in and out, changing mouse mode, and changing the sort of information that is displayed. All professionals make extensive use of key commands in preference to the mouse – it is much faster.

This image on page 39 features different note values on different pitches, with pitch incrementing vertically and time extending to the right on the horizontal. The grid is generally in 16th-notes, but quarter-note positions are also indicated. Along the top, the bar and beat number are stated numerically in the form of 1.1, 1.2, 1.3, 1.4, 2.1, etc.

All of the notes shown here start playing on beat 1. If each note played a drum sound, then all would play simultaneously. If these notes were triggering a pitched instrument, the notes would still start simultaneously on beat 1, but last for different durations as indicated by their lengths. There are also dedicated software editors for drums that do not represent the duration of the note, only the start point. Your DAW manual will have much more specific detail on your own editor.

SIGNAL TYPES

In a hardware studio, any device that can generate or capture sound will output an audio signal. Such devices might be a microphone, an electric guitar, a synthesizer or a computer audio interface, and they will have specific audio cables to connect their outputs to other elements of the studio. In addition, there are also MIDI (Musical Instrument Digital Interface) connections, and these use a particular type of physical connector. MIDI signals are specific to electronic musical instruments and carry instructions for synthesizers and drum machines, to play notes and control their performance, etc. But they not carry the actual sound itself, which is generated by the target device.

The hardware studio has formed a convention for signal types that still exists within the computer DAW environment. In a software system, there is no distinction in physical connectors to tell the signals apart, yet they have completely different parameters associated with them. Therefore it is important to understand what sort of signal is being used for what.

WHAT IS A PLUG-IN?

A plug-in is a piece of software that can either generate sound or produce an audio or MIDI effect on signals that are sent to it. All DAWs ship with a number of native plug-ins that might be synthesizers, drum machines, samplers or special effects. Different manufacturers use different formats of plug-in, for instance Apple uses AU, Steinberg uses VST and Avid uses AAX. Other DAW manufacturers offer their choice of these principal formats too. In addition to the native plug-ins, many third-party examples are available for purchase separately.

CHAPTER 2

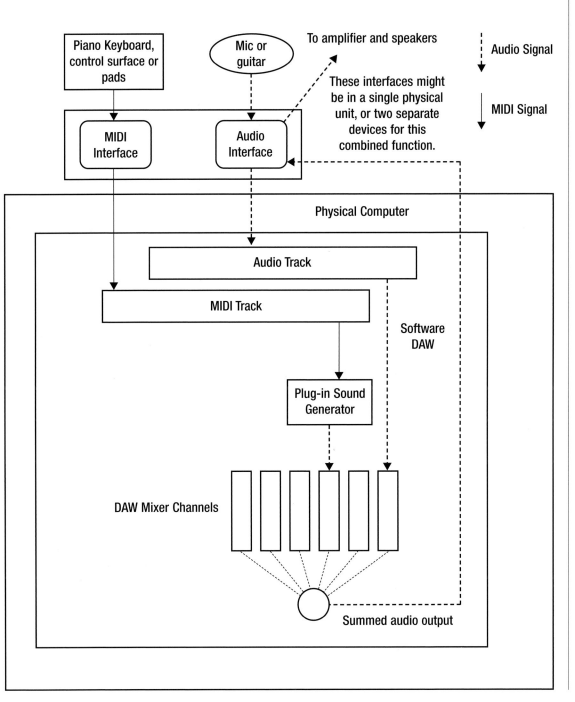

Piano Keyboard, control surface or pads

Mic or guitar

To amplifier and speakers

These interfaces might be in a single physical unit, or two separate devices for this combined function.

Audio Signal

MIDI Signal

MIDI Interface

Audio Interface

Physical Computer

Audio Track

MIDI Track

Software DAW

Plug-in Sound Generator

DAW Mixer Channels

Summed audio output

A block diagram of signals into and within a DAW. Only a single audio and a single MIDI track are shown, but there can be many .

In a DAW, audio will be generated by a digital recording on an audio track, or the output of a given plug-in inserted on an instrumental track, and routed to the DAW mixer for subsequent processing, combining with other audio signals, and then monitoring (listening). A MIDI piano keyboard or control surface will produce MIDI information that is routed to a track of the DAW for recording in its MIDI form. Any such MIDI track will in turn be able to send its information to a plug-in which will then generate the sound as above. Signals and their routing will be discussed further in Chapter Nine.

A typical piano-roll editor (opposite) with a version of the classic velocity display along the bottom.

In the hardware world, a single MIDI cable can transmit 16 MIDI channels (named 1–16) simultaneously, and again this system continues to be implemented in DAWs, although DAWs often feature multiple banks of 16. Each channel can communicate with a different software (or hardware) instrument. Some instruments are capable of producing a number of different sounds simultaneously, usually with each under control of a different MIDI channel, and such instruments are said to be multi-timbral. Sometimes it is necessary to assign specific channels to specific sources and destinations; it is easy, but you will need to read the relevant manuals if you wish to implement this. Remember that we are talking about control signals here, and this has no bearing on the audio outputs of a given instrument.

Within a MIDI signal, there can be several different types of MIDI event that we need to identify.

Notes

In addition to specific pitch, each MIDI note also contains velocity information (as well as the duration and position of notes, as defined elsewhere). The velocity indicates how hard a note was struck, which is usually associated with the volume of the note, as you would expect from playing a note on an acoustic piano. The velocity has a range of 0–127, with 127 being the loudest. The corresponding velocity information might be represented in a bar graph beneath the piano-roll, or in some sort of graphical representation within the block itself. Each note also has a specific MIDI channel associated with it.

Most DAWs have a display along the lines of this one opposite; study your manual to understand exactly how it represents and controls pitch, duration, position, and velocity. The problem with this kind of representation is that it is not always easy to see which velocity belongs to which note, or indeed control them independently as you will often wish to. It is more common and more necessary to do this when programming drums than (for instance) a piano part. It is essential to learn how to read and control the piano-roll editor fluently since you will be using it every day; but because of these issues, and for clarity, we are usually going to take a different approach in this book. The diagram on page 45 shows the same drumbeat represented differently. Make sure that you understand every aspect of what follows since you will be following many (often more complex) diagrams of this style as we advance. Ensure you can relate this diagram to the piano-roll one on page 39.

CHAPTER 2

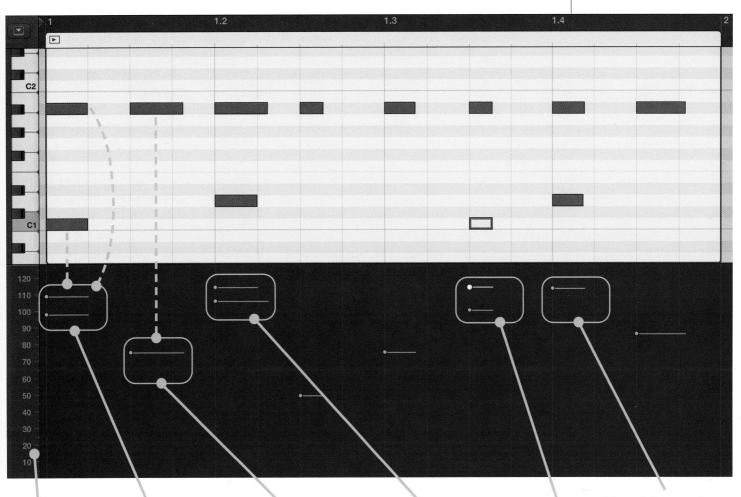

The velocity area. You can see the scale of 0-127 on the left.

The representation of the velocities of the two notes directly above in the piano-roll, on beat 1. Because both notes are the same length, it is not possible to tell which velocity belongs to which.

The indication of the velocity of the note directly above – it is around 75. The length of the horizontal line aligns with the length of the note block.

You can tell which velocity belongs to which of two simultaneous notes by their different durations.

Although there are two notes on beat 4, because they are at the same velocity, there is only one horizontal line.

You can tell which velocity belongs to which note by the highlighting.

CHAPTER 2

The way that notes are usually represented in this book (opposite), showing position and velocity in a single event, but ignoring duration.

As before, time and the grid run from left to right. Vertically, there are a number of lanes, each of which represents a different part of the drum kit. Events can be placed on these lanes in order to trigger the appropriate sound at the appropriate time. These events do not represent duration of the notes, since most MIDI drum kits do not respond differently to how long you might hold your finger on the key. (Indeed, the same is true of acoustic drum kits when struck with a stick.) The width of the events might change in order to accommodate different note values. Importantly, the events do indicate velocity. Each event has a frame that fills the lane, top to bottom, but the amount by which it is filled gives only an indication of the velocity on a scale of 0–127. There is no precise numerical indication in these diagrams.

The grid timing can be different for each lane. Note events are not tied to the grid, and in fact if a note is manually placed on the grid and then the grid is changed to a different note value, the note will remain locked in time, but the grid may not align with it visually. Such functionality is very useful for creating complex phrases, although sometimes these do not appear very tidy once complete. Bar and beat numbers may be featured along the top. Sometimes, patterns represented in these diagrams are extracted from much longer sequences, and so the bar numbers should always be considered only relatively to related featured excerpts. For example, you might encounter bar 36 and bar 37; this is a two-bar phrase extracted from 36 bars into a longer passage, possibly elsewhere in the book.

In this diagram, we have only represented a single bar. If we wished to represent a greater number, the note events would appear thinner in order to fit that number of bars horizontally on the page. Similarly, if we need to display a greater number of drums, for instance when notating fills that use a number of tom toms, we might need to compress things vertically. Neither of these changes affect the musical meaning; it is all about the placement of the note event on the grid, and its velocity. When we need to represent duration of notes accurately, we will use a more traditional piano-roll form.

CONTROL CHANGES (CC#)

There are 128 different control changes numbered 0–127 and categorised by that number. These events can control different parameters such as vibrato (#1), pan position (#10), or filter cut-off frequency (#74). Control changes can typically be sent to the DAW by the modulation wheel on the piano keyboard, other specific physical knobs, or perhaps from a tablet device; these can be assigned to the control change number of your choice and recorded. Alternatively they could be programmed in the DAW using a mouse. Each control change has a value range of 0–127, and again is associated with a specific MIDI channel.

When recorded, they are represented graphically as a series of lines connected by breakpoints often resembling a mountain range, with the value ascending on the vertical axis, and time represented on the horizontal; it is a graph of value against time. Typically, an editor displays one or

Each horizontal lane carries events that represent a different drum.

There may or may not be bar and beat numbers included here, depending on context.

The full velocity range of 0-127 is represented in each lane and again by the frames around each note.

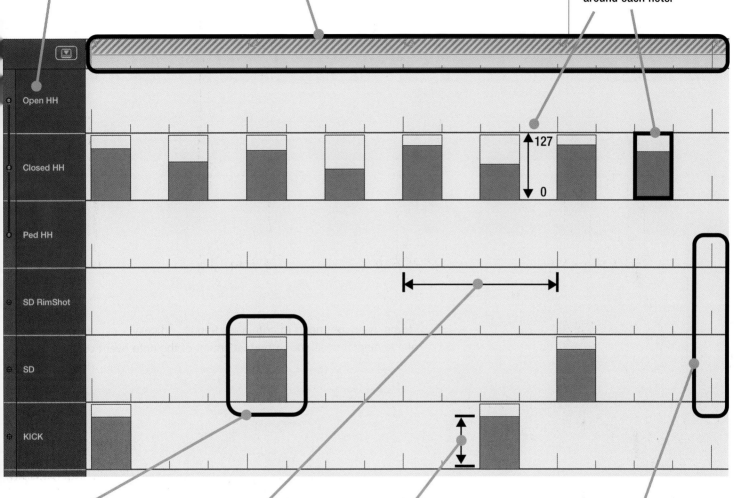

A note – in this case a snare (SD) on beat 2.

The grid here is in 16th-notes, but it could appear differently for each lane – note events do not have to snap to any visual presentation and so can appear "off the grid".

The actual velocity value is indicated by the height of the solid area relative to the frame.

Sometimes the limitations of screen capture mean that you might see the edge of a note just before or after the bars of interest – ignore these.

CHAPTER 2

more control changes beneath the piano-roll area, often one at a time. You might also be able to view these in the track area of your DAW.

You can see that this control change (it does not matter which it is) starts with a value of 126 and immediately starts reducing. It drops to 52 at beat 2 before rising to 95 just before beat 2&, and then continues to change for a while before staying constant at a value of 41 from beat 4& to the end. These numbers are not important since you will almost always program control changes by ear. The point is to demonstrate how a parameter can vary continuously (or not) and how it will look in this book. Spend some time understanding how your own DAW represents this kind of thing and the mode of editing that it offers.

An example of a single control change that fluctuates over the duration of this bar.

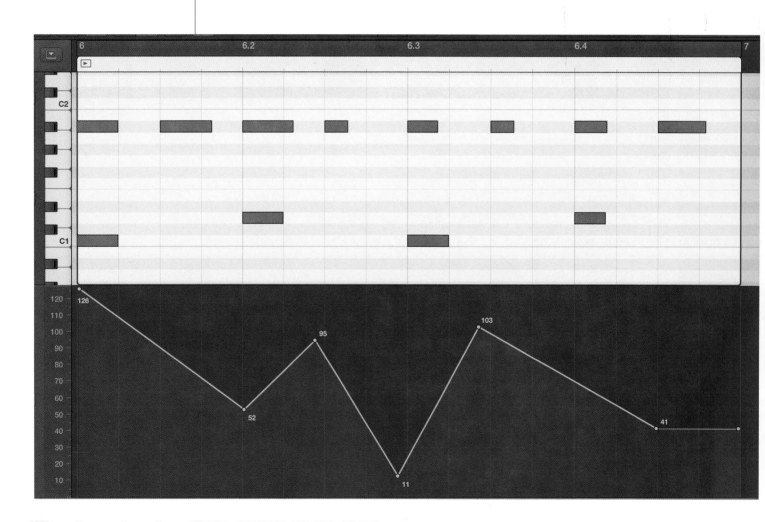

PITCH BEND

This is also control information, and is sent to the DAW by the pitch-bend wheel on the piano keyboard and recorded (or indeed mouse-programmed), and will typically bend the pitch of the note either up or down from a central resting position of the wheel – although it can be made to do other things instead. Pitch bend uses a much larger value range than CC#s, but will be represented similarly in the DAW, bidirectionally above or below a zero point. The actual amount of pitch bending that you hear is a separate parameter that is set on whatever device is responding to the control, typically defaulting to ± two half-steps (semitones); remember that the pitch bend information itself is only an indication of how much of this range to apply.

PROGRAM CHANGE

Software instruments typically feature a number of preset sounds, and you can choose the one that you want from this palette. Each preset is likely associated with a given program change, again numbered 0–127, and sending a program change message to an instrument will force it to select that particular sound, just like doing it manually. This can be handy when programming. Some instruments feature many presets, and have multiple banks of 128 program changes each; these banks can be selected with a MIDI control change. Sometimes plug-ins need time in order to initialise a new program change request, especially if they need to load fresh audio, and you might need to take account of this if working with program changes.

There is actually quite a lot more to MIDI than this, but it is beyond the scope of this book to discuss it. Read further afield if you are interested in developing even more exotic control and technique – it is not to be underestimated. The representation of audio is very similar in all DAWs and so does not need further explanation here, but there is more information in Chapter Six.

KIT CHOICE

Each of the sections in this book will be demonstrated with a particular drum kit and the software that hosts it will generally be named for your reference. You do not need these tools in order to work with the examples in this book. Just use whatever sound sources are available to you. The range of kits used in the audio examples does not change too much, in order that the focus on programming is maintained, but there will be times when we take an already-programmed pattern and develop it with a different drum kit. None of these choices is by any means definitive, and you should always experiment with how the patterns translate to different sound sources. But do understand that simply switching sound might not provide an instantly perfect result, and often adjustments then need to be made, possibly to the relative balance of the parts of the kit, velocities, mapping of notes to kit parts, and even tempo.

CHAPTER 2

THE DRUM KIT

In this book we will use the term kick drum; although it is legitimately also called the bass drum, using 'kick' avoids confusion with any reference to a pitched bassline or bass guitar. We will use the term cross-stick for the action of striking the rim of the drum whilst holding one end of the drumstick in contact with the drumhead to make a click-like noise. Some plug-ins refer to this sound as a rim-click, side-stick or a rim-shot. We will use the term rim-shot to indicate when the drumstick is played 'through the air', hitting the rim and the drumhead simultaneously to produce a loud and sharp-sounding snare sound.

It is extremely useful for any drum programmer to have an understanding of the setup of an acoustic drum kit and the way that a drummer approaches it. An acoustic drum kit might be described as being five-piece if it has five drums; the cymbals are not counted. For a right-handed drummer playing a drumbeat, the snare drum tends to be played with the left-hand, and the kick drum with the right foot. The snare drum has some wires stretched underneath it (called the snare) that give it the characteristic rattling sound when struck.

On the left of the kit (seen from the drummer's position) is the hi-hat, which is a device with two horizontally mounted cymbals that can be hit with a stick or moved together by the left foot, using a pedal. The hi-hat will generally be played with the right hand, thus giving a cross-handed look to playing a drumbeat. The left foot can alter the pressure between the two cymbals and consequently change the sound from a short chick to a sustained rattling. The left foot can also click the cymbals together, which has a slightly different tone from when they are struck with the hand. This sound is sometimes called pedal hi-hat in some plug-ins.

There are three tom toms that make a similar type of sound, but which differ in pitch. These are generally termed the hi tom, the mid tom and the lo tom. The lo tom might also be referred to as the floor tom since it often has legs that allow it to stand on the floor, as opposed to being mounted on a stand.

On the right of the kit is the ride cymbal, which makes a pinging sound when struck with the tip of the stick. It is designed so that when hit repeatedly you can always hear the individual notes, so it is good for playing rhythms. Drummers will often hit the raised and curved area in the centre of the cymbal – the bell – with the shoulder of the stick to get a louder and more pronounced clanging tone. On the left of the kit is the crash cymbal, which tends to be hit in unison with the kick drum or the snare for a sudden explosion of sound.

Not all kits are the same, and many have different numbers of cymbals or tom toms, or even extra kick drums and snares. In addition, all these drums and cymbals can be different sizes and shapes, which gives them different sounds; however they all tend to be used in similar ways.

CHAPTER 2

A typical five-piece drum kit. This example features a double kick-drum pedal.

CHAPTER 2

PROGRAMMING EXAMPLES

This book contains numerous examples of drum programming. Many of these are represented diagrammatically. Use these diagrams as instruction templates in order to enter the notes into your own DAW.

Where you see a symbol in the margin of the book, the audio patterns is available as an MP3 from the book's accompanying website at www.halleonard.com/mylibrary. When you enter your 16-digit access code, found at the front of the book, you will be taken to the right web page. There you will find music files for each chapter, available to stream from the site or download on to your computer. The pattern numbers in the book correspond to the file numbers on the mylibrary site. If you are using an iPad or iPhone, you may need to use a third-party browser rather than Safari.

Shorter examples of the music might be played two or four times. Longer ones will typically only be played once, although on some occasions more than this. You might wish to run these up against your own programming, or indeed use them differently in the accompanying exercises. Do take care to trim your edits accurately (see the discussion of audio editing in Chapter Six); the supplied MP3s are not 'ready to use' in the fashion of a sample library. If you are running the supplied audio patterns alongside your own to compare, keep them muted except when you are checking something.

Some of the examples are simply described in text, perhaps with an accompanying image. There are numerous exercises that will require a little of your own thought, too. If you are feeling creative then you can do these a number of times with different approaches; you will learn even more that way. The idea is that you attempt to replicate all the examples in order to absorb the underlying techniques. When you have recreated the examples as accurately as you can, try out your own ideas to develop them. There are many ways you might experiment, and some of these are listed in specific chapters, although there is no reason why you cannot translate the ideas between different chapters too. Of course, the experiments that you devise yourself are likely to be even better.

CHAPTER 2

MIDI
PROGRAMMING
WITH
ONE-SHOTS

Inputting Notes

Editing Notes

Quantisation

Making Beats

Editing Velocity

Eighth-Note Groove

Kick And Snare Patterns With 16th-Notes

When we use the term one-shot, we mean that a single MIDI note triggers a single drum hit. Sometimes people just call this MIDI programming. Nowadays, many people's first introduction to drum programming comes from sampled loops. The notion of having to construct your own beat from individual drum hits could seem labour-intensive, cumbersome, and primitive. This is not true. By learning to construct beats with one-shots, you will develop an intimate understanding of rhythm and the role of individual sounds in beat-making, with precision control. Many of the audio loops that you might have heard have been crafted by skilled programmers from one-shots in the first place.

Furthermore, there are many things that you can do when programming one-shots that are simply not possible if using audio loops. For example, when using audio samples, people go to great lengths to vary the tempo while keeping the sound clean; but with MIDI, all you do is change the tempo and it still sounds perfect. What's more, audio loops and one-shots can coexist to great effect in the same beat, and all the techniques around one-shots can also be applied to sampled loops with a rhythmic content. So we are going to start programming with one-shots.

INPUTTING NOTES

First, let us consider a number of different ways of getting your notes into the DAW. There are several approaches, each with its own advantages and disadvantages. It is useful to know them all, so that you can select the right input method in a given context. We are going to assume that the song you are working on has a steady tempo and was, or will be, recorded with a click (we will look at other contexts in a later chapter).

You will need to select a DAW track on which to record, and have that track routed to a MIDI drum kit. Make sure that you can hear the kit correctly balanced with whatever you intend to play along with, be that pre-recorded music or a click, and that your system will give you a count-in.

REAL-TIME RECORDING FROM A PIANO KEYBOARD

This is perhaps the most obvious way of inputting notes; you hit the record button and perform on the keyboard. Sometimes, as with any instrument, you will have to perform multiple takes until you get one that is satisfactory. Less obviously, it is often good to get an idea of what you need to play before you start. This involves listening, thinking, and perhaps practising. It is a good idea to practise with record enabled, since it is common to come up with a killer idea when you are not expecting it.

Many DAWs have a 'retrospective record' function (possibly buried amongst the key

MIDI PROGRAMMING WITH ONE-SHOTS

commands), and this can be very handy too. If the transport is running, even if you're not actually recording, it allows you to capture anything that was played recently. The next consideration is whether to try to play all the parts of the drum kit simultaneously, play them one at a time into a single region, or use separate tracks for each part of the kit. Playing all parts simultaneously can give a great coherent feeling but requires a certain amount of keyboard dexterity; it is certainly worth developing this to a degree.

Playing the groove one part at a time – eg, first pass hi-hat, second pass snare, and third pass kick – into a single region requires a certain splitting up of your thinking. It will probably lead you towards thinking of shorter repeating patterns rather than longer performances, but it will be easier to edit the final result as a whole.

Taking the same approach, but with separate tracks dedicated to each component of the kit, can be handy if you might need to repeat and mute different elements of the kit; this can be done at a region level, rather than within a MIDI editor, and it also helps you 'see' the arrangement. You might even find that you like working in this way, and then merging all the tracks to render them into a single editable performance after some structural arrangement.

There is a time and a place for each of these approaches, and you should be familiar with them all, as well as how to combine them.

REAL-TIME RECORDING FROM A QWERTY KEYBOARD

This is very similar to the above, except that a layer of detailed control is removed; qwerty keyboards cannot directly respond to the velocity of performance. However, they do generally have a mode that can control the fixed velocity at any given time by pressing certain keys. Even so, this means that you will record a very robotic and perhaps sterile performance; but this might not be a problem in many electronic genres that require that as a stylistic feature. The great advantage of programming this way is that you can do it without an external keyboard, for instance whilst travelling with only your laptop, and if necessary edit in details at a later stage.

REAL-TIME INPUT FROM A MIDI DRUM KIT OR PAD CONTROLLER

All that was said about the piano keyboard also applies here, but the main difference is that a pad controller (one that is designed for finger use) might feel more natural – like tapping your fingers as you might on a tabletop, as opposed to playing the piano. Many keyboards also feature a pad surface for this very purpose. Each pad will transmit a MIDI note and velocity, just like a piano keyboard. It is often easy to rearrange which drum is on which pad to make performance more customisable.

A MIDI drum kit (or pad surface designed to be used with sticks) gives the ultimate 'performability' – but you do need to be able to play the drums. If you are a drummer, then being able to precisely control your feet and hands at the same time will be a great asset when creating drum performances, and this approach offers unrivalled realism, if that is what you want. MIDI drum kits

TIP
In order to make it easier to place your notes, you can reduce the tempo whilst recording and turn it back up once you have a good take.

TIP
If you have used any elements of real-time recording with a keyboard, the varying durations of notes as seen in a piano roll editor might feel rather untidy. Find a DAW function to fix the note lengths to something quite short. If you can do this via a key command, that is even better. A couple of clicks after each take can offer a much neater (hence faster) environment for subsequent editing.

CHAPTER 3

are also great for creating loops, by jamming whilst recording, and then extracting your favourite excerpts. Price and physical space might be further considerations when deciding if this is for you.

STEP-TIME INPUT FROM THE SONG POSITION LINE

Your DAW will typically have a mode whereby any note that you play will be recorded, and the song position line will move forward by a prescribed note value, awaiting further input. This is a much less natural input mechanism than using real time, but has the advantage that you can take your time to think about which note to select next, or indeed the velocity with which you might wish to strike it. Playing two notes (eg, a kick and a hi-hat) simultaneously can feel rather strange with this approach, particularly controlling the velocities independently, and it might be best suited to a workflow that builds up layers of the kit.

STEP-TIME INPUT FROM A DEDICATED SYSTEM

Another form of step time input is often offered via a dedicated editor in the DAW, possibly linked to musical notation. The approach can be very useful when inputting a part from notation, perhaps something that you saw in a magazine or drum kit tuition book, but obviously requires a certain level of musical literacy. Those formally trained in composition and arrangement often like to work this way, since it might align with their greater workflow.

CLICK INPUT WITH A MOUSE

This is one of the most common modes of programming, and typically involves working with a DAW editor window, either a piano roll or a dedicated drum editor. In a piano roll, note pitches are often edited independently of their velocity, although in dedicated drum editors these might be combined in some way to optimise the speed of typical operations. You will be able to set your mouse pointer to function as a special tool in your DAW editor. For inputting notes, this might typically be a pencil-like icon, and with this you will be able to draw notes directly onto the grid. Although not always relevant to drum editing, this tool will also allow you to change the length of the notes.

This way of working has the advantage of letting you think at your own pace and precisely place and adjust every note, but it is less natural to those more familiar with real-time performance. It is in this mode that you will do most of your editing, and so you need to develop skill in this way of working. People often always use a 16th-note (semiquaver) grid, but it can greatly speed up workflow to be able to change this, especially with a key command.

EDITING NOTES

Those are the different ways to get notes into the system. One of the great strengths of MIDI is the ability to edit things once the notes are entered, and so now we will discuss this.

TIP
Drum kit tuition books are a great source of beats to attempt when programming. They typically feature dozens to hundreds of beats written out in drum notation, often with an accompanying audio recording. If you feel the need for more patterns to try, and can read musical notation, regardless of whether you are an actual drummer, consider using such books to develop your programming.

CHAPTER 3

> **TIP**
>
> The default click on a typical DAW is a quarter-note (crotchet), probably with a cowbell sound or electronic beep, often accented (made louder) on beat one. Whilst this works perfectly well for many people in many cases, it is not always the easiest thing to play along to, depending what you are doing. Your DAW might feature some simple facility to tweak its inbuilt click a little, but you might like to experiment by creating a special loop to use as a metronome instead. Do this in step-time or click input to ensure that the notes are exactly in time and make sure that the region that you are working with is an exact number of bars long. Otherwise, when you repeat it, it will gradually move out of time.
>
> You might like to program quarter-notes with the sound of your choice, but also have eighth-notes (quavers) or even 16th-notes, perhaps more quietly or with a different sound. Using an easily recognisable sound like a triangle only on beat 1 can help as well. Sometimes it is useful to have such a 'cue-sound' happening on beat 4 to give you warning that beat 1 is coming up next.
>
> Some people like to program a simple pattern with congas, etc, and play along to that. Your special loop does not have to be one bar long, but however long it is, simply repeat it for as long as you need to play along with it in your song. If you like to work this way regularly, save the loop in a default template that can launch with your DAW.

Regardless of how you have entered the notes into your system, the mouse can be used as described above to input any additional notes you need. In most DAWs, it is possible to select other mouse pointer modes too, and setting the pointer to erase can be handy. In practice, however, it is probably faster to erase by using the pointer in selection mode, selecting either one or a number of notes by 'rubber-banding', and then hitting delete on your computer keyboard. Aside from rubber-banding, it is possible to select multiple non-adjacent notes using keyboard modifiers: [Shift], [Control], [Alt/Option], or [Command]. Check your DAW manual for details of this. Most edits can be applied not just to single notes, but also to selections. For example, several notes can be simultaneously dragged either horizontally on the timeline or vertically on the piano roll to transpose them; however, setting up a key command for transposition is often faster and can be more accurate when subtle timings need to be maintained.

There will also be a modifier key – [Option] on Mac, [Alt] on Windows – that you can hold down to make copies of the selected notes when dragging. This is an essential function, but investigate how the clipboard and cycle marker can help with copying as well. Something that you will be doing a lot is editing the velocity of your notes, and there is often a particular tool dedicated to this. You will find this tool useful sometimes, perhaps when working with one of a number of densely packed notes, but very often it is quicker to use the general-purpose selection tool on the velocity indicators (vertical bars) in your DAW.

Similarly, there is often a quantisation tool (see the next section), but again, it is often quicker to select and then use a key command. Many DAWs feature mouse pointers that automatically change function depending on their position relative to a note or region. Make sure that you understand all possibilities here, since it will greatly speed up your workflow. In addition, it is often possible to set particular tools to different buttons on your mouse, and they can also respond to particular modifier keys. Check the manual. Before setting up those tools, think about the automatic mouse tools, and how you might best augment these with others that you set. You might wish to override your 'standard' settings if you know that you need to do numerous edits of a particular kind and so would prefer to have access to a different subset of mouse tools.

QUANTISATION

Your DAW keeps time with computer precision, and represents notes on its grid, which aligns with its internal metronome. Whenever a human makes a recording, there is a greater or lesser degree of precision, and the recorded notes will not be precisely aligned with the grid positions. It could well be that you are quite happy with the sound of the performance, and if this is the case then think twice before letting your eyes persuade you to adjust things. If however you wish that the performance was better, specifically 'tighter', then quantisation will assist you.

Applying this function will move the notes to the closest grid position, or in special cases closer to this position or to create a particular 'groove-feel'. You will be able to change the grid to which quantisation is applied, eg, from eighth-notes to 16th-notes; understanding when and how to do this relative to a given performance is crucial. Furthermore, this often needs to be done for sections of the performance, sometimes even very short phrases. Rather than attempting to describe this in detail here, you are advised to study your manual and also look at a number of specialist tutorials on this subject. However, later in this book there will be a discussion of advanced quantisation techniques as applied to drums.

MAKING BEATS

To start programming, we are going to use a basic acoustic kit with a tight piccolo snare, three toms, a ride, a crash, and a splash cymbal, but you can try these beats with any kit for a different musical impact. In this chapter and the next, we are going to work towards emulating a human drummer, and for this reason a number of references to human performance will be made. Even if this is not your preferred musical style, this approach provides an excellent platform for learning.

CHAPTER 3

MIDI PROGRAMMING WITH ONE-SHOTS

Pattern 03_01: An ultra-simple classic beat.

Pattern 03_01

KICK AND SNARE PATTERNS WITH EIGHTH-NOTES

PATTERN 03_01: Kick on 1 and 3, snare on 2 and 4, eighth-note hi-hat. Repeated four times at 100bpm. This is the ultra-simple all-time classic, and it will fit more songs in more genres of music than any other. This beat is important, since it defines the characteristic sound of many songs; eighth-notes, with a backbeat (a snare on 2 and 4). The kick defines the places where we naturally expect a musical accent, beats 1 and 3.

With the grid set to 8 (although visible as 16 in this picture), all the notes have been inputted with the mouse, and all have the same velocity, although your system might offer different options, which of course you should explore. The hi-hat here seemed a little loud, and so the velocity of all those notes was reduced simultaneously until it sounded more balanced.

You could just as easily create this beat through any of the other note input approaches described above, should you prefer. Starting with an empty one-bar region, program this beat into your system, experiment with adjusting the velocities of each part of the kit relative to one another, and listen to it playing back at several different tempos. The feeling of the kick on 1 and 3 gives us a great starting point to do a number of kick drum variations, something that is very common in many genres of music.

> **TIP**
> Many DAWs allow you to select all the notes of a given drum by clicking on the appropriate key in the piano roll editor. Once you have done this, you can simply drag the velocity indicator of one note, and all other velocities in the current region will move with it.

Pattern 03_02: Some kick drum variations.

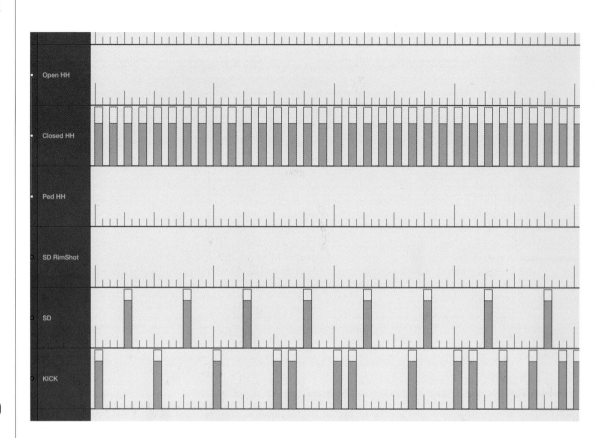

Pattern 03_02

Pattern 03_03

PATTERN 03_02: Pattern 03_01 plus three kick variations. Four bars repeated twice at 120bpm. Here, we have made three copies of Pattern 03_01 to form a four bar sequence. We have added a number of further kick drums, and edited some of those already there. In the second bar you see that another has been added on beat 3&. In the third bar, we have added yet another kick on beat 1&, and moved the original that fell on beat 3 forward by an eighth-note. This gives an interesting effect – that of creating a small tension in the groove since the listener expects to hear a loud note on both beat 1 and beat 3. Adding the bass drum on the next eighth-note pulls the feeling of the groove back with some urgency. The last bar emphasises this even more by having the hit on beat 2& as well.

PATTERN 30_03: A mix of all eight bars of Pattern 03_02 in a different order to form an eight bar phrase at 120bpm. Copy all four regions so that you now have eight in total. Mixing up the order, perhaps starting randomly but then using some musical preference, is a great way to form longer and more complex phrases. There is no need to try and replicate the order in the audio

MIDI PROGRAMMING WITH ONE-SHOTS

example – just mix them up. Do not feel bound by any phrases that you do not like, just edit them or delete/replace them.

Pattern 03_04

The second four bars of the performed Pattern 03_04.

PATTERN 03_04: A four bar hi-hat and snare ostinato with real-time kick input. The first four bars are exactly as recorded, but the second four are quantised, both at 120bpm. First create an empty four-bar region. Now select only the hi-hat and snare notes from one bar of Pattern 03_03 and copy them to the clipboard. In the empty region that you have created, and making sure that the song position line is exactly at the beginning of the region (because this will likely set the paste destination), paste the notes into the region. Check that they have aligned with the grid as you would expect. Repeat this phrase to fill the full four bars, either by continuing to paste at the beginning of each successive bar, or using a repeat function.

Now, either using a separate track routed to the same MIDI instrument, or overdubbing onto the same region, perform an improvised kick drum part aiming for an eighth-note feel; we are doing this in preference to mouse input because sometimes the kick drum might sound better spontaneously phrased to fit with the bass guitar or the track in general. You'll notice in the audio example that the first four bars have a degree of human timing-error. You might like this, thinking

TIP
One thing to watch is that everyone has a different perception (or resolution) of timing accuracy. What seems okay to one person might sound rather rough and ready to another, and so you have to consider your target audience when making decisions as to whether your performance is good enough. Now you are becoming a producer as well.

CHAPTER 3

Ostinato (plural ostinatos or ostinati).
This is a musical phrase, usually quite short, that is repeated. It is a very common technique in drumming, for instance played on the hi-hat while other parts of the kit vary.

Pattern 03_05: Some snare drum variations.

that it gives a more realistic feel, but depending on the accuracy of your performance it may need to be tightened up; the second four bars has the same performance, but quantised to eighth-notes.

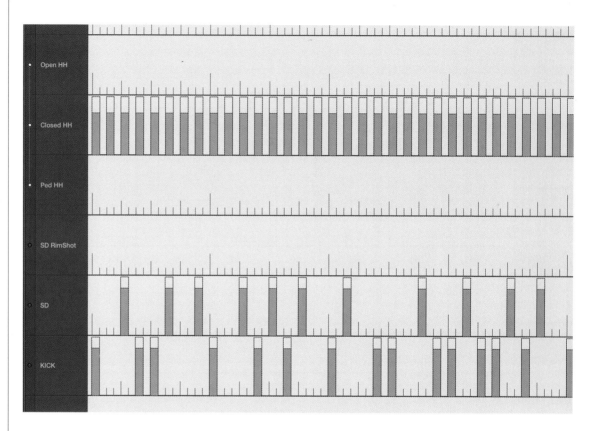

PATTERN 03_05: Some snare drum variations away from 2 and 4. Four bars, repeated twice at 96bpm. Here, we have used a simple kick drum pattern, but in each bar we have modified the snare drum pattern to move away from just playing the backbeat on 2 and 4. In reality, when you do this you might move a snare and find that it then becomes necessary to move a kick; this is normal. Notice that in this example, we do not have snare and kick playing simultaneously; this aligns with what many drummers do naturally. The resulting pattern is certainly very mobile, and will not fit with tunes that require something more solid.

CHAPTER 3

PATTERN 03_06: An edit combining all of the above to form a long sequence at 160bpm.
This long pattern is a mixture of both the preceding kick drum patterns and the Pattern 03_05
snare variations, which have been split into four individual one-bar regions. These have been
jumbled together to form four-bar phrases; that is, patterns that seem to reset or resolve every four
bars, which aligns to song structures in many genres. We have used each of the snare drum
variations towards the end of the four-bar phrases, and this adds interest and also tells the listener
that we are about to enter a new four-bar phrase.

 Pattern 03_06

   You will notice that this example does not simply use a snare variation every fourth bar;
sometimes the variation is on the third bar, and sometimes it might be both the third and fourth
bars, and towards the end of the sequence becomes even more varied. This has been done in
order to demonstrate some extended possibilities of this approach. As the listener locks into
expecting a four-bar phrase, you can take more liberties with it and their ears will follow.

Exercise One: Create a number of your own eighth-note based kick and snare variations of
   different lengths; there are many other possibilities.
Exercise Two: Reorder the sequence of various different bars; try including both those
   recommended here, and some of those that you made in Exercise One.
Exercise Three: Try a kick and snare ostinato over a few bars, and input the hi-hat in real-time.
   Consider how different the effect of this is to inputting the kick in real time. To quantise or not to
   quantise? Try repeating the four-bar phrase with a different snare variation on every fourth bar.

> **TIP**
> Your DAW might have a
> shuffle-edit mode, whereby
> dragging a region
> automatically displaces the
> adjacent regions, allowing for
> a speedy reordering; find out
> if yours has this function. You
> might find it helpful to use a
> different colour for the snare
> drum variation regions.

CHAPTER 3

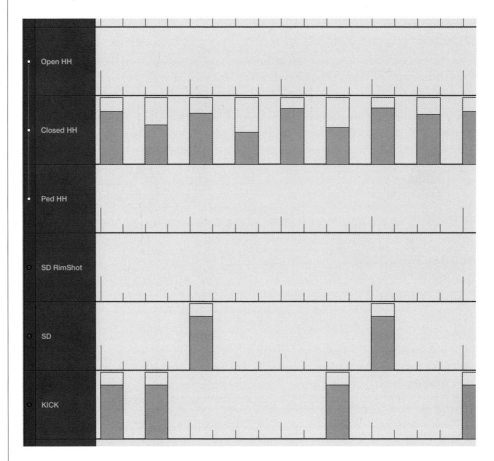

*Pattern 03_07: Velocity
variations in the hi-hat
part.*

Pattern 03_07

EDITING VELOCITY

**PATTERN 03_07: A version of the third of the previous Pattern 03_02 variations with edited
hi-hat velocities at 112bpm. Four repeats of a one-bar pattern.** Hi-hat velocities have been
changed one at a time. The onbeat notes are generally louder, which is something that drummers
often do, although notice both the volume and effect of beat 4&, which is 'in between'. The simple
act of varying these hi-hat velocities has made the beat sound much less mechanical. Be careful of
turning velocities up to 127, since if you need a little bit more later on (maybe whilst mixing), then
you will have nowhere to go.

CHAPTER 3

EIGHTH-NOTE GROOVE

PATTERN 03_08: The Pattern 03_07 hi-hat used as an ostinato on the longer sequence from Pattern 03_06. Once through at 140bpm. In order to make this groove, first create a new track routed to your MIDI instrument alongside your version of Pattern 03_06, and create an empty one-bar region at the beginning of it. Using the same process that you used to create Pattern 03_04, paste only the hi-hat notes from Pattern 03_01 into the empty region that you have created. Now repeat the new region for the same duration as Pattern 03_06: your DAW will have a function to make this easy. Merge all the regions of Pattern 03_06 together so that you can see them in a single editor window. Select the hi-hats and delete them all.

You should now have an arrangement whereby the one-bar hi-hat pattern plays back repeatedly on one track and a single long region with kick and snare variations plays back on the same instrument from another. Have a listen and think about how you might apply this workflow in other situations.

Let's now program a 'gear change', of the sort a drummer might play when moving from verse to chorus in a song. Firstly repeat the entire Pattern 03_08 arrangement so far. At the

TIP
You might prefer to edit the hi-hat ostinato into the merged Pattern 3.6. Use of the clipboard/repeat functions in this fashion can be slightly more intricate, so please refer to your DAW manual.

Pattern 03_08

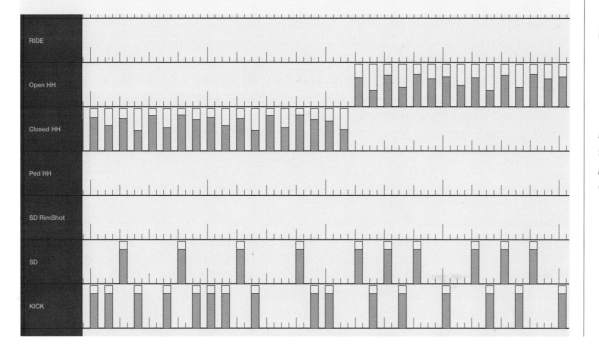

Pattern 03_08: Just the transition from closed hi-hat to open hi-hat, with velocity variations in both.

CHAPTER 3

point of repeat (halfway through the new whole) until the end, select all the hi-hat regions and transpose them until they play with an open hi-hat sound; you might prefer doing this in the region information/parameter box. This gives the effect of a transition in the music, with a louder and rather more aggressive second half. You might need to adjust the velocities of all the open hi-hat notes in order to balance them against the closed ones.

For a bit of (non-essential) musical interest, the audio of this exercise has been edited so that the open hi-hat comes in on the snare drum variations just before the halfway point; it starts on beat 2, so that it aligns with the change in snare drum phrase to set up the following section.

Further, you will notice that some more loud/quiet hi-hat phrases have been placed towards the end of this audio. If you listen carefully to the first of the two quiet (closed hi-hat) ones towards the end, you might notice that it sounds rather different. In fact, here we have transposed the part to play the pedal hi-hat sound instead of the normal closed hi-hat. This would probably be impossible for a human to replicate with their foot, but would anyone even notice this in the mix, if you like the sound of it?

So, if we are trying to emulate a human, can we only do things that a human can? Maybe, but there are times when you can take production liberties too. It often depends on the context, and how exposed the drum part is in the full instrumentation of the track.

Pattern 03_09

PATTERN 03_09: Like Pattern 03_08, but moving the hi-hat pattern to the ride. Once through at 140bpm. Assuming that you have used the two-track approach outlined above, apply the transpose again to move the hi-hat parts onto the ride cymbal. If you had integrated the hi-hat notes into the region with kick and snare, then select and drag within that region, or use your key command as mentioned earlier. Notice how the velocity variations might affect the tone of the cymbal. The audio excerpt features some moves to the open hi-hat and back as well. Listen for how the last two bars of ride have had the velocities evened out for a more insistent feel.

Exercise One: Edit the hi-hat velocities over the whole of Pattern 03_03; experiment to see what range of effects you can create.

Exercise Two: Read your DAW manual for different ways of editing velocity. Every system offers a number of different approaches suited to different situations, so by learning each of these your overall workflow will improve. Do not be afraid of 'numerical' systems that might add to or multiply the velocity values of a selection. Such systems can take a little longer to learn, but can be a very powerful addition to your editing toolbox.

Exercise Three: Take the kick and snare pattern that you created in the previous real-time hi-hat exercise, and replace the hi-hat part with one programmed using step time. Experiment.

CHAPTER 3

KICK AND SNARE PATTERNS WITH 16TH-NOTES

Now that we have mastered numerous eighth-note based patterns, we shall develop the intricacies of the phrases that are available to us by adding intermittent 16th-notes to the sort of eighth-note structures that we have already formed. First of all we will look at a number of kick drum variations, and then include snares. Set your grid to 16.

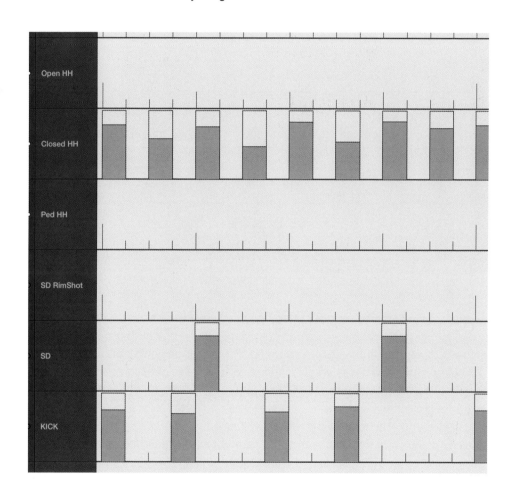

The first pattern of Pattern 03_10.

PATTERN 03_10: Four 16th-note kick patterns. Each is played twice at 100bpm. This pattern features kick drum hits on beats 1a and 2a, and has a fairly relaxed spacing between the notes; the absence of a note on beat 3 gives it a funky feel.

*The second pattern of
Pattern 03_10.*

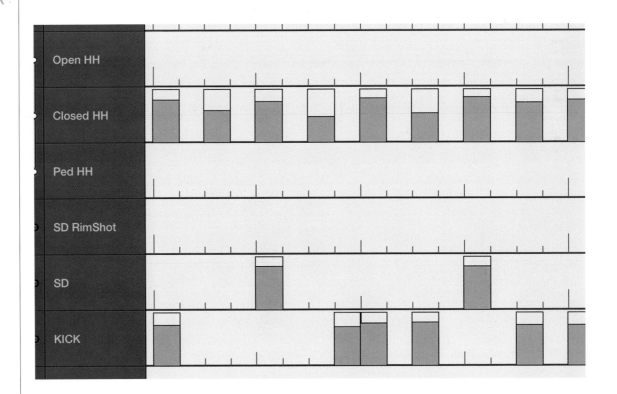

This pattern is perhaps less relaxed; has two kick drum notes only a 16th-note apart. That feels quick, but it is something that good drummers can do surprisingly fast. Look closely at the velocities. If you program them both at the same volume, it will have an unnatural robotic feel. A human drummer will typically play the notes at two different volumes, and here you can see that the first note of the pair is slightly quieter when compared to the following note and indeed all the single hits.

There will be times when you wish to have the relative volumes the other way around too; experiment. This subtlety makes a massive difference! Be careful not to overdo the difference in velocity, though, since doing so will lose the double-hit feel in the final mix. A good plug-in like FXpansion BFD3 will also offer a slightly different tone for each note in this situation, which emulates a real kick drum.

*The third pattern of
Pattern 03_10.*

Whereas the previous pattern had a fast double hit that landed on the beat, this one now has a pair on beats 1& and 1a, coming 'off' the eighth-note pulse, thus sounding rather different, regardless of its placement in the bar. Again, you will see the velocity trick. Look at the last three kick drum notes in this beat. Do you notice anything about the way that they are spaced?

CHAPTER 3

The fourth pattern of Pattern 03_10.

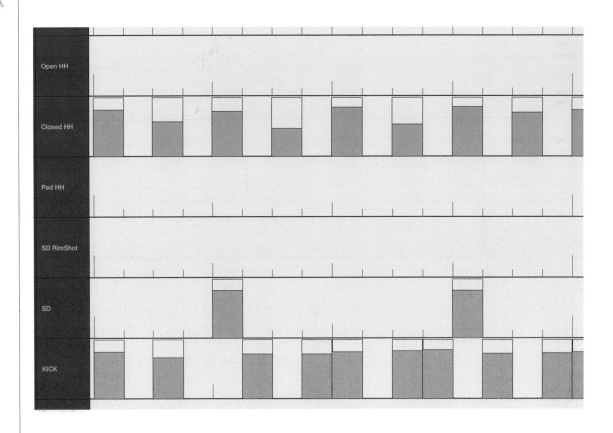

This is a busy pattern that features three lots of double hits on the kick drum as it repeats round to beat 1 again. It might sound impossible to play, but for generations, drummers have been developing their kick drum technique and many have taken it to extreme levels, especially with double hits. Three hits in a row however, is much more difficult!

■ **CHECK OUT**

Listen to what real drummers can do with good kick drum technique and phrasing (with one pedal): Ian Paice, Dennis Chambers, and Jo Jo Mayer amongst many others.

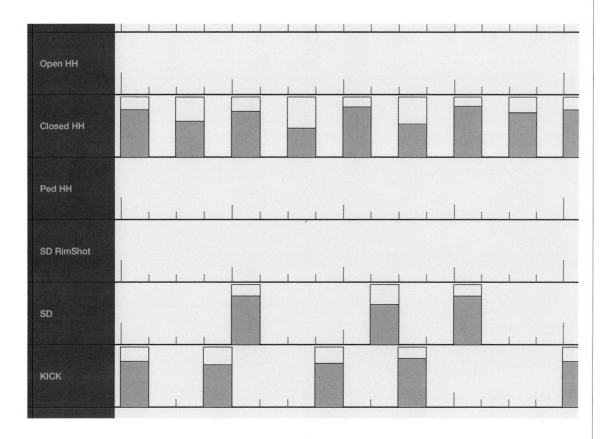

The first pattern of Pattern 03_11. The snare drum adding different 16th-note embellishments.

Pattern 03_11

PATTERN 03_11: 16th-note snares added to the previous four beats. Each is played twice at 100bpm. The addition of another single snare hit on beat 3e is a funky addition. Notice that its velocity is slightly less than that of the backbeat. This helps drive the beat forward and stops it becoming lumpy with too many loud snares.

The second pattern of Pattern 03_11.

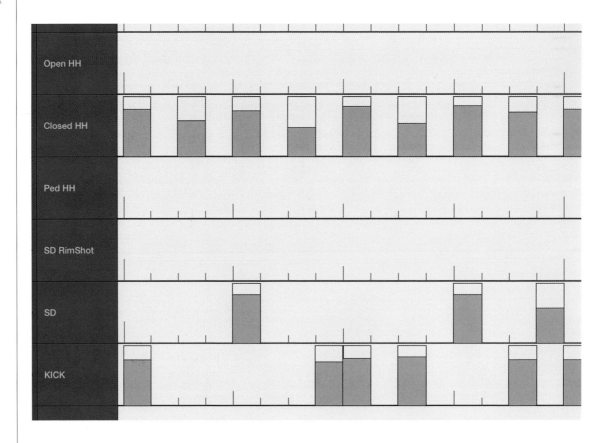

Here, we have added a different single snare on beat 4a, but this time being tucked between two kick drums gives a fast flurry of three notes.

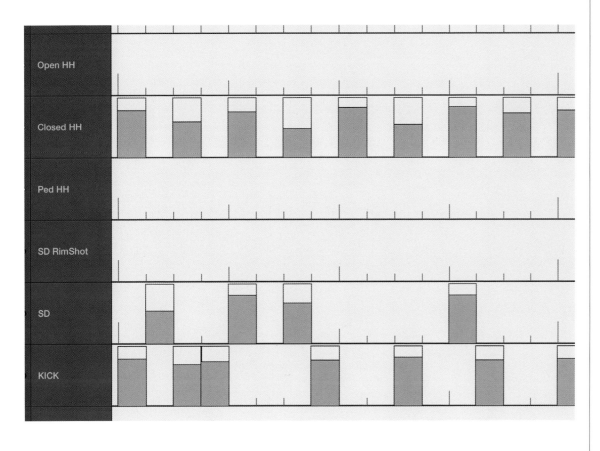

*The third pattern of
pattern 03_11.*

The snare drum on beat 1e this time gives us a fast flurry of five notes: beats 1e&a2. This is still quite possible for a human to play, since we are spreading the effort between the kick and the snare. In addition, this beat has an interesting funky phrase on beats 2&a.

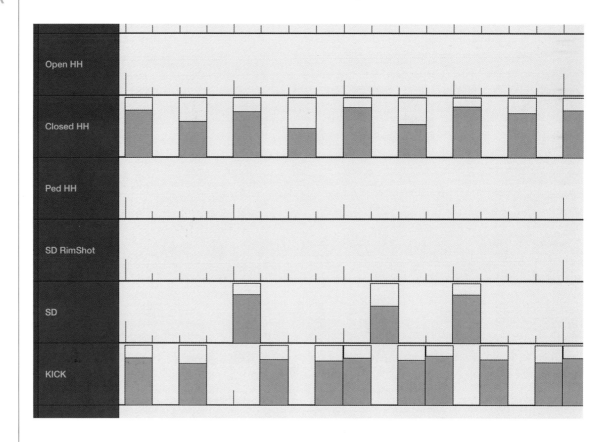

The fourth pattern of
Pattern 03_11.

Our fast flurry has now been extended to seven 16th-notes in a row from beats 2a to 4e, but yet there are still no more than two rapids kick hits consecutively, and therefore it is still quite playable for a human.

These four phrases are only scratching the surface of what is possible when alternating kick and snare with 16th-notes. You must listen out for patterns that you hear in music you enjoy and try to replicate these when programming. Remember drum kit tuition books too. Also experiment in an abstract or even mathematical way, and often you'll come up with great beats. Try to remember the phrases that you enjoy, but also be mindful of what does not work so that you can avoid it another time. It is just like practising an instrument.

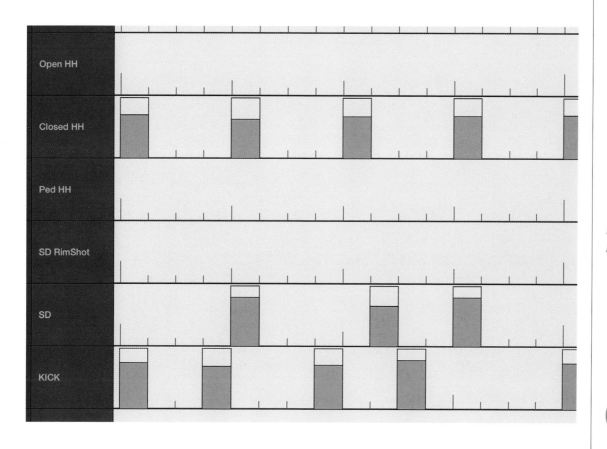

Open HH	
Closed HH	
Ped HH	
SD RimShot	
SD	
KICK	

Pattern 03_12: Quarter-notes on the hi-hat.

Pattern 03_12

PATTERN 03_12: Quarter-note hi-hats with the previous four-bar phrase, Pattern 03_11. It is played twice first with a closed hi-hat and then with open hi-hat sound: 16 bars at 120bpm. Instead of eight-notes, playing quarter-notes on the hi-hat gives a sense of space, even with quite a busy kick and snare combination. This approach simply adds to the range of feels available to you; however, if the quarter-notes are played on something more noisy such as an open hi-hat, the effect changes yet again with the open hi-hat stating the quarter-note pulse with quite an aggressive attitude. You could simply delete every second hi-hat from the previous pattern, although this will probably take more time than deleting all, then reprogramming one bar and copying it throughout the region.

This hi-hat style works just as well on eighth-note-based kick/snare patterns too. You might wish to try using the bell of the ride in this fashion, perhaps with a simple eighth-note kick pattern and turning the tempo up.

CHAPTER 3

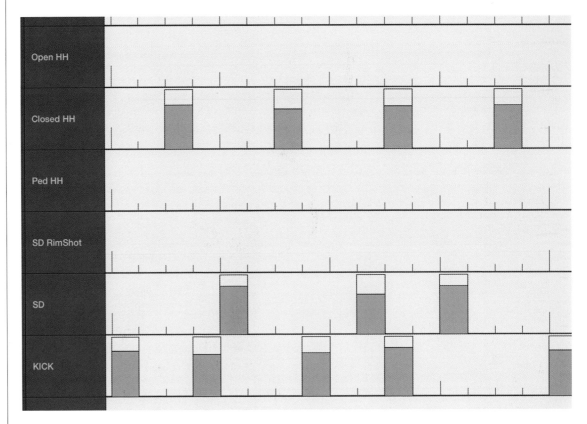

Pattern 03_13: Offbeats on the hi-hat.

PATTERN 03_13: Offbeat quarter-note hi-hats with the previous four bars from Pattern 03_11. This time there are no repeats of the four bars, and there is a change in the order of the grooves between the third and fourth bar. Twice through: eight bars at 120bpm. Placing the hi-hat on the offbeat gives an interesting and bouncy feel. If you wish to replicate the order of the bars in the audio for example, you can slice into single bar regions and rearrange. But there is nothing precious about this particular order: you can choose your own. You can create this hi-hat pattern by simply selecting the quarter-note hi-hats from Pattern 03_12, and dragging them forward in time by an eighth-note. Think about the workflow here. In terms of slicing and removing every repeated bar, reordering regions, and applying this simple adjustment to the hi-hat, what would be the fastest order in which to realise this edit?

CHAPTER 3

MIDI PROGRAMMING WITH ONE-SHOTS

PATTERN 03_14: A version of Pattern 03_13 with a ride cymbal bell sound. The hi-hat has simply been transposed to play the bell. This gives a very clearly defined offbeat field with a distinctive quality: eight bars at 120bpm.

PATTERN 03_15: A quarter-note pedal hi-hat has been added to Pattern 03_14, and half-bar slices shuffle-edited: eight bars at 120bpm. Most human drummers have four limbs. One foot tends to reside on the hi-hat pedal although sometimes other things are played, for instance a

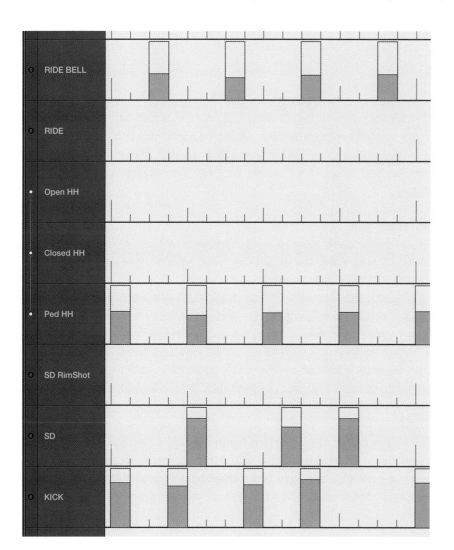

*Pattern 03_15:
A combination of pedal hi-hat and ride cymbal bell.*

second kick drum. Up until now, our grooves have typically used both hands and one foot. We can add another layer to Pattern 03_14 by adding the pedal hi-hats on all the quarter-notes. It is easy to generate this, by copying, time-sliding, transposing, and adjusting the velocity of the ride bell part. The effect of this is a slightly more textured and fluid groove.

To add interest at this point, the whole pattern has been chopped into regions that are exactly half a bar long, and these have then been shuffle-edited (reordered). The trick with using half-bar regions is that the backbeat on beat 2 juxtaposes with that of beat 4 maintaining a consistent backbeat, but allowing the kick patterns to move between the first and second half of the bars of the reordered pattern, thus offering many more phrasing variations for very little effort. Of course, if you doing this in a track where musical structure and phrasing need to align with other instruments, you have to be judicious!

Exercise One: Using the hi-hat and snare ostinato of your choice, program a 16th-note kick drum sequence of your own.

Exercise Two: Using what you created for Exercise One, delete the snare part and copy the kick drum pattern to the snare, then create a new and simple kick to go with it.

Exercise Three: For the beat that you created for Exercise Two, edit the velocities of the new snare part to create a different feel.

Check that you can:
- Program in both step-time and real-time modes.
- Apply a variety of mouse-based editing techniques to your patterns.
- Repeat specific selections of notes and regions.
- Combine multiple regions to form extended phrases.
- Set up a DAW where multiple tracks control a single plug-in drum kit.
- Program both eighth-note and 16th-note patterns.
- Control velocities of notes.

Things to experiment with
- Try to devise systems for developing new phrasing ideas: for instance, only allowing the kick drum on offbeats, using visual patterns, creating a complex longer phrase and then deleting every third kick drum, etc.
- Program an eight-bar sequence with each drum on a different track, then slice each region into smaller regions of different lengths and reorder them.
- Duplicate a given region a number of times, but edit the velocities differently in each region.
- Again with each drum programmed on a different track, slide just one of the regions forward by a fraction of a bar and listen to the effect. Try this with different fractions.

CONCLUSION

We have established a number of ways of working. Use the checklist below to make sure that you are comfortable with all of the key concepts from this chapter. In the next chapter, we will extend these techniques to produce much more intricate and exciting beats, and also start studying how to program fills.

MORE DETAILED ONE-SHOT PROGRAMMING

CHAPTER 4

■ **CHECK OUT**
Omar Hakim on the Daft Punk
track 'Beyond' from *Random
Access Memories*. You might
also notice the open hi-hat on
beat 4& every second bar; see
'Decorations' later in this
chapter.

Now we are going to build on the techniques discussed in the previous chapter. We will consider 16th-note hi-hat patterns in the ways that a real drummer might play them, and learn about triplets and shuffle to give completely different feels. We will also look at repeating short phrases throughout a given beat and think about how to decorate a basic beat with open hi-hats and crashes. Things will get funky when we learn about ghost notes, and lastly we will investigate a number of approaches to creating drum fills.

HI-HAT 16TH-NOTES

Let's now start looking at what 16th-notes can do for hi-hat patterns. When a tune is slightly slower and the drummer wants to fill the space and drive it along, he or she might choose to play 16th-notes on the hi-hat in place of the kind of patterns we have seen so far. If it is possible at a given tempo, the first option for doing this is to use one hand.

Pattern 04_01

*Pattern 04_01: A 16th-note
hi-hat groove.*

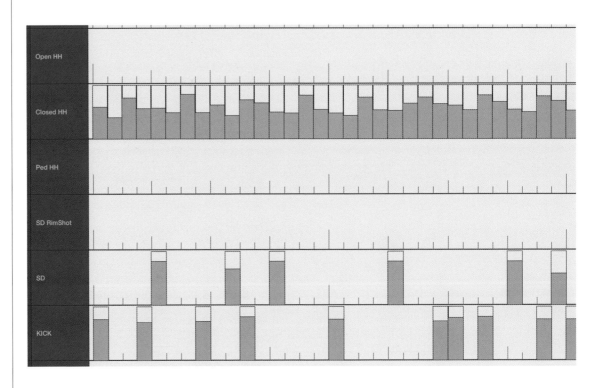

MORE DETAILED ONE-SHOT PROGRAMMING

PATTERN 04_01: 16th-note hi-hats with the first two kick/snare combinations from Pattern 03_10. Twice through at 86bpm. You can see that all available 16th-note spaces have been filled with hi-hats. Velocity is absolutely crucial here; if you draw in the hi-hats all at the same volume, the result will be akin to that of a dreadful old-fashioned drum machine. You will notice that there are accents on all the offbeat eighth-notes (quavers), and in combination with some subtle velocity variations leading onto and from these accents, there is a lilting feel to the groove akin to a relaxed funk track. Listen carefully to the audio whilst studying the picture, and try to really tune in to the hi-hat velocity variations.

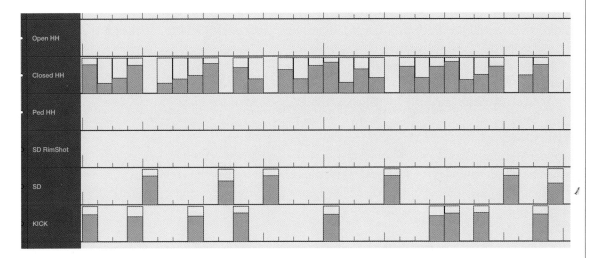

Pattern 04_02: The hand-to-hand hi-hat style misses the hi-hat as the snare is being hit.

Pattern 04_02

PATTERN 04_02: Using the hand-to-hand hi-hat style with velocity interest at 116bpm. Twice through. If a tune is faster and the drummer cannot manage to play all the 16th-notes with one hand, but still wants something like that feel, the hand-to-hand hi-hat style offers some options. This involves alternating the two hands on the hi-hat to play the 16th-notes; what this means is that it is not easy to play the snare simultaneously with a hi-hat as we have done previously. Where a snare drum is required, one hand will come back from the hi-hat whilst continuing the hand-to-hand playing action, strike the snare drum instead and then return to the hi-hat. This means that there are little gaps in the continuity of the hi-hat pattern, but these gaps are not too drastic when you listen.

Another thing that often happens in this style of playing is that accents are added with either hand to give life to the overall pattern; these accents may fall with, or in between, kick drum hits. You will notice that the hi-hat accents are tending towards beats 1 and 3, although there are a few elsewhere, and the hi-hats have been removed from the snare drum hit points for authenticity.

TIP
The accents in this example are only one of many possible variations, and each will impart a very different feel. You might like to try editing this so that the accents fall on all the eighth-notes, the onbeat quarter-notes, or even adjacent pairs of 16th-notes in each beat.

Pattern 04_03

PATTERN 04_03: the second kick drum variation of Pattern 03_02, adding a moving succession of accents in the hand-to-hand style. This is a one-bar kick/snare pattern with four bars of changing hi-hat, repeated twice at 116bpm. The effect is of a simple, ostinato basic beat, in this case eighth-note based, but with a subtle, bubbling flow of 16th-note accents that keeps it feeling alive. If you are working on a track that demands a simplified kick/snare pattern, but you want more from the drum part without getting in the way, this can be a good strategy.

Exercise One: There are a large number of possible combinations using kick and snare, even in a single bar. Using the 'one-handed' style, create another five single-bar patterns of your own, experimenting with hi-hat accents too.

Exercise Two: Starting from only one of the previous five, create a four-bar phrase with subtle variations between the different bars, simply adding or removing a note here and there and keeping the overall feel the same.

Exercise Three: Create your own hand-to-hand hi-hat drumbeat with some syncopated snare drum placements, trying to imagine how a human might play this.

TRIPLETS

We mentioned earlier that some songs divide each quarter-note (crotchet) into threes. These are called eighth-note triplets (triplet quavers), and this sound is sometimes referred to as twelve-eight or six-eight (written 12/8 or 6/8, for technical reasons). We will now develop some beats with this approach.

MORE DETAILED ONE-SHOT PROGRAMMING

Pattern 04_04

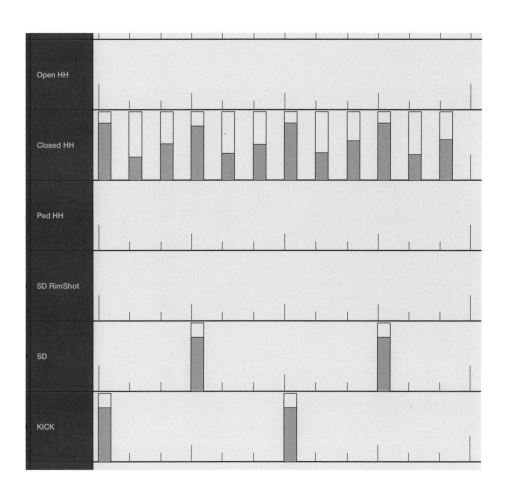

Pattern 04_04: Notice the distinctive appearance of the triplets.

PATTERN 04_04: A simple triplet beat at 90bpm. This beat is the equivalent of Pattern 03_01 and has the same kick and snare, but with the triplet style on the hi-hat. To achieve this, you will need to set the grid on your DAW to 8T (12). This will clearly show three subdivisions per quarter-note, as opposed to the more familiar twos and fours. By filling up all of these spaces with hi-hats, you will have created a triplet beat. As ever, a little attention to the velocities will give a much better feel, and as you can see in the example, accenting the quarter-notes is a good place to start. Keeping the middle note of each triplet a little quieter is also useful.

NOTE
The diagrams of Patterns 04_04 to 04_09 appear slightly different to each other because the width of the note-blocks is narrower. This has been adjusted in order to make the 16th-notes easier to see in the later examples. The width itself is not important and does not change anything; it is the position of the start of the block on the grid that counts.

The last two bars of Pattern 04_05 where the beat 'turns around'.

 Pattern 04_05

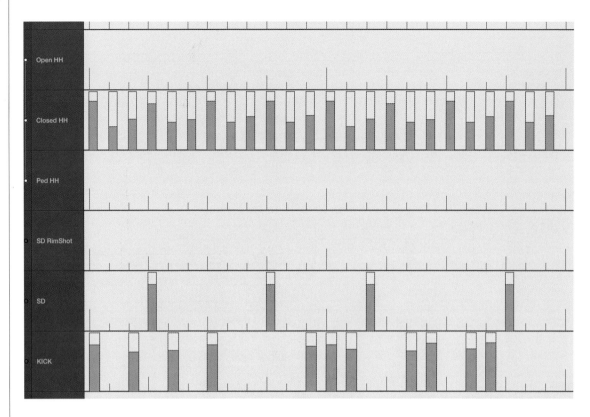

PATTERN 04_05: **Some kick drum variations on a triplet beat. Eight bars at 90bpm.** This pattern features a number of combinations of kick patterns and one or two decorative snare drum notes. It is a case of ensuring that the grid is set to 8T for all components of the drum kit, using Pattern 04_05 as a starting point, and then simply experimenting by adding and removing kicks, steering away from the middle note of the triplet as a rule of thumb. The last two bars are shown in the screen grab since they complicate the phrasing slightly by actually using the middle note of the triplets, and also by deviating from the strict backbeat.

MORE DETAILED ONE-SHOT PROGRAMMING

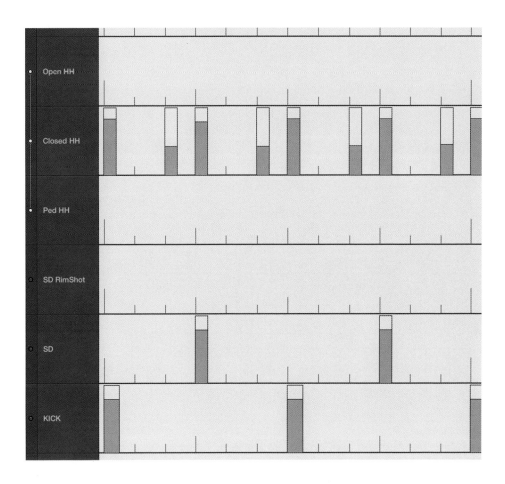

Pattern 04_06: the shuffle.

PATTERN 04_06: A simple shuffle. One bar repeated four times at 90bpm. It is very common to completely miss out the middle note of the triplets all the time. This produces a unique musical groove known as the shuffle (which has absolutely nothing to do with the shuffle-edit technique). The shuffle features in all genres, but is often manipulated and disguised. To create a basic shuffle, take Pattern 04_04, and delete the middle note of each triplet on the hi-hat. Adjust the velocities so that there is a definite quarter-note feel with the last note of each triplet rolling into each of the quarter-notes – this gives an authentic sound.

Pattern 04_07: Kick drum variations in the shuffle style.

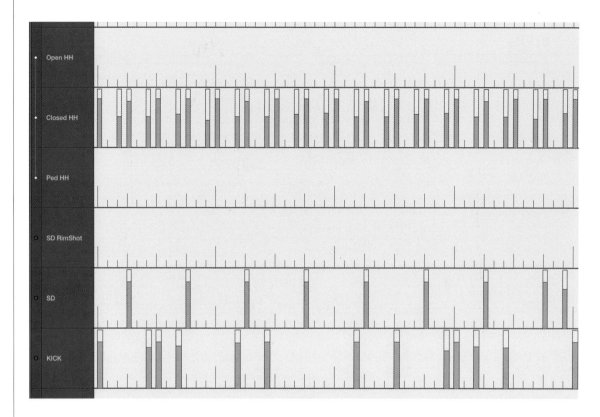

PATTERN 04_07: A four-bar shuffled kick and snare pattern. Twice through a four-bar phrase; first at 90bpm, then at 150bpm. This pattern demonstrates some possible kick drum phrasing, and also the shuffle at a much higher tempo, which is quite common.

PATTERN 04_08: Kick/snare shuffle with ostinato ride cymbal bell on quarter-notes at 150bpm. Just as when we played quarter-notes on the hi-hat in Pattern 03_12, we can do this and maintain a shuffle feel from the kick pattern.

MORE DETAILED ONE-SHOT PROGRAMMING

PATTERN 04_09: 16th-note triplets (triplet semiquavers) in a 12/8 style. **Eight-bar phrase at 98bpm. This pattern demonstrates 16th-note triplets in a groove.** The grid is in 8T for all of the kit components except the kick, where it can be seen to be in 16T. In bar 1, the double kick-hit that that leads 'onto' the last 8T before beat 4 gives a double time feel, and this form of phrasing is replicated throughout this extract.

You might notice a curious timing between beat 4 of bar one, and beat 1 of bar two. The kick is playing on the 16T between the second and third 8T positions; in other words on the eighth-note, beat 4&. It sounds slightly strange because your brain is in 'triplet-mode' due to the way the hi-hat is reinforcing this as the main subdivision. Again, this phrasing is used elsewhere in this excerpt.

There is a curious fluttering of notes from bar five into bar six. This is being driven by fitting some 16T notes in between those of the 8T hi-hat ostinato, and is further reinforced by the rather quiet 16T snare drum between beats 3 and 4 of bar five. You might also notice the snare 'turnaround' in the last bar. This is modelled on the phrasing of Pattern 04_05, but simply is decorated with some 16T notes.

Pattern 04_09

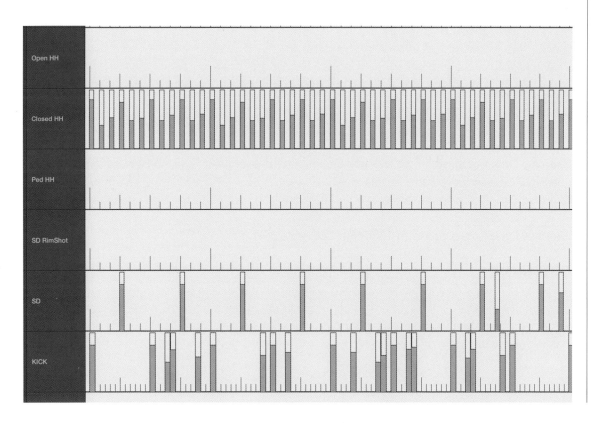

Pattern 04_09: The first four bars.

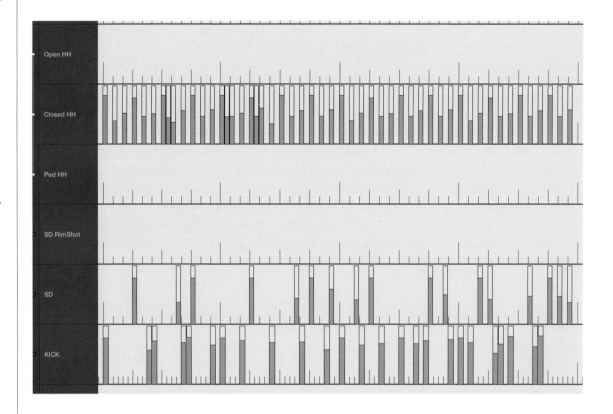

Pattern 04_09: The second four bars.

Exercise One: Create your own kick and snare patterns in a triplet style, some busy and some spacious. Convert these into a shuffle style.

Exercise One: Try using a quarter-note hi-hat or ride with your patterns. Turn up the tempo on the spacious ones.

Exercise One: Create your own 16th-note 12/8 style beat.

OSTINATOS

As we have already mentioned, the ostinato is an important musical phrase in drumming and drum programming. In this section, we are going to look at a number of hi-hat/cymbal ostinatos; later in this book, other types will be revealed too.

MORE DETAILED ONE-SHOT PROGRAMMING

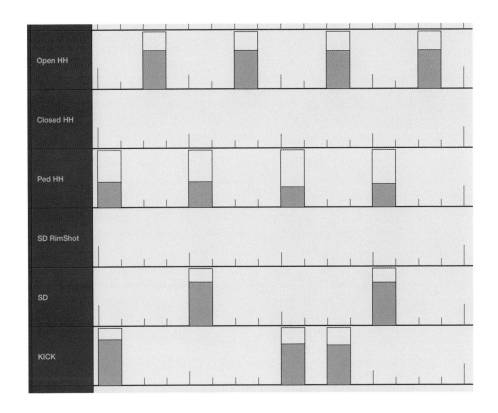

*Pattern 04_10: An open
and closed hi-hat groove
with a simple kick drum
pattern.*

PATTERN 04_10: An ostinato open and closed hi-hat on an eighth-note beat. A single bar repeated three times at 100bpm. Here we have a very simple kick/snare pattern, with the hi-hat opening and closing continually on eight-notes. Notice the velocity of the pedal hat, which is fairly quiet. A drummer might sometimes hit the pedal hard to make a 'chick' sound, but when simply choking the hi-hat as it sizzles will probably play it more softly, and we do not want to hear this note articulated too strongly.

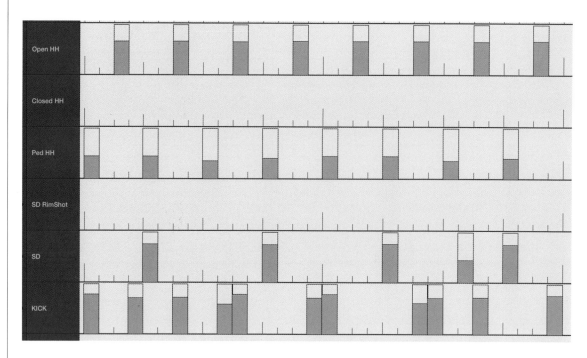

*Pattern 04_11: An open
and closed hi-hat groove
with kick drum variations.*

**PATTERN 04_11: An ostinato open and closed hi-hat on a 16th-note beat. A two-bar phrase
played twice at 100bpm.** To create a pattern like this, simply copy and paste both open and pedal
hi-hats from Pattern 04_10 into any 16th-note groove from earlier. Experiment by playing it back at
different tempos; you might think that it 'sits' best in the range of 90–130bpm. The optimum tempo
is always something to consider with any beat. The effect that we have achieved has been very
widely used, and you can hear it in various guises from 70s disco classics, through The Red Hot
Chili Peppers, to a huge proportion of house music, from way back until now.

■ **CHECK OUT**
Chad Smith on the first half of
'Funky Monks' from *Blood
Sugar Sex Magik* by Red Hot
Chili Peppers. This is a 1/16th-
note kick/snare pattern with
this very ostinato.

MORE DETAILED ONE-SHOT PROGRAMMING

  Pattern 04_12

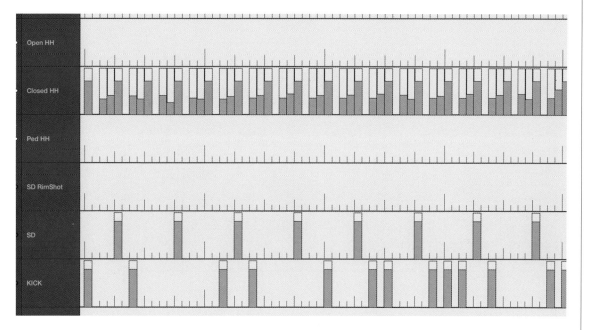

Pattern 04_12: A new ostinato 16th-note hi-hat pattern.

PATTERN 04_12: This example takes the kick and snare of Pattern 03_04 and uses an ostinato 16th-note hi-hat. Four bars played twice at 100bpm. In this we have spiced up a straightforward eighth-note-based beat from earlier and used a cluster of three 16th-notes that recur each quarter-note. The accent is on the quarter-note, but this pattern will work just as well with the accent on the upbeat instead. To create it, use the mouse to enter three notes in the first beat, paying attention to relative velocities. Use the repeat function of your DAW to fill up the rest of the region. You might wish to make some velocity adjustments over the duration of the region in order to stop it sounding too mechanical.

An alternative to this is to copy the initial cluster once by dragging and dropping, change a couple of velocities, drag and drop all six notes you have just created to form a full bar-long pattern, tweak the velocities again and then repeat this pattern throughout your region. You might also use real-time recording to get a genuine human performance of this, played over its entire duration. Of course, you may or may not wish to quantise this.

TIP
You might like to try unusual lengths of phrase to repeat back to back, eg, one-and-a-half beats or three beats. These will move in and out of phase with your kick and snare pattern, but the ear will derive its pulse from the latter, and the effect will be simply a much more varied and possibly interesting movement of hi-hat velocities. When you reach the end of your kick/snare pattern, you will very probably need to edit the hi-hats, either adding (or copying) in a few extra to fill the region or trimming any overshoot.

CHAPTER 4

*Pattern 04_13: The
ostinato 16th-note hi-hat
pattern, now incorporating
the ride bell.*

Pattern 04_13

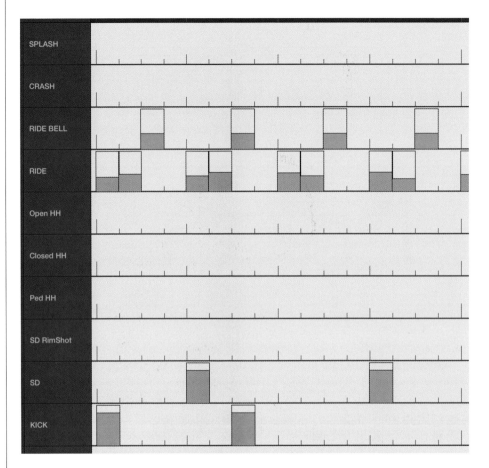

PATTERN 04_13: Again with the kick/snare of Pattern 03_04, an ostinato ride cymbal bell,
first 16th-note on the quarter-note with an accented bell on the upbeat. Four bars played
twice at 100bpm. This pattern is very similar to the last one, except backwards in a sense. What
does 'backwards' mean in this context, and what other sorts of backwards might there be?

Exercise One: Create your own kick and snare patterns with the hi-hat/ride ostinatos from above.
Exercise Two: Invent three of your own ostinatos and try them in the patterns you have just
created.
Exercise Three: Thinking of ostinatos, program a beat using three different tracks assigned to the
same plug-in for kick, snare, and hi-hat. Consider the advantages and disadvantages of
working this way.

CHAPTER 4

HI-HAT AND CYMBAL DECORATIONS

PATTERN 04_14: This is Pattern 03_01, repeated with added open hi-hats. Four bar phrase played twice at 112bpm. Eighth-note open hi-hats can be thought of in four simple ways: played on their own and closing on their own; played on their own and closing whilst hitting a kick or a snare; played simultaneously with a kick or a snare and closing whilst hitting another kick or a snare; or played simultaneously with a kick or a snare, and closing on their own. Here we have the basic Pattern 03_01, spiced up by adding open hi-hats in various parts of the bar.

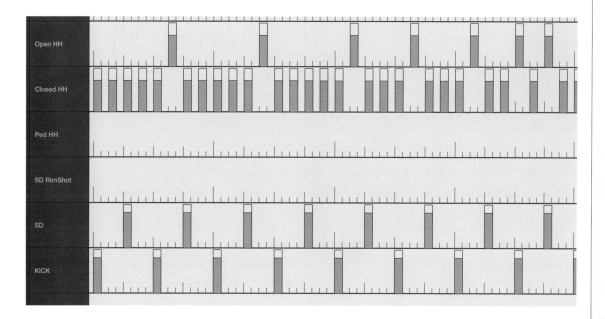

Pattern 04_14: An eighth-note pattern with irregular open hi-hats.

PATTERN 04_15: The long phrase of Pattern 03_08 with added open hi-hat to decorate the kick/snare phrasing, at 130bpm. You will hear numerous examples of phrasing in this excerpt, but they still largely follow the basic rules above. There are occasions when the hi-hat is held open for a quarter-note, which gives the impression of a slight pause in the groove, there are syncopated snare drums that have been emphasised by opening the hi-hat simultaneously, and towards the end of the passage, ostinatos with open/shut hi-hat.

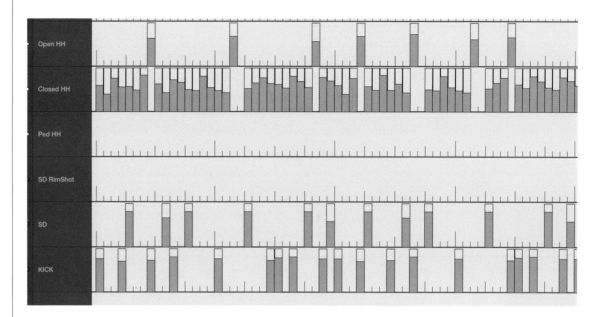

Pattern 04_16: Open hi-hats in the hand-to-hand style.

PATTERN 04_16: Pattern 04_01 is played twice and open hi-hat is added. This two-bar phrase is repeated once at 86bpm. This funk beat has particular kick hits emphasised with the open hi-hat. Notice that sometimes the hi-hat is only held open for a 16th-note, and other times for an eighth-note. In a 16th-note groove, holding it open for an eighth-note gives the effect of a slight pause. This is similar to a quarter-note in the previous example; basically, opening for longer than the main subdivision of any groove will do this. In the context of a track, it can be very effective to add open hi-hats that land with other instruments' syncopated accents.

MORE DETAILED ONE-SHOT PROGRAMMING

PATTERN 04_17: Pattern 03_12, shuffled half-bar groups and added ride cymbal bell
randomly at 120bpm. Once through. In this extract, Pattern 03_12 has been sliced into half-bar
groups and these shuffle-edited in order to form new phrases from that palette. This ride-based
groove has had the normal ride hit substituted with a bell in a similar fashion to how we used the
open hi-hat instead of the closed; occasional notes or sometimes clusters of notes are played on
the bell in order to form phrases running alongside the kick and the snare, or to emphasise
particular notes. In addition, some clusters of 16th-notes have been played too, although never
more than three, since that is tricky for humans to play.

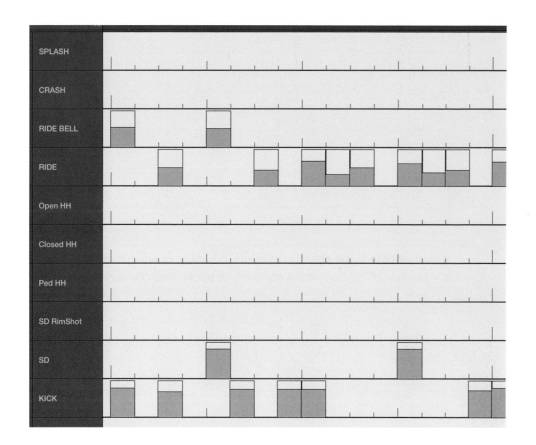

Pattern 04_17: Bar three.

Bar three of the Pattern 04_17. You can see a bell being struck concurrently with both kick and
snare, and also clusters of three 16th-notes, coming 'off' the beat.

Pattern 04_17: Bar five.

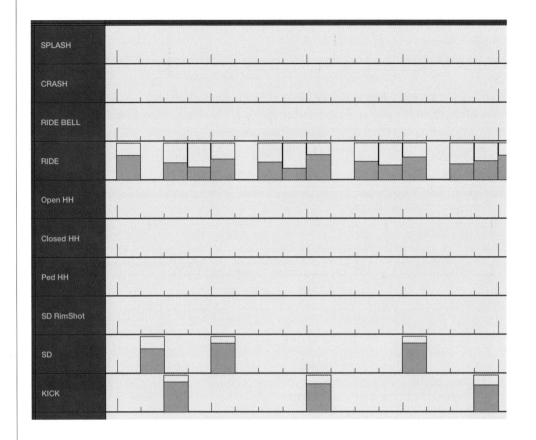

This is bar five of Pattern 04_17. Here we have consecutive clusters of three 16th-notes, but this time coming 'off' the & and landing on the beat.

MORE DETAILED ONE-SHOT PROGRAMMING

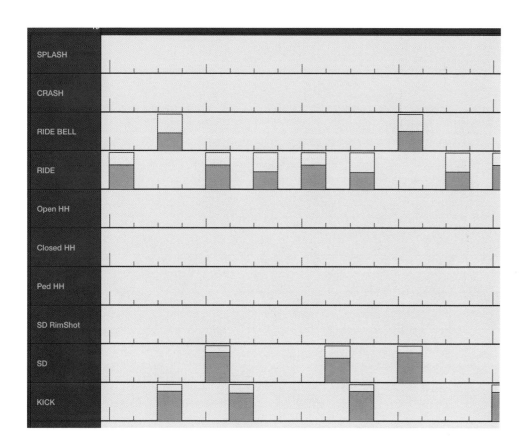

Pattern 04_17: Bar eight.

This is bar eight of Pattern 04_17. Notice the placement of the first bell on 1&.

Pattern 04_17: Bar 12.

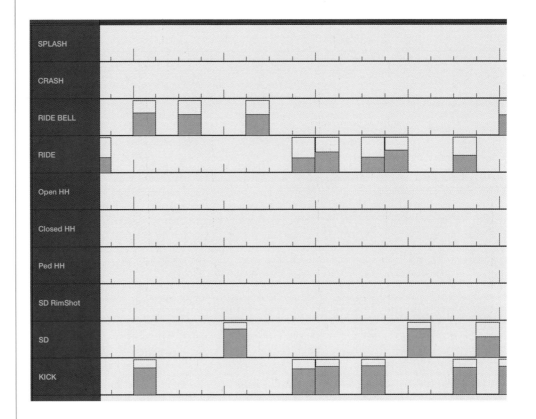

This is bar 12 of Pattern 04_17. The cymbal pattern does not conform to an ostinato, and moves quite independently of the kick and the snare. It does not generally land concurrently with any snare hit, which is representative of a technique sometimes used by drummers, with a syncopated pattern between the hands.

MORE DETAILED ONE-SHOT PROGRAMMING

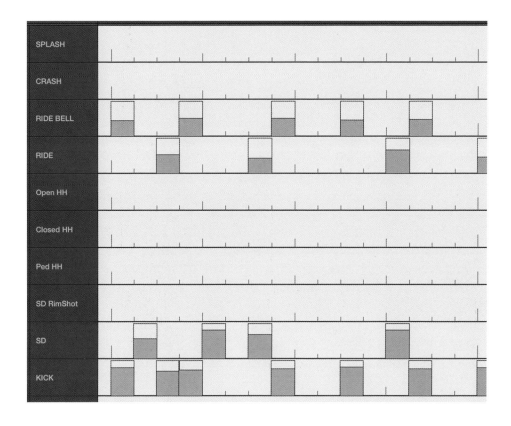

Pattern 04_17: Bar 14.

This is bar 14 of Pattern 04_17. The combined ride and bell pattern mostly aligns with that of the kick drum. Again, this approach is quite natural for many drummers since both are played by the same side of the body; one hand and one foot. The drummer's hand would simply be moving between the ride and the bell, which are after all different areas of the same cymbal.

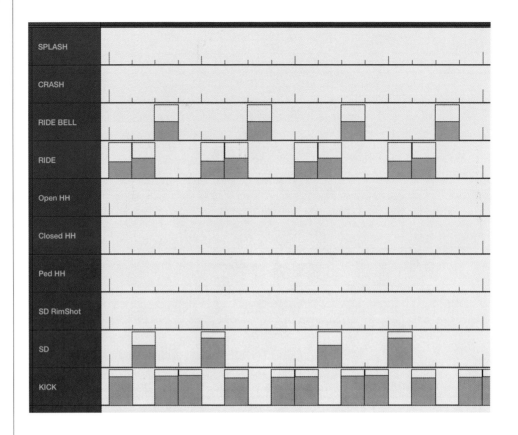

Pattern: 04_17: Bar 15.

■ CHECK OUT

Irregular or 'broken' cymbal patterns are often associated with Latin music, but really can be applied in all genres. Listen to the verse section of Beyoncé's 'Crazy In Love' from *Dangerously In Love.*

This is bar 15 of the Pattern 04_17. We have another 16th-note ostinato, coming 'off' the beat with a bell on every &.

When all these are played consecutively, it gives the impression of a drummer improvising with three limbs, and has a 'complicated' feel compared to a steady ostinato.

MORE DETAILED ONE-SHOT PROGRAMMING

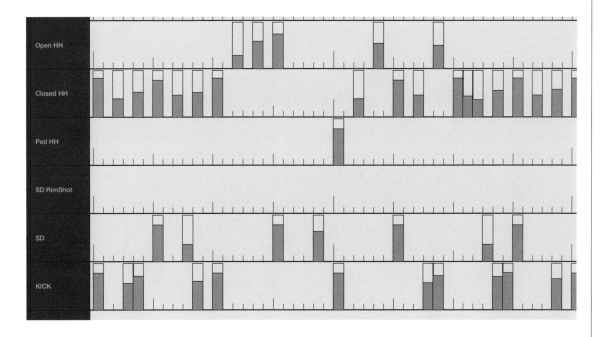

*Bars four and five of
Pattern 04_18: 12/8 open
hi-hat variations.*

Pattern 04_18

PATTERN 04_18: This is the 12/8 Pattern 04_09 with added open hi-hat hits. Eight bars long at 98bpm. Note the little crescendo on the open hi-hat leading on to beat four of bar four. The hi-hat is held open for a quarter-note as we have heard before, but there is a snare drum playing during that sustain, and the hi-hat is closed with a pedal sound only, which adds another subtle yet nice texture to the phrase. The open hi-hat leading onto beat 3 of bar five further develops the 16T phrase that follows.

100

THE
DRUM
PROGRAMMING
HANDBOOK

MORE DETAILED ONE-SHOT PROGRAMMING

Bars seven and eight of Pattern 04_18: more 12/8 open hi-hat variations.

By adding open hi-hats to the syncopated kick drum pattern on beat 3 of bar seven, the kicks are turned into punchy accents. Although they sound great on their own, this is the sort of technique that you might like to use in unison with certain phrases in your track to really emphasise those notes. Again we have used the pedal hi-hat to close off the longer opening, just for texture.

PATTERN 04_19: **This is derived from Pattern 03_12 with the closed hi-hat transposed to the ride, and adds crashes intermittently. It was then sliced into half-bar sections and randomly shuffle-edited. Eight bars long repeated twice, but with different crash variations throughout at 130bpm.**

Once again, shuffle-editing has provided a new slightly chance-based sequence. At the beginning of this excerpt, there are relatively straightforward single cymbal hits that coincide with both kick and snare, but as the phrase progresses, the syncopations develop.

Pattern 04_19

Crescendo (plural crescendos or crescendi).
This term is used to describe a musical phrase that gets louder over its duration. Getting quieter is termed either diminuendo or decrescendo.

MORE DETAILED ONE-SHOT PROGRAMMING

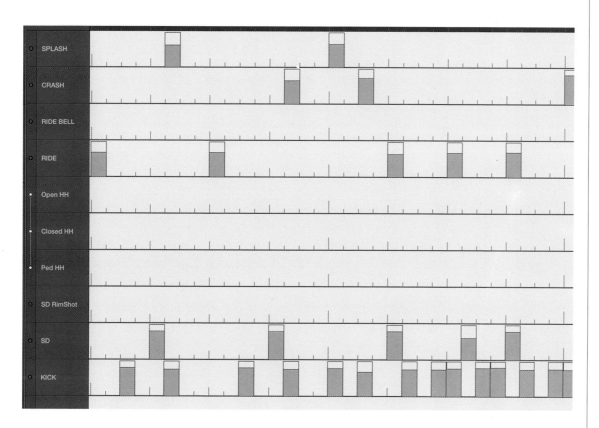

Bars seven and eight of Pattern 04_19: crash and splash variations.

The hi-hat on beat 2 of bar seven has been deleted. This is because there is a splash on beat 2e, and at this tempo, a human would find it difficult to play both hands on the backbeat on beat two immediately followed by a cymbal, one 16th-note later, and would likely sacrifice the hi-hat at this point. This technique is repeated on beat 4.

Notice that there is a 'double crash' on beat 1 of bar eight and the following eighth-note. Including the preceding beat 4e, we have actually played a crash, a splash followed by another crash, and it is generally a good idea to orchestrate rapid successive simple accents between multiple cymbals. Although an acoustic cymbal can respond to fast double hits, when programming one-shots, a more natural result is obtained by spreading the load. The note on beat 1& might seem unusual at first, but clusters of cymbal hits such as this can provide great little explosions in your music if placed tastefully.

TIP
Most DAWs have a one-
click function for cutting
regions into many sections
of the same length; find out
if yours has these functions
and practise using this
technique along with
shuffle-editing.

*Bars 12 and 13 of Pattern
04_19: crash and splash
variations.*

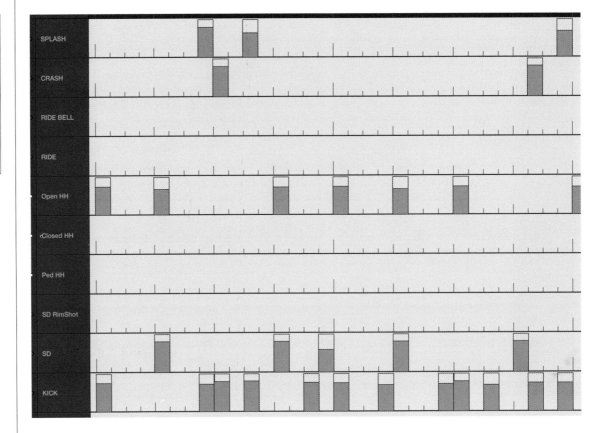

Pattern 04_20

Bars 12 and 13 feature similar techniques, but with different phrases, and indeed this approach is used through to the end of the excerpt.

PATTERN 04_20: Derived from Pattern 04_12 in the hand-to-hand style, with added splashes, crashes, and open hi-hats. Four repeats of the original two-bar pattern at 116bpm. Again, notice the use of the pedal hi-hat. In general, when closing an opened hi-hat we have simply struck it again with the closed sound. When drummers are doing this however they very often hit the hi-hat simultaneously as it is closed, but the difference in sound from just hitting it whilst closed is very subtle. For this reason, we have not generally bothered adding pedal hi-hat parts. Here however, for an extra touch of authenticity when playing in the hand-to-hand style, we have added pedal notes when the hand would be striking either the snare drum or the splash.

Once again, the effect is subtle, but programming in this fashion will help you to develop the ability to think like a drummer. Besides, subtle is good.

CHAPTER 4

MORE DETAILED ONE-SHOT PROGRAMMING

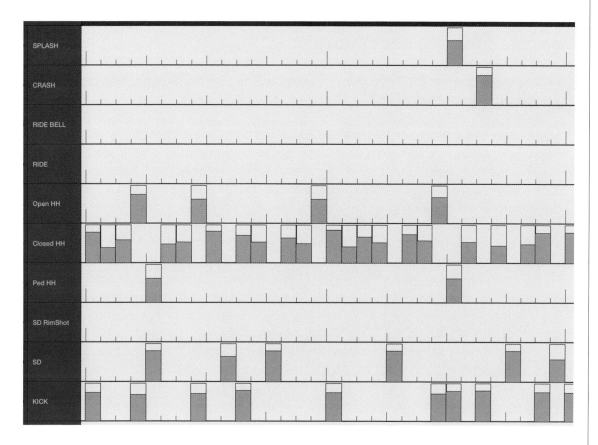

Bars five and six of Pattern 04_20: punctuating the hand-to-hand hi-hat style with open hi-hats and cymbals.

Exercise One: Pick one of the beats that you have programmed from an earlier exercise, repeat it several times, and experiment with a number of open hi-hats in different placements over its length.

Exercise Two: Now, in this new sequence, select all the open hi-hats that landed simultaneously with either a snare or a kick, and transpose them to become crashes for a different effect.

Exercise Three: Take another of your own beats, make a copy of it, then repeat it a few times. In the repeats, break up the ostinato of the hi-hats by adding a mixture of crashes and open hi-hats that align with the kick/snare pattern. Edit together a longer sequence of the original beat interspersed with some of these new variations every so often..

104

THE
DRUM
PROGRAMMING
HANDBOOK

MORE DETAILED ONE-SHOT PROGRAMMING

FINDING THE FUNK: GHOST NOTES

Have you ever noticed that drummers often seem to be playing quiet notes on the snare as they play a groove? Often, you cannot even seem to hear these notes, and you might wonder why they are bothering…

These notes are called ghost notes, and are a slick trick used by pro drummers to make relatively simple beats bounce along and give a great feel that the band play off and the audience dance to, even if they cannot hear the actual notes! Strange? Well, programming these notes is a great way to spice up your basic patterns, so let's experiment with adding ghost notes to one of the earlier beats, and you can make up your own mind. The thing to remember is that ghost notes are really quiet. You should only just be able to hear them, and they should not alter the main kick/snare pattern. If you make them too loud, then the whole thing will get very lumpy.

We'll start with the first bar of Pattern 03_11 from earlier. It has straight eighth-notes on the hi-hat, and we are going to fill in some of the 16th-note 'spaces' in between them with ghost notes to try to get a more rolling, funky feel. Using the mouse, just click in some more snare drum hits on the e's and the a's. In the following example, we have done most of the available spaces, but avoided the ones immediately before the backbeats for the reason that drummers often find this difficult to play, but you can put them in there if you wish. It will sound fine.

The same often applies to any kick hits that land on beats e or a. Of course, depending on the way your system is set up, the mouse might enter all these notes at a set velocity, and this is very probably going to be too loud for our purposes here and the result will be pretty horrible. Do not worry, we will fix this in a minute.

■ **CHECK OUT**

The Usher song 'Caught Up'. Its sparse arrangement is underpinned by ghost notes that drive the groove, and they are quite easy to hear, which is not always the case.

CHAPTER 4

MORE DETAILED ONE-SHOT PROGRAMMING

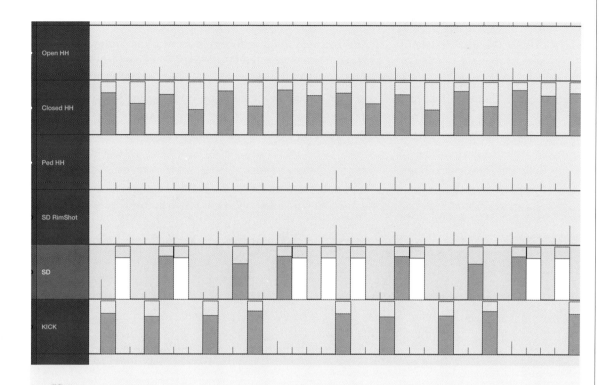

Pattern 04_21: Extra snare drums added on the 16th-note offbeats. The newly input notes are highlighted.

Pattern 04_21

PATTERN 04_21: First of all twice through pattern 03_11 for a re-cap, then twice with the added snare drum hits at 116bpm. For now, you should have something like the above.

PATTERN 04_22: Pattern 04_21 with the velocities reduced to form ghost notes. Two repeats of a two-bar phrase at 116bpm. Now select all the snare drum notes except those on beats 2 and 4. An easy way to do this on most DAWs is to select all the snares, then shift-click beats 2 and 4, which will remove them from the selection, leaving you with only 'all the others' selected. Now you can click on one of these 'others' and drag the velocities down until only those notes become ghosts; do not be afraid of going too quiet for this; it is all about feel!

Suddenly, the beat is getting more professional sounding, and certainly funkier. Notice that we have also reduced the volume of the snare in bar one on 3e, just to keep the smooth feel going and to create a two-bar phrase by virtue of keeping the loud note in the second bar.

Pattern 04_22: The extra snare drums with greatly reduced velocities.

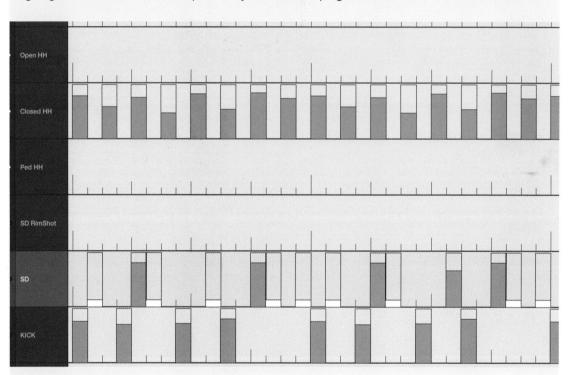

Now for another trick. Something that drummers often do is to play the ghost notes at slightly different volumes, partly because they are humans, and partly because this is another way to deliberately add life to the pattern, perhaps even allowing some of the ghosts to get a bit

CHAPTER 4

MORE DETAILED ONE-SHOT PROGRAMMING

THE
DRUM
PROGRAMMING
HANDBOOK

107

louder than ghosts should really be – we can do this with editing. This could even start to change the main impression of the kick/snare pattern, but we will be sparing with our edits here so as not to be too disruptive.

With your mouse, adjust the velocities of all the ghost notes a little bit up or down, just one at a time. Try to keep them all very quiet on the whole, but you might like to make just the occasional one quite a bit louder. Choosing the notes right after the backbeats for this can sound a bit unnatural, but as ever, it is up to you.

■ **CHECK OUT**
Omar Hakim – Listen to the second half of the Daft Punk track 'Giorgio By Moroder' from *Random Access Memories*. Ghost notes, open hi-hats, syncopated snare patterns, accented 16th-notes on the hi-hat… it is all there!

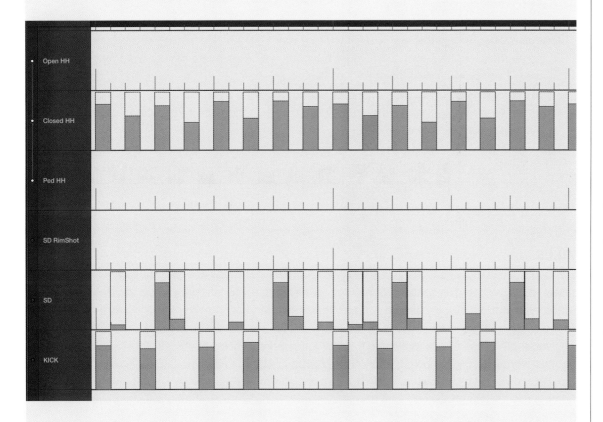

Pattern 04_23: Human-like variations in the ghost-note velocities.

 Pattern 04_23

PATTERN 04_23: Four repeats of Pattern 04_22 with the velocities modified over the duration, to form a single eight-bar phrase at 116bpm. You can see the subtle velocity adjustments – a little goes a long way with this technique. Also notice the extra note that has been added on beat 1& every second bar. There is a natural two 16th-note space between

the kick drum hits here, and a drummer might respond to this by filling that space. Also look at the snare every second bar on 3e. We have reduced the volume of this to not exactly a ghost note, but a quiet note that gives a little bounce to the pattern.

So, compare what you have now created to the beat that you started with. It is the same beat, but there is something magical and funky about it, something that is quite hard to put your finger on, even when listening carefully. This technique forms the basis of many, many programming approaches in almost all styles of music, and the more you develop it, the more 'pro' your programming will sound.

Exercise One: Recreate something similar to Pattern 04_23. After saving what you have done, make another copy of the eight bars, and edit the ghosts slightly differently this time. Perhaps even delete one or two. This could even be used to make a long flowing 16-bar phrase if combined with the earlier eight bars.

Exercise Two: Change the occasional kick drum note in the pattern too, either adding to it or removing one that is already there.

Exercise Three: Try this approach with different patterns altogether, and think about ways to optimize your workflow in such procedures. Reading the MIDI editing section of your DAW manual will often reveal great shortcuts and tricks.

FILLS

A drum fill, also known as a fill-in or just fill, is a flurry of notes to raise the intensity level of the music, possibly between sections of a song, for instance going into the chorus. An important thing to remember about fills is where they finish; it is very often beat 1 of the first bar of the next section of the song, and this is often a kick drum and crash hit, played simultaneously.

The length of the fill is a matter for musical judgement. A good starting point is two beats long, in other words starting on beat 3 in order to finish on beat 1 of (say) the chorus. Having said that, one beat, three beats or even a whole bar or more can be completely appropriate in the right context too. Drummers usually love fills and spend a large amount of their lives learning new and ever more complicated variations.

We are now going to learn to program a few fills. These however, are just starting points and many more approaches in different genres will be discussed later. In order to keep the focus on the fill, we will use Pattern 03_08 for this at the moment.

CHAPTER 4

MORE DETAILED ONE-SHOT PROGRAMMING

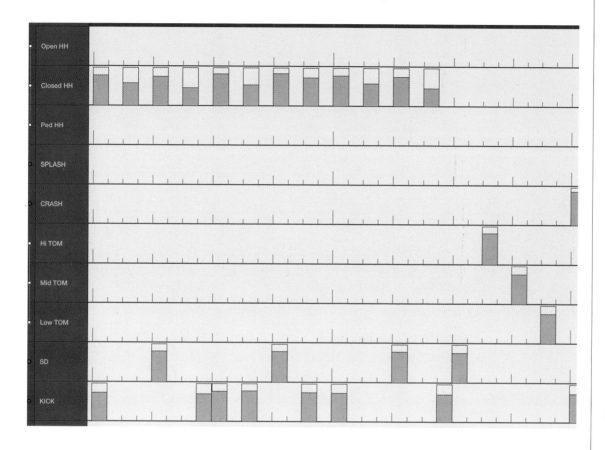

Pattern 04_24: An eighth-note drum fill.

PATTERN 04_24: This is a two beat long fill that uses a succession of eighth-notes, which have replaced all other elements of the groove for their duration. A two-bar phrase played twice at 120bpm. Although simple it is very effective; try sequencing the four 'fill notes' in a different order too.

110

THE
DRUM
PROGRAMMING
HANDBOOK

MORE DETAILED ONE-SHOT PROGRAMMING

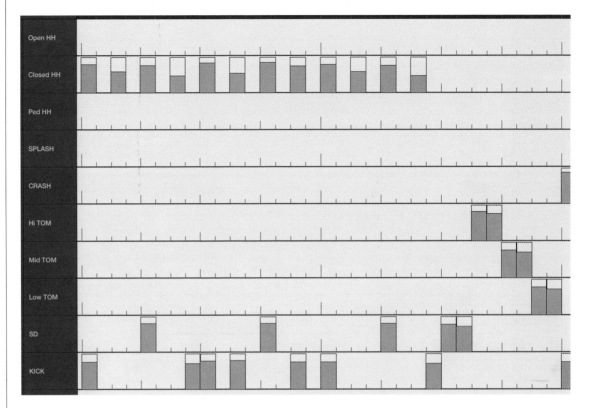

Pattern 04_25: A 16th-note drum fill.

PATTERN 04_25: This fill is similar to the previous one except that it uses 16th-notes – two on each drum. Notice that the second of each pair has a slightly lower velocity, which helps it to sound a bit more realistic. The phrasing could be considered natural for a human drummer going 'round the drums'.

Exercise One: Starting with Pattern 04_25, try deleting the kick drum on beat 2a, or making it a snare instead; notice the musical effect of each.

Exercise Two: Delete a number of different combinations of the eight 'fill notes' and consider the musical effect in each case.

Exercise Three: Scramble the order of the eight hits in a number of different ways, and try to remember your approach if you stumble upon any particular patterns that you like.

CHAPTER 4

MORE DETAILED ONE-SHOT PROGRAMMING

PATTERN 04_26: Here we have the same groove looped, but with different 16th-note fills after every two bars. You will be able to listen to the audio and follow it sequentially through the next six diagrams.

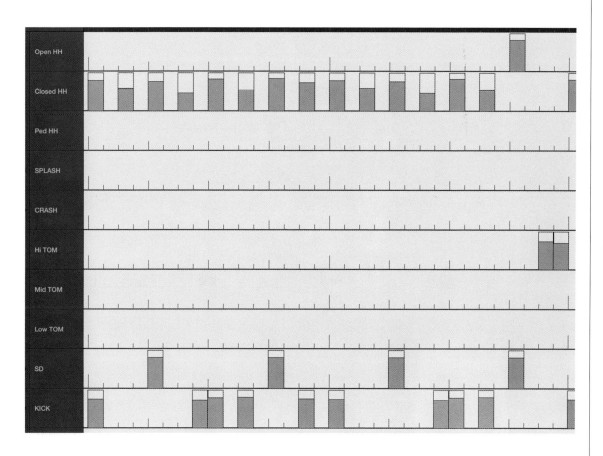

Pattern 04_26

Pattern 04_26: Bars one and two.

The first fill at the end of bar two is simply an open hi-hat on beat four, held open, and then the last two 16-notes on the hi tom, giving a very short and punchy fill.

CHAPTER 4

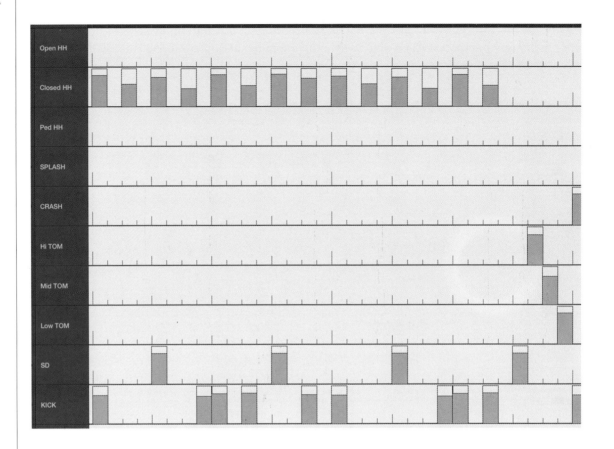

Pattern 04_26: Bars three and four.

The next fill at the end of bar four is the last four 16th-notes of the bar, each on a different drum.

MORE DETAILED ONE-SHOT PROGRAMMING

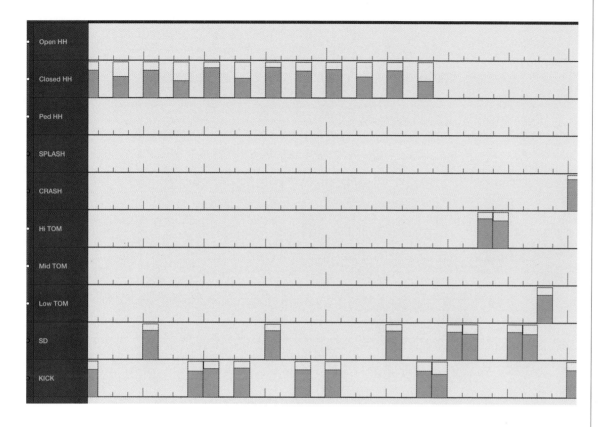

Pattern 04_26: Bars five and six.

The fill in bar six is similar to the one from Pattern 04_25, but it adds an extra kick drum on beat 2&, giving a double kick hit to set things up, and then plays pairs of notes in the sequence: snare, hi tom, snare, and then a single hit on the lo tom, creating a slight tension before beat 1.

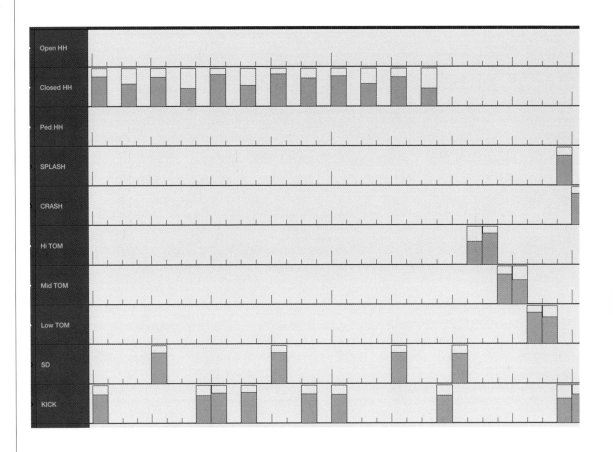

Pattern 04_26: Bars seven and eight.

Again we have a 16th-note round-the-drums fill, but after a single snare-hit on beat 3, pairs of tom notes are displaced by a 16th-note, and beat 4a is a kick drum and splash, giving a double crash effect as we land on beat 1. Overall, this gives a more rolling feel.

MORE DETAILED ONE-SHOT PROGRAMMING

THE
DRUM
PROGRAMMING
HANDBOOK

115

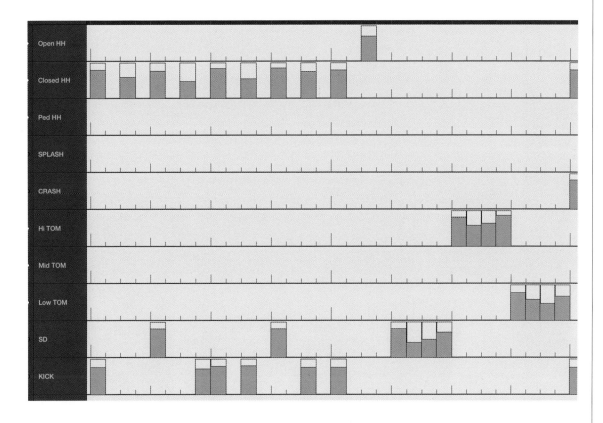

*Pattern 04_26: Bars nine
and ten.*

This fill plays groups of four 16th-notes starting on beat 2, in the order snare, hi tom, lo tom. Notice the velocities in the clusters of 16th-notes. Such phrasing helps stop the fill sounding too mechanical; experiment with other velocity patterns too.

LINEAR PLAYING

In mathematics, linear means 'in a line'. In drumming it means that only one thing is hit at a time, in other words there will not be the familiar hi-hat and snare simultaneously on the backbeat – for instance, there could only be one or the other. There have been many systems of linear playing devised to produce both beats and fills on the drum kit.

*Pattern 04_26: Bars eleven
and twelve.*

POLYMETRES

A polymetre can be
implemented when we have an
odd-numbered grouping of
notes repeating whilst playing
note values that have a
different 'natural' grouping. An
example of this would be using
groups of three 16th-notes,
which of course naturally occur
in groups of four in each beat.
Four groups of three (a total of
12 notes) can fit
mathematically into three
quarter-notes, thus giving us
what might be called 'four
against three', which will sound
as if it could be four beats-
worth of triplets playing at a
different tempo, thus creating a
rhythmic tension that resolves
after the three quarter-notes.
The longer that the group of
three repeats for, the greater
the rhythmic tension that is
created. This mathematical
approach is a commonly used
technique (although often by
'feel' alone), and many other
combinations of groupings are
possible.

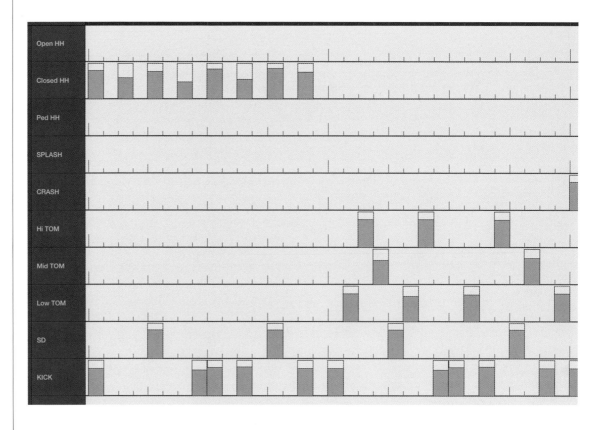

The last fill in this pattern uses a concept called linear playing. In the last bar, the kick and snare
pattern is exactly the same as it would have been in the groove. All available 16th-notes that do
not have a drum hit are filled with tom notes, just one hit on each tom. The particular order of toms
is quite similar to what a drummer might play without crossing their arms over; try to figure this out.

The effect is that of a punchy fill with a mixture of kick drum and toms, and an element of
groove from the backbeat that is still embedded in there. This sort of technique takes years for a
drummer to develop, but programming linear phrases is very easy indeed once you understand the
concept.

MORE DETAILED ONE-SHOT PROGRAMMING

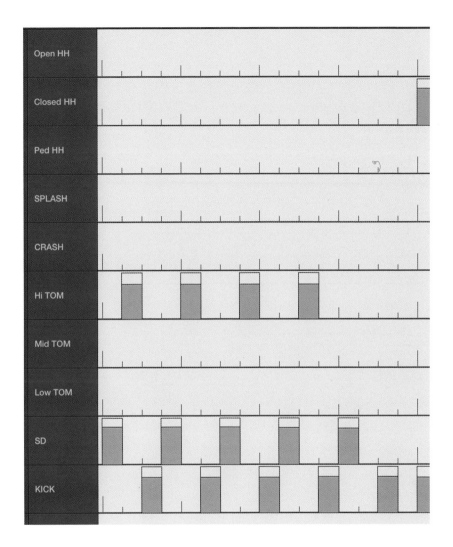

Pattern 04_27: Various applications of a four-against-three polymetric fill. Bar two.

PATTERN 04_27: An eight-bar passage at 120bpm constructed from four two-bar phrases. Each phrase has one bar of the previous beat, then one bar of a 'four against three' polymetric fill. The first fill uses the three 16th-note sequence: snare, hi tom, kick drum. This is repeated four times, and finishes naturally back on a snare on beat four. A single kick drum on beat 4& fills up the rest of the bar. If you tune in to listen to the snare you will hear that it plays a steady pulse, but moving against the actual beat, and similarly with the kick drum.

Pattern 04_27

118

THE
DRUM
PROGRAMMING
HANDBOOK

MORE DETAILED ONE-SHOT PROGRAMMING

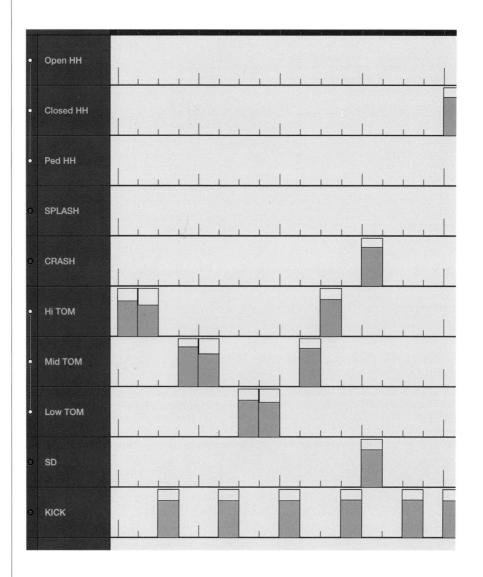

Pattern 04_27: Bar four.

This fill uses a sequence of: tom, tom, kick. Again, it is repeated four times, but this time we play on a different tom on each repeat, with the last cluster of three split between two toms (since we had technically moved all the way round the drum kit after the third group). A snare and crash give a solid resolution on beat four.

MORE DETAILED ONE-SHOT PROGRAMMING

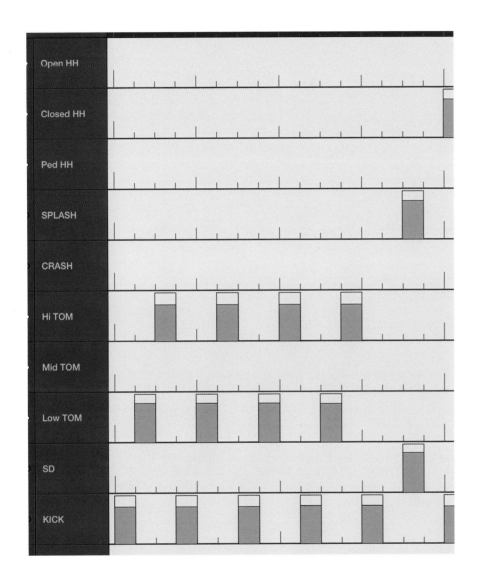

Pattern 04_27: Bar six.

This feels slightly different, since we are starting each three-note group on the kick drum, and indeed it is the kick that resolves onto beat four. Again, we play a note on beat 4&, this time with snare and splash cymbal.

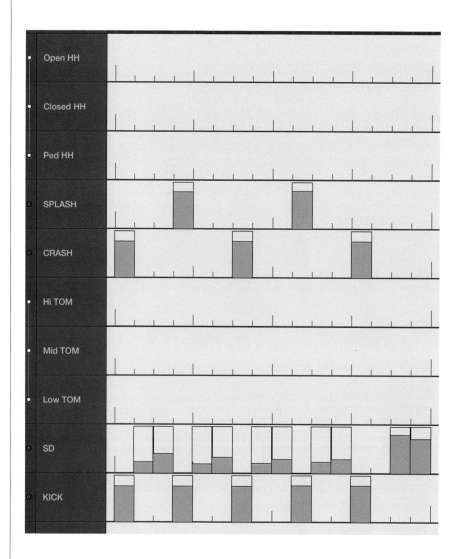

Pattern 04_27: Bar eight.

The last fill takes a slightly different approach that you might imagine the drummer playing with his hands in a sequence of: 'right, left, left', doubling up the right hand with a kick drum. The left-hand plays ghost notes on the snare, whilst the right moves between two cymbals. This fill is rounded off with two 16th-notes that would flow nicely into the following bar.

Any group of three notes will work well in this context, but be aware that if you want the polymetric tension, then at least one note of each group will have to be on the same drum and played loudly.

CHAPTER 4

MORE DETAILED ONE-SHOT PROGRAMMING

THE
DRUM
PROGRAMMING
HANDBOOK

121

Exercise One: Create a one-bar fill of 16th-notes, and delete a single 16th-note from each beat. Try the same 16th-note in each beat, and also different ones in each. Think about the musical effect.

Exercise Two: Take some of your fills, and edit them so that they finish on beat four rather than running all the way to beat 1. Think about ways to make this work, for instance having either a kick or a snare with a crash on beat 4, and rest until one.

Exercise Three: Either by taking a kick drum pattern from another groove, or using one of your own, create a linear fill in the style of the above in a two-bar phrase. Copy the result, and in the repeated instance, edit the linear bit differently to achieve a different result. Play back both in sequence to hear the contrast between the two.

Things to experiment with

- Try different tempos
- Choose different drum kits
- Transpose individual components of the beat to different drums
- Add notes
- Remove notes
- Program variations on a given theme
- Add subtle embellishments over a number of repeats
- Develop fills that roll out of the phrasing
- Try to fit crashes, open hi-hats and fills into the kick and snare pattern
- Push the beats into a number of different genres
- See if you can develop a groove using polymeters.

CONCLUSION

We have developed our rhythmic feels through 16th-notes, triplets and shuffle, and discovered the usefulness of ostinatos and polyrhythms, and the musical punctuation of crashes, open hi-hats, and fills. In the next chapter, we will move towards more synthetic sounds and discover the power of the sampled loop.

Check that you can:
- Construct 16th-note based grooves, and control the dynamics of the hi-hat to provide interest.
- Produce interesting beats using both triplet and shuffle feels.
- Understand what an ostinato is, and be able to use such a phrase creatively in a number of different ways.
- Use crashes, open hi-hat, and the ride cymbal bell in many different parts of the bar to create special effects to decorate your grooves.
- Create a number of different lengths of fill using several different techniques to different effect.
- Understand how to use simple polyrhythms.

CHAPTER 4

SAMPLERS

CHAPTER 5

SAMPLERS

THE
DRUM
PROGRAMMING
HANDBOOK

123

We are now going to look at the possibilities offered by samplers. These devices offer an infinite palette of sounds and allow rhythmic phrases to be played back from a single note. Not only can we build upon the techniques developed so far with one-shots, we can start to manipulate audio loops – the name given to a single recording of an entire beat. The creative possibilities are exciting.

THE SAMPLER

A sampler is a device that can play back pre-recorded audio triggered from a MIDI note; we will refer to this audio as a sample. This sample might be a recording of a single acoustic drum hit (as indeed we have been using so far), a recording of a more synthetic drum-type sound, or a recording of an entire rhythmic phrase, perhaps played by a human, perhaps programmed or just recorded from somewhere. The manufacturer might supply the sample, but a defining feature of the sampler is that you can also use your own. Many samplers can also change the pitch of the recording in piano-like musical intervals by playing it back on different MIDI keys; samplers are not just for drums. Samplers typically offer a large array of tools for manipulating their samples to generate all manner of sound design and performance possibilities.

Some DAWs come with their own native samplers; examples of this are EXS24 in Logic Pro, Simpler and Sampler in Ableton Live and Groove Agent SE4 in Cubase. There are also numerous third-party applications such as Native Instruments' Kontakt and Battery, and iZotope's Iris. All such devices have unique features, although at their most basic level they do the same sort of thing. Some are optimised for working with drums whereas others are designed for broader applications. Unlike their hardware predecessors, modern software samplers are generally unable to record audio themselves; recording is generally done in the host DAW, and the resulting audio file found by browsing or dragged into the sampler.

It does not matter which model you use or prefer, it is how you use it to realise the principles discussed here that matters. So please be prepared to read the relevant parts of your sampler manual and perhaps look at some tutorials online.

ONE-SHOT SAMPLES

With any acoustic-style drum kit, the sounds will be generally more or less appropriate to a given context. Once you start experimenting with synthetic sonic textures that can range from the shortest click to a cataclysmic explosion (and with each described as some sort of snare), it is possible to get it very wrong. You need to audition lots of sounds with care, whatever you are doing.

We are going to start by using some sounds from PlugInGuru's Mega Macho Drums plugin. As well as 'instant production', it gives you quite a head start with organisation and playback too. You can use whatever plugin you have or prefer.

SYNTHETIC SOUNDS

Here, we are using the term 'synthetic sound' to mean something that does not sound like a natural-sounding acoustic drum kit. Synthetic sounds might be derived from an acoustic kit but subsequently processed in some way so that they sound different (perhaps even to the point of being unrecognisable). Or they might come from an old drum machine or synthesizer. They might be audio recordings, not terribly similar to the parts of a drum kit that they represent, yet able to function in this capacity. For example, the sound of a car door slamming can be used as a kick drum.

CHAPTER 5

124

THE
DRUM
PROGRAMMING
HANDBOOK

SAMPLERS

ASSIGNING DRUMS TO MIDI NOTES

There is a standard way of assigning particular drums to particular MIDI notes. It is called General
MIDI (GM). Many manufacturers comply with this keyboard layout, and it ensures for example that
a kick drum always plays on note C1. This means that if you have a sequence that is sending out
C1, when you change the kit or instrument you will get a different kick drum from these notes, and
not a triangle. Not all manufacturers subscribe to this, particularly as some kits feature multiple kick
drums, for instance, and GM can only specify two. As we start working with alternative drum kits
on existing sequences, it is worth being aware of this. It can also influence us when we build our
own kits in a sampler.

GM STANDARD DRUM MAP

*The GM drum map shows
how drums are assigned
to MIDI notes.*

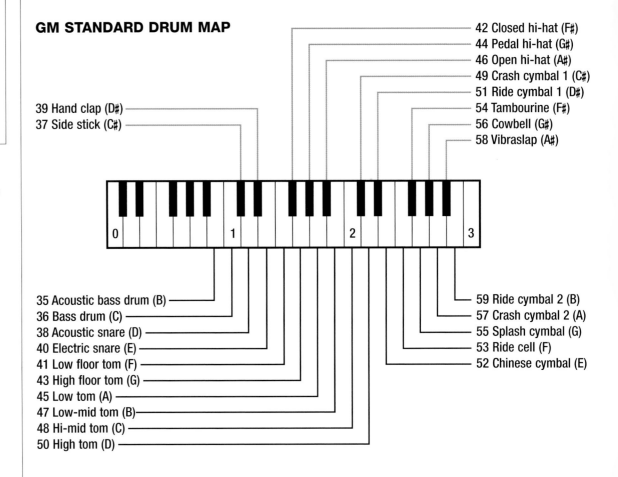

SAMPLERS

PATTERN 05_01: This is simply the eight-bar Pattern 04_23 played with a sampled kit (instead of the original acoustic one – see p107) at a tempo of 170bpm to give a drum & bass feel. The hi-hat sound has a chiptune quality to it, the snare is huge and processed and the kick has an electronic punch to it. It plays back with a machine-like quality by design.

Pattern 05_01

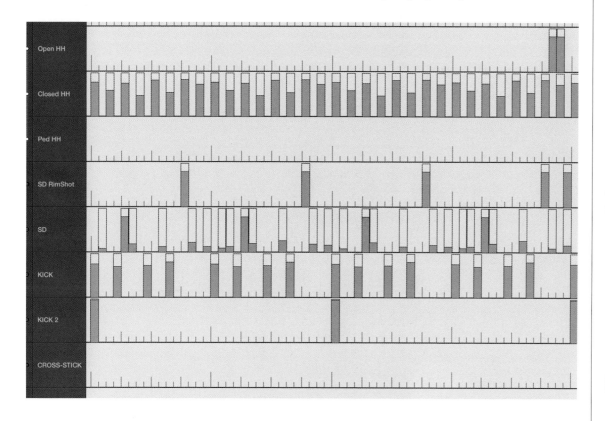

Pattern 05_02: Bars one to four.

Pattern 05_02

PATTERN 05_02: Pattern 05_01 with some added embellishments. One repeat. Funk is turned into drum and bass just by changing kit and tempo. Notice the extra notes here and there.

We have added a second kick drum on the lane labelled Kick 2: a long subsonic sound reminiscent of the Roland TR-808 on beat 1 of every second bar. There is also a second processed snare drum on beat 4 of each bar in the first half, on the lane labelled SD RimShot, but only once in the second half to give an asymmetric feel over the eight-bar duration. This sound also combines with a metallic noise that is shown on the lane labelled Open HH at the end of bar four. Finally, there is a high-pitched snare drum, on the lane labelled Cross-Stick, playing a fill in the last bar.

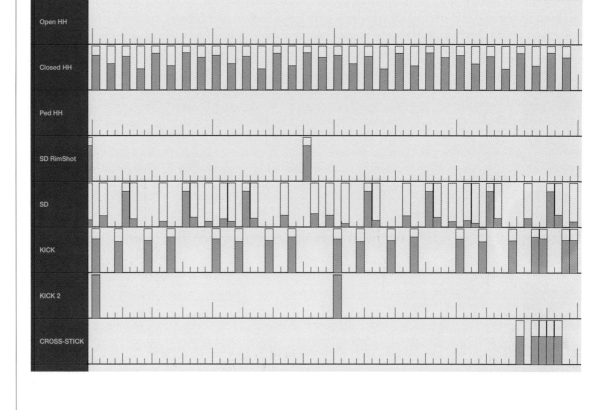

Bars five to eight of Pattern 05_02.

TIP

When working with synthetic drum kits, you often have to get used to having the 'wrong sounds' represented on your grids since synthetic kits do not always map onto the more common acoustic name-sets precisely. You can usually customise the displayed names in the DAW if you wish.

SAMPLERS

THE
DRUM
PROGRAMMING
HANDBOOK

127

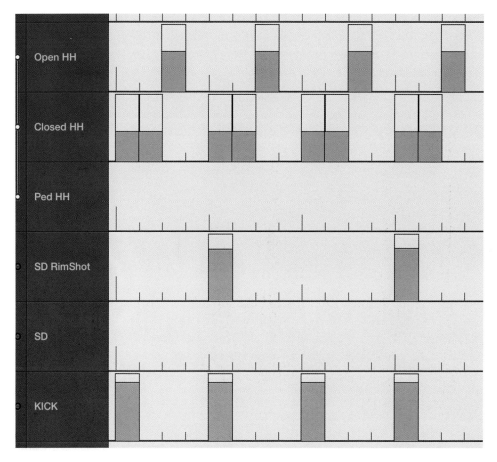

Pattern 05_03: The distinctive visual framework of a house beat.

Pattern 05_03

PATTERN 05_03: An outline of the classic house pattern with three repeats at 126bpm. The velocities of each component of this beat are identical, giving an unashamed mechanical feel; this is a common stylistic feature of electronic genres. The kick drum pattern on every quarter-note (crotchet) is known historically as 'four on the floor' regardless of genre. The sound on every offbeat is an open hi-hat, although it is common to take liberties with the authenticity of this. It is often offset with some closed hi-hat sounds, here on the two 16th-notes preceding each offbeat. The backbeat sound is often a clap, shown here on the lane labelled SD RimShot. In a musical arrangement, it is common to bring in this house beat in layers, one instrument at a time, playing for multiples of four bars before introducing the next drum.

Since we are working with one-shots in electronica, it is a good moment to introduce the idea of the machine-gun drum roll. This is a programming technique that makes no effort to sound human, and quite often plays much faster than any human could. It is common in many electronic genres, but we will use it here in the fashion of a build in a house tune.

Pattern 05_04

Pattern 05_04: Notice the angular appearance of the rolls and the way the notes get closer and closer together over the two bars.

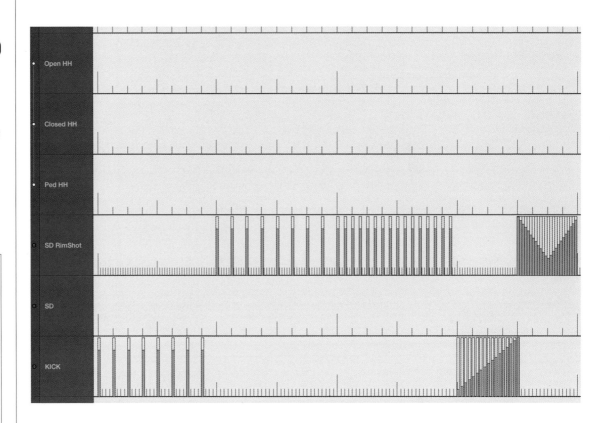

TIP
If you want to build up/break down your house beat in layers and keep easy visual control of this in the arrangement, then you might wish to use a number of tracks in your DAW all pointing to the same plug-in, programming only kick drum on one track, snare on another, hi-hat on another, etc. A common trick is to start with the offbeat hi-hat, which on its own fools the listener into feeling it as the onbeat, thus giving a rhythmic lurch when the kick comes in, apparently moving the beat by an eighth-note (quaver).

PATTERN 05_04: Two bars of Pattern 05_03 followed by a two-bar synthetic roll, and then another two bars of Pattern 05_03, all at 126bpm. At first glance, this diagram appears rather strange. Visually, the notes feature very thin bars. This is because we use some extremely fast note-values towards the end of the phrase and if they were the typical 16th-note (semiquaver) thickness that we are more familiar with, they would overlap dramatically and look messy in the fastest bits. Notice that the grid is still in 16th-notes in the upper part of the diagram; this helps our eyes keep track of the timeline, but is not essential. To change the note-values that you are inputting, alter the grid in the editor of your DAW.

The first two beats have 16th-notes on the kick, followed by 16th-notes on the snare for the

SAMPLERS

THE
DRUM
PROGRAMMING
HANDBOOK

129

second half of the bar. These all have identical velocities. You will have some sort of tool in your DAW to help create these; you can probably set the mouse to be a pencil or line tool that draws multiple notes as you drag it. In the second bar, the first two beats on the snare are 32nd-notes (demisemiquavers). Beat 3 is 64th-notes (hemidemisemiquavers) on the kick drum and you will notice the crescendo that has been drawn over the top of the phrase. Finally, the snare is played at 96th-notes (triplet hemidemisemiquavers) over the last beat with a rather geometric-looking velocity ramp. The overall feeling is of accelerating into the following section of the tune.

Exercise One: Try using a number of different one-shot sampler kits on these beats. Experiment by transposing various parts of the kit to different notes (many sampler kits have multiple kick or snare drums for instance).

Exercise Two: Add a number of rhythmic phrases using interesting sounds in your kit to the basic phrases given here, for instance percussion-type sounds or second kicks or snares; experiment with velocities.

Exercise Three: Experiment with creating machine-gun rolls in a drum & bass style and tempo. Use all the different grid values (including triplet options, if you have them) on different drums and work with velocity ramps. Try some very short phrases in the midst of beats as well as the more obvious longer ones.

TUNING A SAMPLED LOOP

If an audio version of an entire rhythmic phrase is assigned to be triggered by a single MIDI note, it might be termed a sampled loop, or just loop.

PATTERN 05_05: The eight-bar Pattern 05_01 once through at 95bpm. To make our own custom loop, we need to play back and record this pattern as audio. This is sometimes referred to as bouncing, or bouncing to disk – consult your DAW manual if you are unsure of how to do this, and be careful of file formats to ensure optimal compatibility with your sampler. The sonically inferior MP3 is not a good idea. Supposing we wish to play back one bar of Pattern 05_05 in a tune that is at 136 bpm; the sampler provides one option for doing so.

■ **CHECK OUT**

Aphex Twin on 'Bucephalus Bouncing Ball' from *Come To Daddy*. You will hear lots of glitching and stuttering noises that were programmed in the machine-gun roll style.

Pattern 05_05

TIP

When you are bouncing to disk in order to create an audio file to be used in a sampler, it is vital that the sample starts, and possibly ends, in the right place. There are a number of approaches for this. For the moment, we will only ensure that the bounce starts precisely at the beginning of the phrase that you are recording; thus the resulting audio file will start there – at the beginning. You can also specify the end of the sample in a waveform editor often with a marker labelled 'E', and further, you can even crop the audio to form a new audio file that starts and ends as you have specified. Be very careful here, since this process can be destructive. In other words, it can permanently affect the source audio, and you might find that you wanted that end portion at some point in the future. Always be generous when defining the end of your sample. The end can generally be specified by either the length of MIDI note that triggers the sample or a designated end-point, and this is non-destructive. If you edit just a little bit too tightly, then it can cause problems when repeating the sample. It is probably better to include a little bit of the following downbeat In the raw audio; once tuned, you will not hear this.

Samplers have virtual containers that hold and trigger the audio associated with each MIDI note, and these are frequently called zones or keyzones. Each zone might be associated with any number of MIDI notes, from one to many, and the actual number of notes that a zone spans is called the key-range. If a zone has a key-range that covers several notes, then it is likely that each playing each key within that range will transpose the sample. The key on which the note sounds at its original pitch is generally termed the root (or root key), and is typically assigned when you import audio into your sampler. Playing a key above the root will make the sample higher-pitched and faster, and playing below the root will be lower-pitched and slower.

If a zone is only associated with a single key, then that key will play back the sample at a pitch and speed proportionate to the key's interval from the designated root – which could even lie outside the key-range. Of course, if that key is designated as the root, then it will play back the sample unaltered. Samplers also offer the ability to tune a sample's playback relative to its root, independently from key-range transposition.

PITCH AND TIME

Our perception of pitch is derived from the number of times that an object vibrates per second. Consider a guitar string; if you pluck it, it vibrates back and forwards moving the air around it, and the speed of these vibrations tells our ears which note is being played. Imagine that this string vibrates 500 times per second. If you were to finger higher up the neck, effectively shortening the string, then we would perceive this as a higher pitch; in fact, the laws of physics mean that the shorter string must vibrate faster, in other words moving back and forward more times per second.

If we were to sample the original note (that is, record it) for one second, we would capture all 500 vibrations. If we were then to play it back on the piano keyboard on a higher key, it would sound at a higher pitch; samplers are designed to do this by playing the sample back faster, just like shortening a string. Because we have recorded exactly 500 vibrations, if they happen faster, then the duration of the note must be shortened (imagine how long it takes to walk 500 paces and compare this with how long it takes to run 500 paces). In this scenario, pitch and time are inextricably linked.

Suppose now that we sample a rhythmic phrase, for example a recording of a drummer playing a beat. If we play this back on a higher key, then two things will happen; it will be faster and also higher-pitched. The converse is also true, that is, if we play it on a lower key then it will be slower and lower-pitched. An interval of an octave represents a doubling or halving of pitch, and speed will also be doubled or halved accordingly.

SAMPLERS

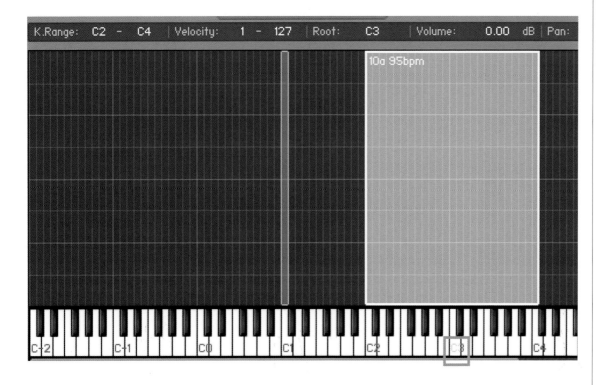

| K.Range: | C2 - C4 | Velocity: | 1 - 127 | Root: | C3 | Volume: | 0.00 | dB | Pan: |

How zones might typically appear on your sampler.

The above diagram illustrates how zones might appear on your sampler. On the left, on the key C1, only a single sample will play back. The broader zone on the right will play back samples spread over the two octave key-range, up and down from C3 (marked). Since this zone is currently selected (hence highlighted) its parameters can be seen along the top. Its root note is designated as C3, and so this key will play at the correct pitch and speed; C4 will play back with the pitch raised by an octave and twice as fast, and C2 down an octave at half-speed. Notice the parameter labelled as 'K.Range' which in this sampler (NI Kontakt) is the numerical indication of the key-range of the zone.

In order to make our loop fit the new tempo exactly, there are several things that we must do. First, enter a note in your piano-roll editor that starts exactly on beat 1 and lasts for a duration of exactly one bar with a pitch of C3 (even though the whole sample is longer). This will play back the sample at its original tempo. With the DAW set to our desired 136bpm, press play. The result will be very ugly; horribly out of time, playing roughly three beats before being forced back to the beginning of the sample. Now drag the note up a tone onto D3. As it plays, you will hear a higher pitch with punchier drum sounds, and the result will be playing back the entire loop except about the last eighth-note. Now move the note up to E3; it will play back in time, but does feel a little lumpy.

CHAPTER 5

It is close, but we are not there yet. What we have done so far might be termed coarse-tuning, in other words in half-steps/semitones, to the closest one. We now need to find the parameter for the *zone* that allows us to fine-tune in cents (1/100th of a half-step). First, in the piano-roll, edit the note to now last and cycle for two bars, and drop it an octave to C2. It will now play back at half-speed with a pleasing industrial feel, but since it is at half-speed, the timing error as it wraps around is doubled and therefore easier to hear.

Using the zone fine-tuning control, increase the tuning by 40 cents. You will hear a characteristic double hit as the note wraps around; this means that the first playback pass has reached the downbeat of the second bar of the sample, and immediately after this the DAW is looping back and re-triggering from the very first downbeat. Too fast! Be aware that after each adjustment you have to let the sample retrigger and play through in order to appraise the tuning.

Setting the tuning to between 20 and 30 cents provides a reasonable groove, and to some extent you can go by feel now since you have achieved reasonable accuracy. If you want to be more accurate than this, but cannot quite hear which way to go, then extend the note to be four bars long, extend the zone down a further octave and play back a C1; retune. Notice that we have not used the metronome. Sometimes in this situation it can be more confusing than helpful. By all means use it as and when you find it useful.

In case you are thinking that you never wanted an industrial 'slow motion' feel, please understand that we went through this procedure simply to get accurate tuning of the timing. Now that we have the tuning offset, go back to the one-bar E3 note playing once. It should be tight and rocking, and the one-bar note can be placed and repeated as necessary in your arrangement.

Of course, there is no reason why you could not have done the entire tuning process with a pitch control knob. Try both to see which method you prefer. In reality, both are useful in different contexts.

TIP

For efficiency of layout, you might wish to edit the key-range of the zone to be only one half-step wide on the E3, but if when building a playable kit, you instead prefer to have this zone playing back from another single key of your choice, you will have to be careful. Suppose you want the zone to now live only on C3. This key also happens to be the root, and so this might seem logical, but actually, you could choose any key. Dragging the zone down four half-steps to C3 will make the sampler assume that you want a transposition, so to override that and maintain your timing, you might also have to edit the root down by the same four half-steps, setting it to G#2. Some samplers will do this automatically when in the appropriate mode, and it is better to action this for such operations; but it is also important to understand how to manually control the relationship between root and zone placement. Organising your zones in this fashion can make space on the keyboard for building instruments with lots of loops on individual keys that play together in perfect time at a given tempo.

SAMPLERS

THE
DRUM
PROGRAMMING
HANDBOOK

133

Pattern 05_06

PATTERN 05_06: The retuned Pattern 05_05 loop, four times at 136bpm.

Exercise One: Practise your sample-tuning by programming a beat with one-shots, bounce it to audio, change the tempo, mute the one-shot track, import the bounce into your sampler and tune it to loop accurately from there. You can unmute the one-shot track to play simultaneously to see how well you did. If you can hear any double-hits (often called flams) especially towards the end of the loop, then there is room for improvement. Practice makes perfect.

Exercise Two: Experiment by sampling slow beats and tuning them up, and sampling fast ones and tuning them down. Trying to develop your ear to anticipate the trends, and think about how you can use this approach for sound design. You might even start off with extreme 'unmusical' tempos and listen to the sorts of sounds that you get after large tuning offsets.

Exercise Three: See if you can build an instrument for your sampler that contains a number of different zones, each one with a different loop, all tuned to fit any given tempo exactly.

RETRIGGERING

Now that we have a loop that plays precisely in time, we can start to exploit the facilities of the sampler that take this approach beyond what we would get simply by placing an audio file in our DAW timeline. We will force the sampler to retrigger from the beginning of the loop, part way through the bar.

The classic original phrase when doing this comes from playing the note again on beat 2&. The effect is to displace all the notes of the retriggered loop into a new part of the bar, giving an instant complexity with minimal effort. When done with a loop featuring a kick on the downbeat and a backbeat, this has the effect of giving a distinctive kick on 2& and a snare on 3&; this was the rhythm of many early drum & bass tracks.

■ **CHECK OUT**
'Saint Angel' by Goldie, from the album *Timeless*. This is often regarded as a seminal jungle album, and although this track features drums that were created slightly differently from the way they are made here, the distinctive 2& 3& rhythm can be heard.

CHAPTER 5

Notes that trigger sample loops giving the classic rhythmic feel.

Pattern 05_07

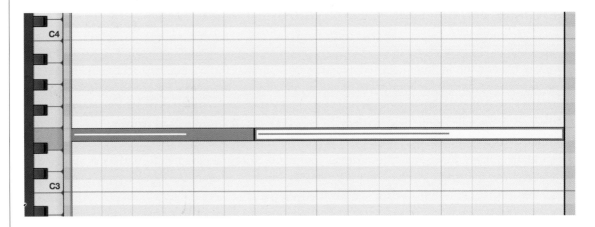

PATTERN 05_07: Pattern 05_06 with a retriggered start on 2&, repeated four times at 136bpm. Whereas with one-shots it is only the onset of a note that counts and so the previous pattern diagrams have only represented this. When playing back loops the duration that the key is held is crucial, playing back more or less of the loop. For this reason we are using a diagram of the piano roll editor here; note-duration can be clearly seen.

CHANGING THE START-POINT

So far, the approach we have taken has been based on playback of the sample from the point at which the bounced recording started. Samplers also allow you to specify where in the audio file you would like the playback to start from upon a key-press. This position is known as the start-time or start-point. If for instance, you wish your sample to commence part way through an actual audio file, then you need to identify the sample start-point on an image of the audio waveform. This is typically done in a waveform editor in your sampler by dragging a marker labelled 'S', but can also be done in a number of external audio editors should you prefer. When you are setting the start-point, make sure that you have a preference activated to snap to 'zero crossings', since this avoids clicking.

To explore this creatively, let's build another zone that starts the sample playing from the snare drum on beat two. Follow the advice in the Tip and set up the zone to play from a single C3 key. Duplicate the zone in the key-mapping section of your sampler to also play back from D3; remember to ensure that the root is transposed as well to keep them both locked in tempo; both keys should now sound identical.

For the D3 zone only (make sure that you are not in an 'edit multiple zones' mode), move the start-point to play from exactly the snare drum on beat 2. Zoom in closely in order to make this as precise as possible, otherwise the entire sample will trigger with a peculiar groove. Some samplers

SAMPLERS

THE
DRUM
PROGRAMMING
HANDBOOK

135

have automatic transient detection that allows you to snap the start-point to the exact edge of the waveform. Some people like to audition start-points by transposing the sample down a couple of octaves, and pressing the MIDI key to hear if there is any 'air' in front of the sample or indeed if there is a click from eating into the transient; adjust the start-point if necessary and then transpose back.

PATTERN 05_08: Retriggering the two loops; a four-bar phrase twice through at 136bpm.

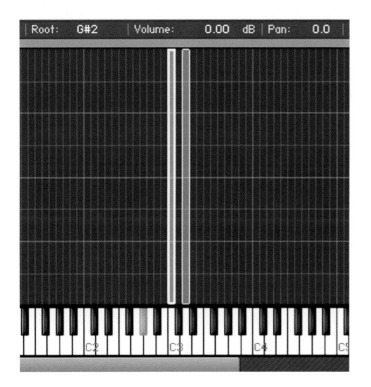

The two zones that play the loop starting with a kick on C3 and a snare on D3. Notice that the root key (highlighted) of the C3 zone is four half-steps below on G♯2.

Pattern 05_08

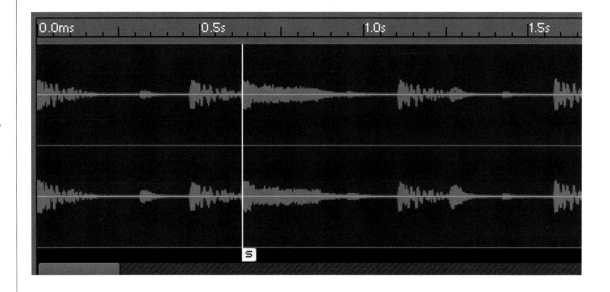

Pattern 05_08: Aligning the start-point to the transient of your choice.

Now that you have 'built' your instrument, try programming a relatively simple pattern to exploit it.

Pattern 05_08 combines the two versions of the loop; notice how it looks similar to what you might expect if just using one-shots of kick and snare.

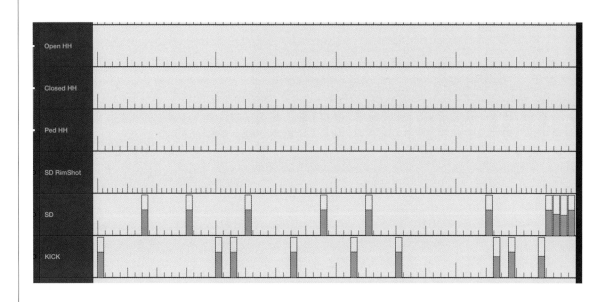

SAMPLERS

THE
DRUM
PROGRAMMING
HANDBOOK

137

Notice the kick drum on beat 3& and this snare on 4&, yet the absence of any backbeat on beat 4. This approach is sometimes called beat-displacement. It creates a rhythmic tension that pulls the listener away from where they naturally expect the pulse to land. Also notice the sound of the snare on beat 2 of bar four; because we have phrased a kick only one 16th-note later, the natural sustain of the snare is chopped and we have a noticeably different sound; this does not usually happen when using one-shots.

What this diagram does not reveal is that because we are playing with loops, the notes need to be edited to the correct length (in the piano-roll) in order to flow into each other.

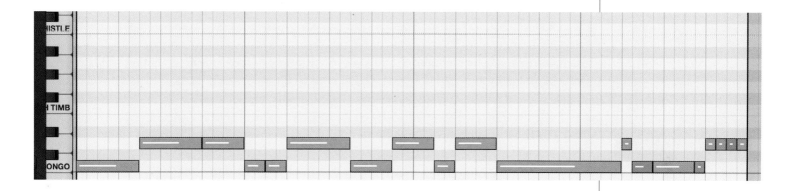

Exercise One: Experiment by programming a number of different rhythms with a retriggered sample. Listen to the phrasing of the sample and use that to help you choose where to place the retriggered notes.

Exercise Two: Using only a single loop, create several different zones, each with a different (beat-aligned) start-point. Experiment by programming these together with different rhythms and durations.

Exercise Three: Using the multi-zone instrument that you built in the last set of exercises, extend it to include further zones, now with different start-points.

Pattern 05_08 again. A piano-roll representation of the same thing reveals the note durations.

LAYERING LOOPS

One incredibly powerful and fun thing that we can do with loops is layering them on top of each other; in other words, having more than one playing simultaneously, although not necessarily starting and stopping at the same time. For this approach to be successful, it is vital that all loops are tuned to play exactly in time.

138

THE
DRUM
PROGRAMMING
HANDBOOK

SAMPLERS

Pattern 05_09

Pattern 05_10

Pattern 05_11

PATTERN 05_09: This is Pattern 05_03 with a layered percussion loop, four bars at 126bpm. We have layered a percussion loop over the top of the rather basic house beat of Pattern 05_03. The effect is to fill all the spaces and it produces a much more authentic sounding house beat. The percussion part is actually playing back from Spectrasonics Stylus RMX – a flexible and powerful loop player that also facilitates layering of its own loops within itself. This particular loop, although predominantly conga drums, also contains a backbeat and some low tones.

PATTERN 05_10: This is Pattern 05_09 with Pattern 05_08 simultaneously, twice through the four-bar phrase at 136bpm. Pattern 05_08 was tuned to play at 136bpm and is four bars long. Pattern 05_03 is only one bar long and was created with one shots, and so is very flexible in terms of tempo. Unseen to the user, Stylus RMX uses pre-sliced loops, and can therefore trigger each slice in sequence over a large range of tempos. Here it is playing a two-bar loop – thus all three parts repeat a different number of times within the cycle, and are locked at 136bpm. It is important to balance the relative volumes of all the loops when layering. It is often best to let one loop be dominant, and tuck the others underneath; here the main feel is house.

PATTERN 05_11: Here we have Pattern 04_03 layered with several loops at 86bpm. Pattern 04_03 was the human-like 16th-note hi-hat beat with an open hi-hat in several places; a four-bar phrase. Here, it is playing with Stylus RMX, which has six synthetic-sounding loops all going at once, although individually they are sparse. Notice the processed snare sound on beat 2 of every bar, but not the other backbeat on 4 – a classic trick. Because Stylus RMX is much lower in volume than Pattern 04_03, it really just contributes a layer of pop music style production without dominating. It is subtly varying its output all the time using its 'chaos' system, and so strictly speaking, there is no definite length to this pattern. If you compare Pattern 04_03 and Pattern 05_11, you will notice that loops can also be powerful when used with subtlety, and can be combined with real humans too.

Exercise One: Using your multi-zone instrument, try layering different samples with start offsets, for instance one sample that plays on beat 1, and another that starts on 2&, each repeating, but out of phase.

Exercise Two: Starting with a one-shot beat, copy it to a new track and edit its kick/snare pitches to trigger appropriate sample zones – the kick sample starting with a kick and the snare sample starting with a snare. Layer the original one-shot pattern over the top, and experiment with relative volumes.

Exercise Three: Using the multi-zone instrument that you built in the last set of exercises, experiment by programming polymetric phrases layered together: eg, a 'main beat' note four beats long, but another sample three-and-a-half beats long, with its triggering notes butt-joined so that the two samples move in and out of phase. Tip: keep the main beat as the loudest.

SAMPLERS

THE
DRUM
PROGRAMMING
HANDBOOK

139

BEATSLICING – FROM AMEN TO NINETIES JUNGLE

Probably the most sampled drumbeat of all time is the so-called 'Amen break'. The original was featured on a 1969 track called 'Amen, Brother' by the Winstons and played by G. C. Coleman, although other versions of the beat (eg, Mantronix) have been sampled too. We are now going to create a programmed (just as funky, and legal) version of the break, then feed it into the sampler, slice up the audio and assign the slices to different MIDI notes, then rearrange the slices. This was the seminal technique that led to the reworking of so many break-beats in the 1990s and defined jungle, the precursor of today's drum & bass. It also gives us a very powerful technique that we can use in many genres and different applications in a contemporary setting.

PATTERN 05_12: This is a version of the Amen break, twice through the four-bar phrase at 136bpm. The first thing to do is to programme your own version of the four-bar

Pattern 05_12

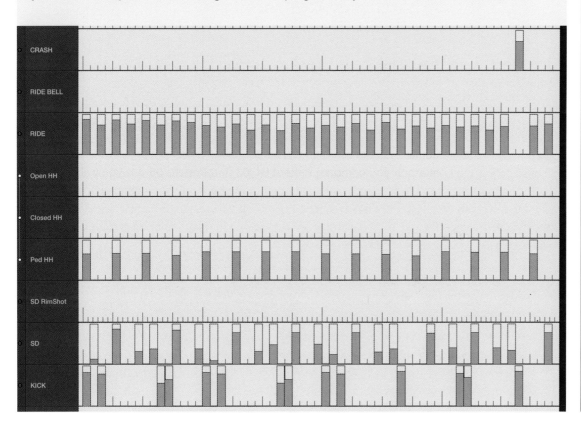

Pattern 05_12: the Amen break in one-shots.

CHAPTER 5

140

THE
DRUM
PROGRAMMING
HANDBOOK

SAMPLERS

TIP

It is best to place the loop on a note near either end of the keyboard. This will make room for the cluster of notes that we will define to play back the slices. Once all the notes have been designated, you can place the original loop adjacent to the cluster if you wish, but remember also to change its root to compensate for the transposition.

Pattern 05_13

Amen break using one-shots at around 136bpm, the tempo of the original. You might need to listen to it a few times since it has both quiet (not quite ghost) snare drums, and some beat displacement – in the third bar the snare plays on 3& and the following kick is on 4&, and in the fourth bar there is a kick and crash on 3&. Do not worry if yours is not exact; indeed, you can take some artistic liberties if you wish. The idea is to get some variations around a theme that can be recombined differently later.

Next, bounce the break to audio and import it into your sampler. Since we are going for an 'old skool' jungle feel, set the DAW tempo to 160bpm. You will need to tune the break to fit this new tempo, and this is a little tricky with a four-bar loop. Start by setting up a MIDI note that is exactly one bar long, and cycling this, tune as before; obviously this is only playing back the first bar of the break. Now double the length of the note, cycle it and refine your tuning; you will likely need to adjust by just a few cents this time. Finally, extend it to the full four bars and adjust again until it is perfect, likely ending up with around +2.8 half-steps – don't cheat! You should now be hearing the full break, but pitched up in that classic jungle fashion.

PATTERN 05_13: This is Pattern 05_12 tuned up by 2.81 half-steps, once through the four-bar phrase at 160bpm. We now need to chop the break into individual slices, each of an eighth-note duration (which for this loop aligns nicely with the ride pattern), giving you a total of 32 different slices. Then we need to make the slices play consecutively to sound as if the loop has not been sliced at all. There are many ways to perform this slicing, and you might need to research the options for your particular system. These approaches all tend to loosely follow the convention pioneered by Propellerhead ReCycle. Each slice must be assigned to its own MIDI note, and it is usual to map these ascending chromatically, often starting at C1, so two things are needed; a number of audio slices and a MIDI region to play them back in the correct order. The correct order in this case means that they sound identical to the original entire loop – for the moment.

Approaches that you might use to implement this include:

- A DAW function that slices an audio region and maps it to the DAW's native sampler while simultaneously generating a MIDI region to play back the regions from the sampler.
- Using a beatslicing function integral to your sampler.
- Using Propellerhead ReCycle to export an .RX2 file if compatibility allows, or just to prepare the slices and MIDI file.

SAMPLERS

THE
DRUM
PROGRAMMING
HANDBOOK

141

- Manually assembling a palette of slices, either by assigning start/end-points in the full sample, or using the sampler's editing function to trim away the unwanted audio, leaving each of the required slices and mapping these to the appropriate zones.

Whichever approach you take, be sure to somehow maintain the tuning shift for authenticity.

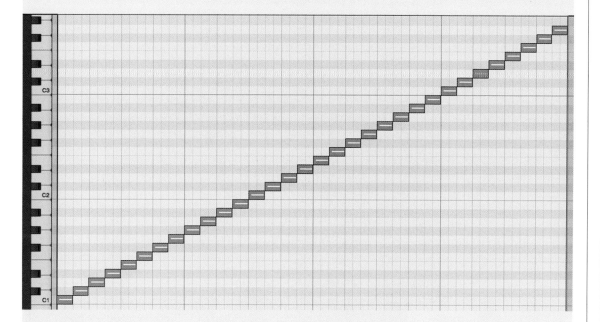

A typical chromatic sequence that plays all the slices in the correct order.

So, now we have a ramp-shaped sequence in the piano-roll editor that plays back the loop unchanged. If you edit this sequence, changing a note's pitch within the range between the first and last note (C1 – G3 in this case) causes a different slice to be triggered at that point in time. When transposing upwards chromatically, each half-step effectively moves the played slice forward in time by an eighth-note, and vice versa. Instead, sometimes it might feel more natural to you to drag a given note horizontally to a particular point in time, for instance to state a backbeat. It is useful to start practising these techniques working with a single bar, but it can be applied to sequences of any length.

> **TIP**
> In fact, most DAWs have more sophisticated (and therefore easier to use) tools for doing this tuning in the audio domain, but be aware that 'match to tempo' time-stretching functions will not usually apply the pitch shift on their own. Not only is the approach here authentic, it is great ear training and will really help your production skills by exposing you to the sound of the tiny timing anomalies that you will often need to rectify in various contexts. Once you can do this sort of thing with ease, use your best DAW tools for speed and to add them to your repertoire.

142

THE
DRUM
PROGRAMMING
HANDBOOK

SAMPLERS

Pattern 05_14: A single bar of the reordered slices; clearly this does not follow the original geometric-looking order.

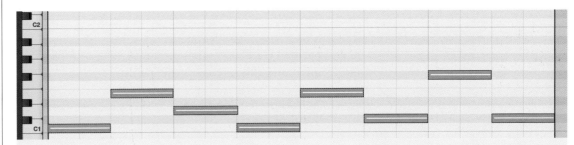

Pattern 05_14

Pattern 05_15: All four bars of the reordered slices.

PATTERN 05_14: This is the first bar of the Amen break with reordered slices, repeated four times at 160bpm. You will see that the single kick drum hits are playing back from both of pitches C1 and C♯1; the C1 has a pedal hat hit, whereas the C♯1 only has the ride, giving it a softer tone. Sonically quite subtle here, but in other scenarios this multi-kick (or snare) technique can be significant. Notice also how the original quaver ride pattern feels largely maintained, despite the edits.

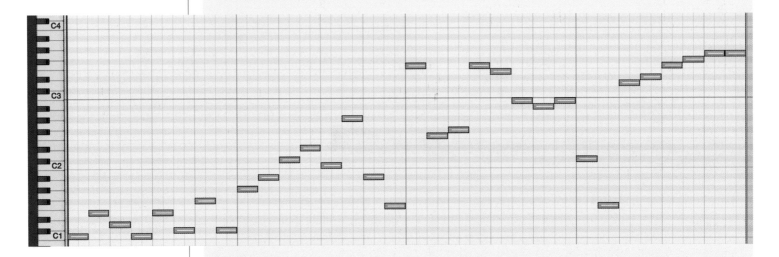

Pattern 05_15

PATTERN 05_15: This is a four bar reordering, played twice at 160bpm. We are really in jungle territory now! This phrase starts with the first bar being Pattern 05_14, but then develops. In bar three, it also features choked cymbal effects through playing only the first eighth-note slice of the cymbal crash, but also two consecutive slices that represent the sustain of the crash, except displaced to beat 3 of bar four. There also appears to be four

SAMPLERS

THE
DRUM
PROGRAMMING
HANDBOOK

143

Pattern 05_16: The four bars of reordered slices with additional MIDI editing.

consecutive 16th-notes on the kick drum, achieved by repeating the original pair of 16th-notes from the break. All this from an eighth-note MIDI sequence!

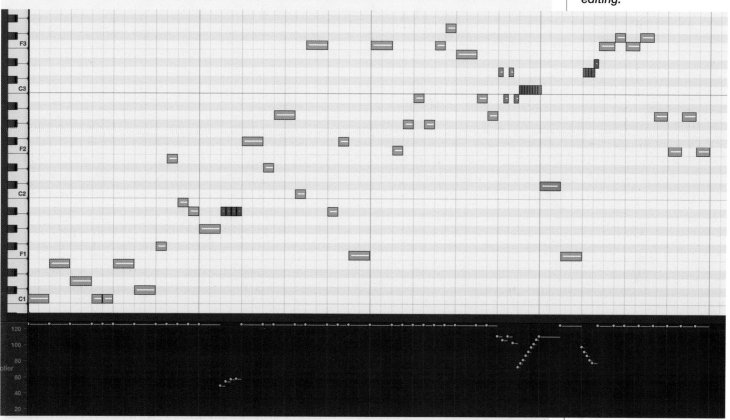

PATTERN 05_16: **This is a four bar phrase with mixed note values, played twice at 160bpm.** This pattern also features a number of 16th-notes. These only play back half of our designated slices before re-triggering, either with the same note or a different one. Because every slice carried a ride hit, such phrases change the impression of the ride pattern regardless of whether there is also a kick or a snare. On beat 2a there is an eighth-note playing 'across' the beat, giving a syncopated feel.

There are a number of machine-gun rolls, for instance on beat 1& of bar two – this phrase using 32nd-notes. But you will also notice the 64th-note roll on 4& of bar three. Preceding the

 Pattern 05_16

latter are four 32nd-notes with snare drums, but here using two different hits to add subtle interest.

Running into beat 4 of bar four, there are four eighth-note triplets (triplet quavers) that create a rhythmic tension, almost dragging against the predominantly 16th-note feel. It is important here to use slices that only have one principal drum-hit in them, since if they carried 16th-notes 'inside', the triplet re-triggering could produce an awkward sound. The double-crash phrase around beat 3 of bar four uses both 'halves' of the crash cymbal; and notice the unusual timing of the first crash, which adds to the rhythmic tension in this bar.

Exercise One: Slice up another loop with a different feel; Pattern 04_16 could be interesting. Rearrange its slices to retain its original feel at the original tempo, but with a different phrasing, and at a new tempo in order to create something new.

Exercise Two: Sequence one of the sliced loops in a quite abstract way over several bars, but then layer it underneath a more regular beat programmed with one-shots; the sliced layer should provide a bubbling and moving interest underneath something outwardly steady.

Exercise Three: Build a sampler instrument with two different sliced loops tuned to the same tempo, and a selection of one shots. Use it to program a mash-up!

Things to experiment with

- Try re-tuning individual drums of a one-shot kit – save the result as a new kit.
- Use the pitch bend wheel whilst playing back one-shot sequences.
- Build your own hybrid loops using all available techniques.
- Layer a number of patterns from previous chapters with patterns from this one, both loops and one-shots.
- Sample the same one-shot loop a number of times from different tempos, playing them back tuned to a single tempo.
- Create sampler instruments that offer palettes of multiple loops all tuned to the same tempo – use the global tuning facility of your sampler to utilise this instrument in songs of different tempos.
- Try different slice lengths, for example quarter-notes.
- Program sequences of slices using step-time.
- Work by slicing on individual kick or snare hits instead of fixed lengths.

SAMPLERS

THE
DRUM
PROGRAMMING
HANDBOOK

145

CONCLUSION

We have now moved away from naturalistic programming into a rather more synthetic world, courtesy of the sampler. Applying existing MIDI programming techniques to one-shots opens many doors and offers a huge sonic vocabulary; extending this to loops multiplies it tenfold. Tuning and slicing loops offer an enormous range of creative possibilities and allow you to create things that you could only conceive of, but not necessarily execute, at a base level. In the next chapter we will explore the possibilities of working with audio without a sampler, in the native DAW environment. It offers a new range of creative possibilities.

Check that you can:

- Load one-shot sample-based kits, and map notes as required.
- Create machine-gun rolls with various note values.
- Tune a sampled loop to play back precisely in time.
- Set up multiple zones on specific MIDI keys on your sampler whilst maintaining the desired playback timing.
- Set start points to different parts of the loop, assign to zones and 're-sequence' the loop.
- Slice an entire loop up and map every slice on a different zone.

WORKING WITH AUDIO

CHAPTER 6

WORKING WITH AUDIO

THE
DRUM
PROGRAMMING
HANDBOOK

147

All of the sounds that we have used so far have been triggered by MIDI notes. We are now going to explore the possibilities offered by direct audio playback and manipulation in the DAW. This will include creative editing, time-stretching, layering, and more.

THE AUDIO ENVIRONMENT

An audio recording is stored as an audio file on the computer disk in one of a number of formats such as WAV or AIFF, denoted by the filename extensions .wav or .aif. These formats are described as being PCM (pulse code modulation) and are capable of playing back audio at optimal studio quality. The two factors that determine the quality are 'bit depth' (also referred to as resolution) which determines how precisely volume is represented, and 'sample rate' which determines the highest frequencies that can be recorded and reproduced. It is recommended that you read further afield on this to better understand the parameters involved.

There are also a number of so-called lossy formats, the most common being MP3. These are designed to save disk space on your portable music player, but have inferior audio quality as a consequence, and should be absolutely avoided at all stages when making your own music.

Stereo audio files can be either split or interleaved. Split means that two separate files (for the left and right channels) exist on disk, but are played back simultaneously. Interleaved is a single stereo file stored on disk. They behave identically once in the DAW.

When recording or bouncing you will often be asked which settings you would like to use. Recommended settings, assuming that your system supports them, are these:

- **File type: WAV**
- **Bit depth: 24-bit**
- **Sample rate: 44.1kHz**
- **Stereo format: Interleaved**

There are notionally higher qualities available, but check them out in a test comparison before you use them, since they use more computer resources and you may not be able to hear the difference.

All DAWs play back audio files from designated audio tracks, and these can be configured as being either stereo or mono.

A DAW will often play back only a part of an audio file, and this is often referred to as an audio region. These regions might typically be a number of bars long. Regions can be repeated, moved, copied, or sliced into smaller regions, just as with MIDI, as we have already seen. It is important to understand that audio regions usually play back at their original tempo unless your system is

---

TIP
Often, the DAW can play both stereo and mono audio files from either kind of track, but using the wrong kind of track is not recommended; mono files on stereo tracks are wasteful of computer resources, and stereo files on mono tracks will not play the intended different sounds from the left and right speakers.

specifically configured otherwise, and therefore altering the playback tempo will force the region to play back out of time relative to the grid; this is of course different from MIDI one-shots, but more comparable to loop playback from a sampler. Regions that play repeating drumbeats are often also referred to as loops.

WORKING WITH AUDIO REGIONS

Let us make a bounce from the last chapter, the eight bar Pattern 05_10. Import this into a fresh stereo track on your DAW.

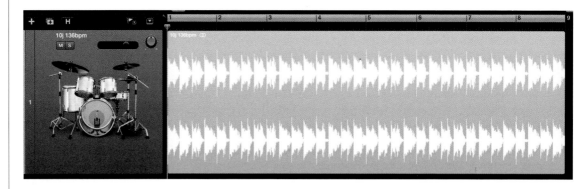

Pattern 05_10 bounced as an eight-bar audio region.

The fourth bar features a 16th-note (semiquaver) fill over its last beat. We have cropped out the other bars, and moved this bar to what will be the beginning of a new pattern and repeated it three further times. Beats two and three have been removed from the last instance, and the fourth beat has been copied into the gaps to produce a three beat fill.

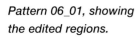

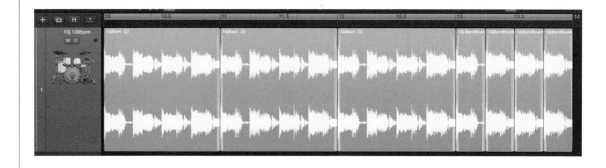

Pattern 06_01, showing the edited regions.

CHAPTER 6

WORKING WITH AUDIO

THE
DRUM
PROGRAMMING
HANDBOOK

149

Pattern 06_01

PATTERN 06_01: A one-bar house beat repeating three times with a three-beat fill on the fourth bar, twice through at 136bpm. When working in this fashion small clicks are often induced where the new regions meet. These are caused by volume changes from non-continuous audio that is now adjacent. You will have a crossfade function on your DAW that can be applied to mask this. Always use the shortest fade that you can get away with, lest you hear other artefacts, although much longer fades can be used to creative special effect. Setting the track to an automatic crossfade mode can often be helpful if doing multiple edits, since each edit point receives its fade automatically. Enabling the audio preference 'snap to zero crossings' can also help by forcing the edit to be made where the volume is instantaneously zero.

Clearly, Pattern 06_01 has a very mechanical and repetitive feel, although this of course is entirely appropriate in certain styles of music. In order to use editing to produce something stylistically different from this, we will now cut the pattern up further at a much finer resolution, using 16th-note slice points.

TIP
DAWs typically have some sort of snap mode by which edits are performed to the nearest bar, beat, or subdivision. Investigate this, and make sure that your snap is set to the appropriate value in order to speed up your workflow and prevent small errors. There are often also intelligent modes that change depending on your viewing resolution. Sometimes you have to be careful with these.

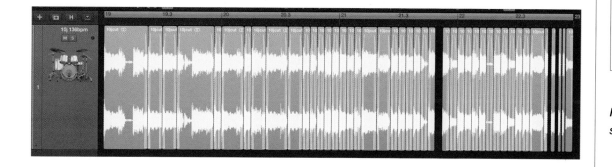

Pattern 06_02: Slicing and stuttering effects.

Pattern 06_02

PATTERN 06_02: Pattern 06_01, sliced and stuttered twice through at 136bpm. Using a 16th-note grid setting, Pattern 06_01 has been further sliced and the resulting regions reordered. The focus was to identify the kick/snare hits and rearrange and copy them to form a more syncopated beat – aiming for particular grid destinations. The resulting regions vary in length from a quarter-note (crotchet) to a 16th-note; this breaks away from the four on the floor sound and produces a different texture. As was the case when we did this with sampled loops, the other components of the beat (hi-hats and percussion, etc) are sometimes subject to beat displacement, breaking the ostinato and providing a more complex layer against the kick/snare pattern. Note the open hi-hat sound, originally from the offbeat, now playing on beats three and four of bar two.

CHAPTER 6

The second two bars of the four-bar Pattern 06_02. Fades have not yet been applied around the gaps.

■ **CHECK OUT**
The *Emotional Technology* album by BT, a superb programmer who is said to have invented the so-called stutter edit, and even holds an official world record for the most number of vocal edits in a song!

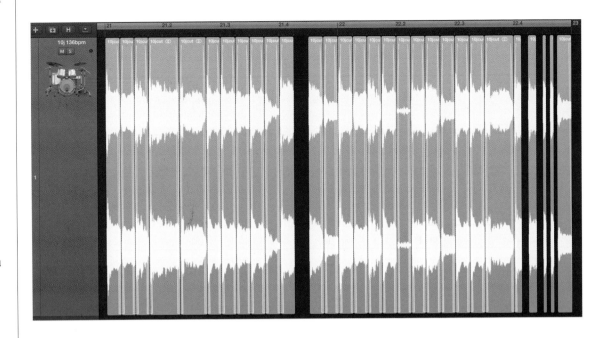

> **TIP**
> Your DAW might feature a shuffle-edit mode. This can be employed to drag a given region to the desired position; all surrounding regions will move precisely to accommodate it. You must be sure that all regions are exact note values in length, otherwise you will incur timing problems due to the butt joining of adjacent regions. When working in this way, it is often better to proceed in only one direction along the timeline otherwise a degree of scrambling will occur. With practice, however, this can be a powerful technique.

You will notice that on beat 4 of the first of these, there is a gap – a silence that gives a staccato snare hit. On beat 4 of the second, there is a cluster of even shorter regions of both 16th and 32nd-notes in length, the latter aligning to a 32nd-note grid to give a stutter effect. When programming in this way you sometimes have to extend the length of the region very slightly to make it feel more musical, and you may also need to add short fades to stop clicking at the beginning and the end of individual regions.

Exercise One: Practise cutting, copying, and slicing audio regions of your own bounced beats. Start with whole bars, and then gradually reduce the note values with a focus on rhythmic phrasing to create new beats.

Exercise Two: Experiment with stutter edits, using the same part of a given region. Use adjacent clusters of different note-values to create acceleration and deceleration effects.

Exercise Three: Develop your stutter edits to incorporate different sounds from different regions, both in clusters and with scrambled regions. Try using shuffle-editing for the latter if your DAW supports this.

WORKING WITH AUDIO

THE
DRUM
PROGRAMMING
HANDBOOK

151

LOOPING AND LAYERING

Playing different audio loops on multiple tracks simultaneously gives us infinite sonic and rhythmic possibilities. As long as all the loops are locked to tempo, combinations of one, two, and four bars will provide many options, as has been seen with MIDI-triggered samples. What can be even more interesting and exciting, when used with control and discretion, is to combine odd lengths of loop together.

To explore this, we have created a two-bar kick and snare pattern in a dubstep style at 140bpm. This pattern will dictate the rhythmic feel and time cycle. As it happens, dubstep usually only has a single backbeat per bar, placed on beat 3. We then added a fairly simple hi-hat pattern – precisely three beats long, and also a simple ghost snare part that is exactly nine eighth-notes long, in other words one eighth-note longer than a whole bar. Lastly, we added a whoosh-like electronic noise that functions rather like a crash cymbal. This sound plays at the beginning of a region that is three and a half bars long. Clearly these do not fit neatly with the original kick/snare pattern – yet.

Pattern 06_03

Pattern 06_04

Pattern 06_05

Pattern 06_06

PATTERN 06_03: KickSnare   **PATTERN 06_04:** Hat

PATTERN 06_05: Ghosts   **PATTERN 06_06:** Whoosh

These sounds are derived from MIDI one-shots with Mega Macho Drums, each once through at 140bpm.

Patterns 06_03 to 06_06: Notice the timing relationship between the four layers.

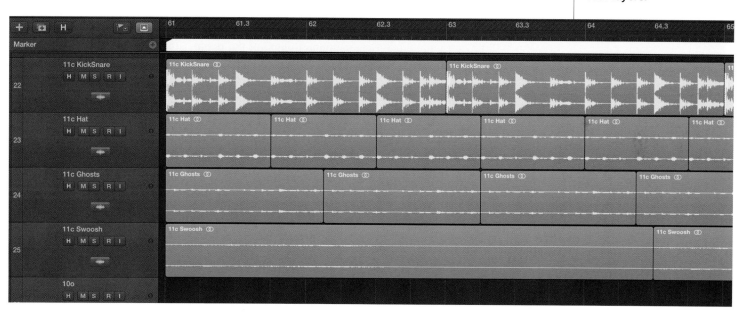

152

THE
DRUM
PROGRAMMING
HANDBOOK

WORKING WITH AUDIO

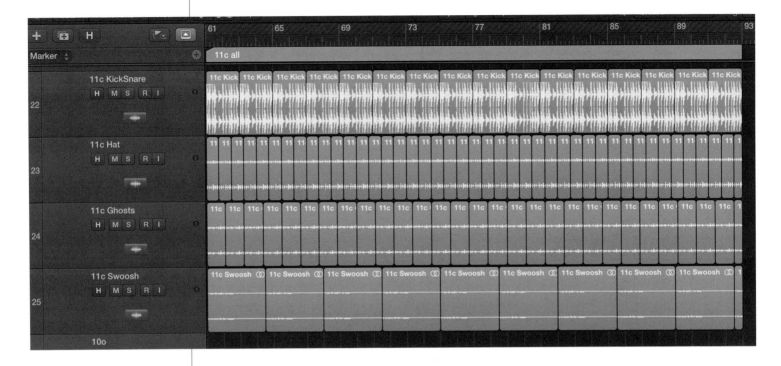

Pattern 06_07: The 32-bar sequence

Pattern 06_07

TIP

If you wish to have your programming regarded as interesting, then try to avoid absolute copies of one or two-bar loops. Even if you wish to create a repetitive feel, the occasional subtle variation makes all the difference, especially if placed tastefully in the musical arrangement.

PATTERN 06_07: 32 bars of the polymetric combination at 140bpm. We will now repeat all of these individual regions on their own tracks; using the kick/snare pattern as a reference and copying it 15 times to make a 32-bar sequence. Each of the other patterns are copied back to back until they last for the same duration as the kick/snare, rounded off as necessary. What we should have is a 32-bar sequence that feels like an ostinato kick and snare. It is accompanied by a hi-hat and ghost part that percolates along, feeling somehow the same, but also subtly different, giving new life to the static two-bar kick/snare pattern; it takes a long time to repeat exactly, a time that is dependent on the mathematical relationship between the lengths of the regions. Each occurrence of the whoosh sound is given by the overall length of its region in bars, but the extra half bar in its duration means that it alternately lands on beat one with a kick, then beat three with a snare. This whole approach could be described as polymetric; notice the phasing movement of the region boundaries in the diagrams.

It takes a bit of practice in order to match the appropriate phrasing of individual patterns to their duration. Broadly speaking, if a pattern is based around eighth-notes, then setting its duration to be some multiple of eighths will probably work. If it has more of a 16th-note feel, then it will still also work with an eight-note based length, but might also in multiples of 16th-notes. As when we did similar things with MIDI, much of the secret is to keep one pattern dominant. Simply editing

CHAPTER 6

down regions of a more regular length is a great way to create a palette of more exotic lengths. We will now take a slightly different approach to layering sounds for a subtle yet musical effect. First, bounce Pattern 05_03 at 120bpm and repeat it to form a four-bar loop.

PATTERN 06_08: **Pattern 05_03, using a different kit from Mega Macho Drums, twice through at 120bpm.** On a different track, we have imported Pattern 04_22 and sliced it into four smaller regions of three quarter-notes in length, each starting on a snare – you can use different snare hits if you wish. With snap set to 16th-notes, the first two instances are placed on the third 16th-note of beat 2 of each of the first two bars. The third region is placed on beat 2& of bar three, and the fourth on beat 2 of bar four. The effect is of the first two bars having a displaced and syncopated feel, with what were backbeats now appearing on the offbeat 16th-notes. The third bar has these backbeats on the offbeat eighth-notes, and the fourth bar is in sync.

We now set up long fade-outs on three of these regions, but for variation faded into the second instance instead. This will likely sound rather strange on its own, but when layered with Pattern 06_08 gives the effect of a driving 'four on the floor' beat with skipping and syncopated textures.

PATTERN 06_09: **Pattern 04_22, sliced into four three-beat long regions with fades, twice through at 120bpm. Played with a metronome click.**

PATTERN 06_10: **Pattern 06_08 layered with Pattern 06_09, twice through at 120bpm.**

Pattern 06_10: you can see the creative use of fades.

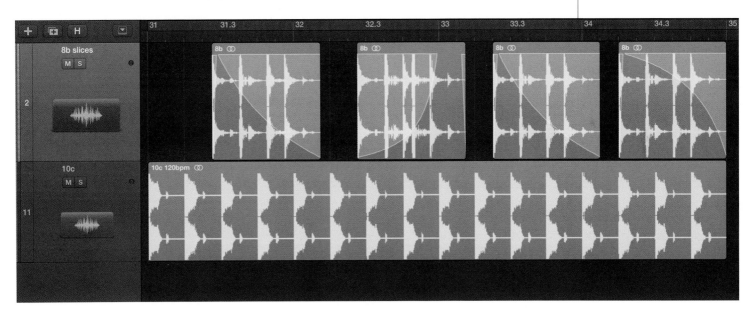

154

THE
DRUM
PROGRAMMING
HANDBOOK

WORKING WITH AUDIO

COMPING LOOPS

PATTERN 06_11: A four-bar loop from iZotope BreakTweaker. BreakTweaker is a loop generation tool that offers, among other things, sophisticated and ultra-easy manipulation of machine-gun rolls and beyond. Played at 136bpm, once through.

PATTERN 06_12: Once through a four-bar stack of four audio regions layered together at 136bpm. The stack of four layered loops in Pattern 06_12 has a certain quality, but it is rather relentless and very busy. The four layers are: Pattern 05_12 (our version of the Amen break), Pattern 05_06, Pattern 06_11 and a loop from Stylus RMX. We will now develop another technique known as compiling, but more commonly referred to as comping. This is a form of detailed editing that is often used to create 'best-of' performance of (say) vocals when recording. Instead of comping multiple recordings of the same passage, we are going to use three of the loops above in order to develop a creative approach for developing new loops that can be used for giving a 'production feel'.

The idea was to make a number of cuts in all three loops at the same point. We then muted two of these, allowing only a single loop to be heard at a given point in time. This had the effect of thinning the overall stacked sound, but also allowing for a complex mixed palette of sounds.

Many DAWs have tools to assist with this approach, but often they are not promoted towards working with drums. For example, Pro Tools has 'playlist comping', Logic Pro has 'quick-swipe comping', and Cubase has 'lanes', but also the 'LoopMash' system which is optimised for up to four drum loops. If you do not have a suitable tool, there is a straightforward manual approach that we will discuss now; and if you do have bespoke tools, the principle still applies.

So, disregarding Pattern 05_12 for the moment, we have the other three loops on their own tracks, and have balanced the relative volumes to give a fairly even blend, but this must be done with region parameters, leaving the channel faders all at unity gain. We have also coloured each region differently. Next, we have muted all three and then sliced them into individual 16th-note-duration regions. We then worked through the four bars unmuting slices on individual tracks as sounds good. We then dragged the regions of each of the tracks onto a new single track – they should now be neatly aligned and their volumes still balanced (this is why we did not initially adjust volume at the faders). It will now be easy to switch on an automatic crossfade for this track, or just work through it manually if you need to. You can also take liberties with the 16th-note discipline if you wish.

WORKING WITH AUDIO

THE
DRUM
PROGRAMMING
HANDBOOK

155

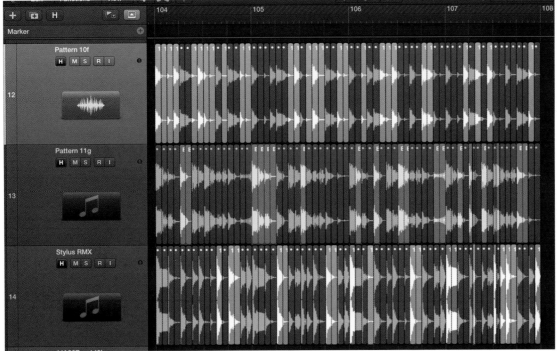

Pattern 06_13: How the three layers were sliced and combined. The highlighted regions play, whilst the others are muted.

PATTERN 06_13: **Pattern 06_12 after comping at 136bpm. Twice through the four bars.** The result is liable to be a quite jarring and staccato pattern that features many different sounds. While this is great if that is what you are after, a slicker 'production' effect can be achieved if you tuck this underneath a more regular beat. This regular beat has the function of smoothing out the abrupt sonic movement, and glues things together. We have added back Pattern 05_12 to play simultaneously at a dominant volume, and you will hear a smoother effect with a transformation of the Amen Break, the effect being of the basic sounds playing consistently, but underpinned with the new choppy pattern.

PATTERN 06_14: **Pattern 06_13 also layered with Pattern 05_12 at 136bpm, twice through the four bars.**

Exercise One: Using either your own loops or those used in the dubstep example, try creating different polymetric effects by adjusting the length of the source regions so that the phase of the repeats changes to produce different effects. Remember that you can crop the beginning of a region as well as the end.

Exercise Two: With loops of your choice (create them if you wish) experiment with the displaced and faded region concept, but use several layers simultaneously, all with different fades and placements. Try to choose loops that will naturally complement each other if overlapping.

Exercise Three: Practise comping together some different loops. If you are working with exact and consistent region lengths, then try shuffle-editing the comped result too.

TIME-STRETCHING

Time-stretching is the facility offered by DAWs to alter the duration of recorded audio independently of its pitch, perhaps to adjust its tempo. Further, there is usually a facility to identify note onsets – the 'b of the bangs' – in the audio. These are often referred to as transients. Audio quantisation stretches an area of audio either side of a given transient to correct the transient's timing towards the grid. The transients to either side of the target transient are anchored in time. Such quantisation is often employed to tighten the timing of a human performance. Before you can do this, you typically have to activate such a facility on a given track. Different DAWs have different names for this, eg, 'Warping' in Ableton Live, 'Elastic Audio' in Pro Tools and 'Flex Time' in Logic Pro. Be prepared to read your manual in order to master the basics such as detecting, adding, and moving transient markers. It is also really useful to know how to jump the song position line between transients with a key command, and how to slice regions at those points. Time-stretching a piece of audio to last for less time might be described as time-compression.

Quantisation can typically only make small corrections before unwanted noises are generated, as the computer tries to 'invent' sufficient musical information for the space it has been asked to fill. This can spoil the authenticity of the recording. Rather than pursue normal quantisation here, we will explore how the normally unwanted artefacts can be used as a sound design tool and turn an acoustic-sounding kit into a glitch sequence.

Starting with the 16th-note-based Pattern 04_16, we activated real-time time-stretching for the track and made sure that all the principal transients were detected. Once done, we were able to drag the notes around to snap to different places on the grid, applying lengthening and shortening as we did so, with corresponding artefacts. When you try this, discard any idea of maintaining an authentic acoustic sound, and experiment with note placements based on rhythmic positioning and the timbres that you are creating; the further you stretch, the more extreme the timbre will be. You will soon get a feel for what sort of moves create which sort of sound on a given drum or cymbal.

TIP

You will probably have a number of different time-stretch algorithms that you might employ. These are typically optimised for working with certain types of performance, but once you have applied some extreme stretches, you will find that the algorithms have quite different sonic effects, so do try them all; you can toggle them after setting up your transient markers. They also often have a small number of parameters that can be adjusted to change these effects still further; try these too.

CHAPTER 6

WORKING WITH AUDIO

THE
DRUM
PROGRAMMING
HANDBOOK

157

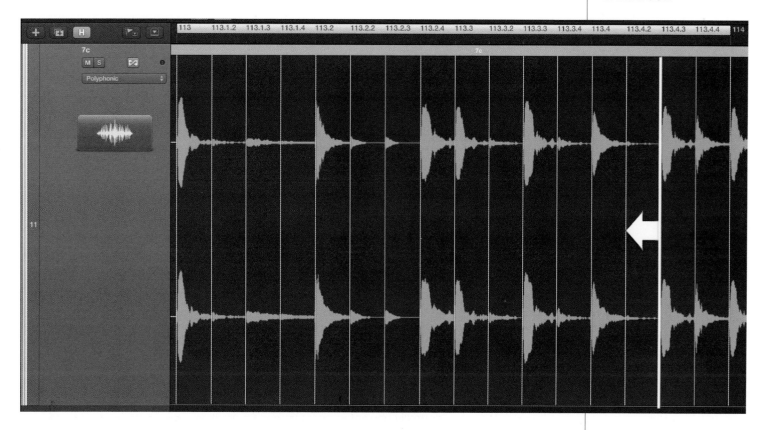

PATTERN 06_15: The fourth bar of Pattern 04_16 before time-stretching at 86bpm. Once through.

This is a single example from the fourth bar of Pattern 04_16. The highlighted transient is to be dragged one 16th-note earlier in time.

Pattern 06_15

CHAPTER 6

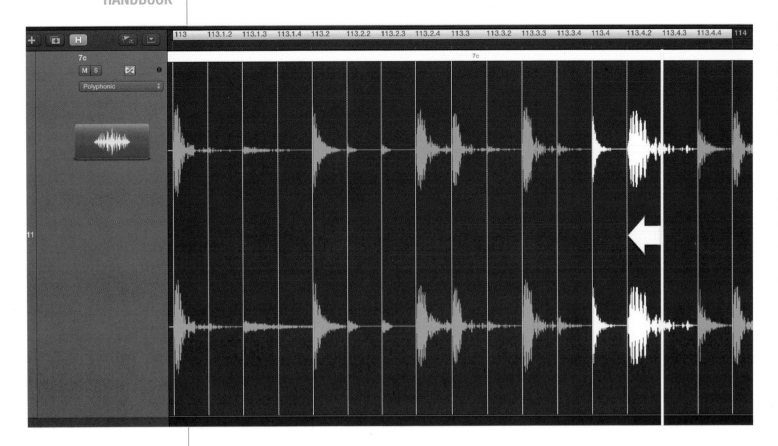

Pattern 06_16: After stretching. The vertical white line indicates where the transient has been dragged to, over the duration of the arrow.

Pattern 06_16

PATTERN 06_16: **The fourth bar of Pattern 04_16 after initial time-stretching at 86bpm. Once through.** After dragging, you can see that the preceding note on beat 4 has been shortened – it could not move since it was anchored by its own transient marker, and the note that was dragged has now been lengthened. The sound here is interesting, but in order to exaggerate it even further, a new transient marker has been defined manually part way through the lengthened note and it has been dragged even further to the left. This is an important sound-design technique when working in this way. The particular algorithm used in the audio example has given an almost machine-gun roll effect.

WORKING WITH AUDIO

THE
DRUM
PROGRAMMING
HANDBOOK

159

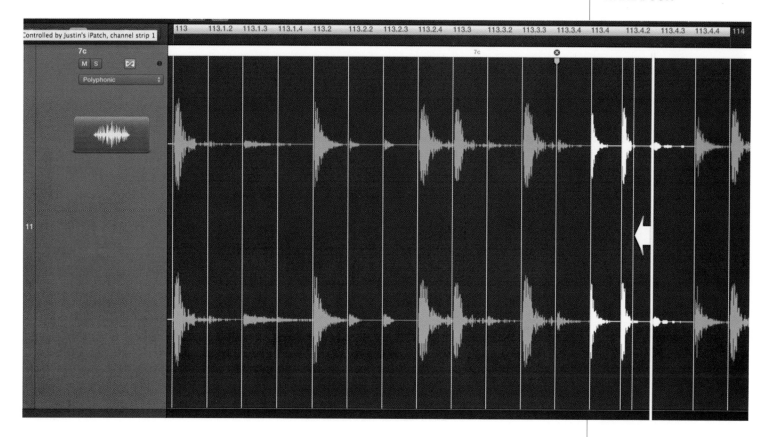

PATTERN 06_17: **The fourth bar of Pattern 04_16 after further time-stretching at 86bpm. Once through.** Again, the vertical white line indicates where the transient has been dragged to, over the duration of the arrow. A gap in the audio is implied visually, but it is actually filled by the stretching algorithm.

Pattern 06_17: After stretching from the newly inserted transient.

 Pattern 06_17

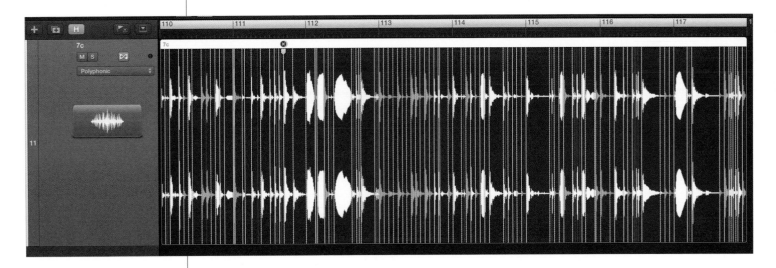

Pattern 06_18: After working through the whole eight-bar sequence in a similar fashion according to taste, the markers might look something like this.

Pattern 06_18

Pattern 06_19

Pattern 06_20

Pattern 06_21

Pattern 06_22

PATTERN 06_18: Pattern 04_16 after time-stretching at 86bpm. Twice through the eight-bar pattern with the polyphonic algorithm.

PATTERN 06_19: Pattern 04_16 after time-stretching at 86bpm. Twice through the eight-bar pattern with the Speed algorithm.

PATTERN 06_20: Pattern 04_16 after time-stretching at 86bpm. Twice through the eight-bar pattern with the Logic Pro X Tempophone algorithm.

PATTERN 06_21: Pattern 04_16 after time-stretching at 86bpm. Twice through the eight-bar pattern with the Logic Pro X Tempophone algorithm with a large grain size.

It could be that you like different hits or phrases of the different algorithms, and so it might be fun to bounce each and then comp the results together to make a 'best of'. The algorithms used here are from Logic Pro X, and are Speed, Polyphonic, and Tempophone at two different grain sizes.

PATTERN 06_22: Pattern 04_16 after comping four versions at 86bpm. Twice through the eight-bar pattern.

Exercise One: Take a different acoustic-sounding drumbeat, and import it onto a track at a very different tempo from its original. Realign the transients with the grid for an interesting effect, but do not be precious about maintaining its original feel and backbeats etc.

CHAPTER 6

WORKING WITH AUDIO

THE
DRUM
PROGRAMMING
HANDBOOK

161

Exercise Two: Bounce the result of Exercise One with your preferred algorithm, and then on a new track, apply further processing with a different algorithm. Note the sonic effects.

Exercise Three: Try comping together both of the above. The hits might now be in different places, but that is part of the creative fun.

STRUCTURING AUDIO LAYERS TO A BRIEF

When working in the context of a tune, a good programmer will typically become involved in the construction of a number of layers of sound, closely bound to the actual arrangement of the song. These layers might include drums – both acoustic and electronic – percussion, special effects, starts and stops, and fills. It is common to create the arrangement based on existing material, working directly in the DAW (bass, riffs, melody, etc). But what we will do here is present an imaginary arrangement and then offer an interpretation using audio, the idea being to think about how to put things together.

Here is a description of the drum/percussion arrangement of the tune – the brief:

Style:	Pop/Electronica
Tempo:	84bpm

Introduction: four bars solo synth, then eight bars of acoustic kit, funky. Fill into next section.

Verse one: 12 bars, electronic and percussion layer on top of acoustic kit. Fill into next section.

Link one: four bars, strong hits (to go with band).
Bar one: beats 1 and 4&.
Bar two: none.
Bar three: beats 1 and 3.
Bar four: building electronic fill – crescendo into next section.

Chorus one: 12 bars, electronic four on the floor with hints of double-time feel. Four bar phrases and louder.

Link two: four bars, strong hits (to go with band).

> **TIP**
> If you have a time-stretch algorithm that uses discernable grains of sound (tiny excerpts only a few milliseconds in duration that can be overlapped or pulled apart), then choosing a grain size that relates to the tempo can be useful. Divide 7.5 by the bpm to get the duration of a 32nd-note in fractions of a second (remember that 0.001 second is one millisecond), and choose the closest value that you are allowed in your DAW. The stretching will then emulate machine-gun rolls. Halving your number again will give you the time for 64th-note rolls. If you also have an adjustable crossfade parameter, then it is worth experimenting with this too.

Bar one:	beats 1 and 4&.
Bar two:	beats 2 and 3&.
Bar three:	beats 1 and 3.
Bar four:	building electronic fill – crescendo into next section.

Add special effects.

Verse two: 12 bars, electronic and percussion layer plus minimal acoustic kit. Fill into next section.

Chorus two: 16 bars, electronic four on the floor with double-time feel. Four bar phrases and louder.

Link three:	four bars, strong hits (to go with band).
Bar one:	beats 1 and 4&.
Bar two:	beats 2 and 3&.
Bar three:	beats 2 and 3&.
Bar four:	dropping electronic fill – decrescendo into next section.

Jungle groove throughout.

Outro: to fade. Eclectic electronic with special effects. Repeating hits as for the first two bars of the last Link section.

DISCUSSION OF SECTIONS
INTRODUCTION

 Pattern 06_23

PATTERN 06_23: The eight bars of the Intro section including the set-up fill. The instructions for the first four bars of this arrangement are solo synthesizer, so we do not need to do anything in this section. After this however, an acoustic drum kit is required to play something funky. One of the first things that you have to do when assigning audio to a song is to make a judgement about both the content and the sound, be prepared to find something aligned to the artistic vision in your head, and then maybe customise it in some way, or better still, create bespoke audio.

When you find an appropriate audio excerpt, it would be a great coincidence if it

CHAPTER 6

WORKING WITH AUDIO

THE
DRUM
PROGRAMMING
HANDBOOK

163

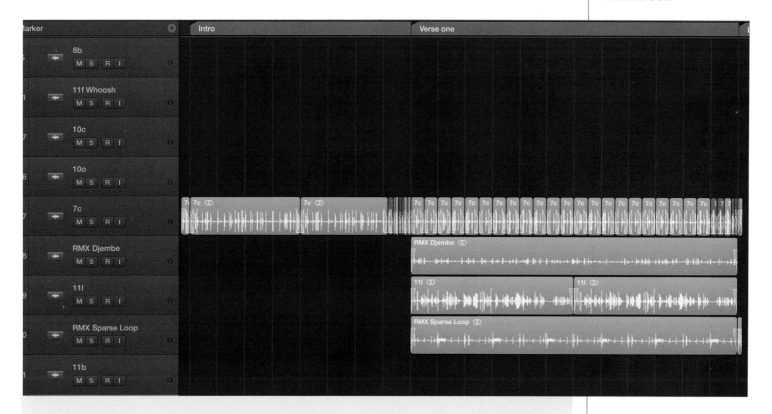

happened to be at the correct tempo. It needs to be fairly close if you wish to use it, otherwise unwanted artefacts could creep into any tempo conversion. Your DAW might automatically match the tempo to that of the tune, or you might have to do this yourself, for instance by dragging the end of the region to an appropriate bar line, so again, read the manual on this. Remember to match the number of bars that you can hear in the region to the same number on your grid. Let us use Pattern 04_16: you will have to match its tempo to the required 84bpm, but this is not a huge difference from the original. Repeat it once to fill the required eight bars.

To give it an interesting entrance, copy beats 3 and 4 of bar three to start just before the groove. Using beat displacement, align the open hi-hat eighth-note (that was originally on 3&) to land on beat 4, and keep the preceding 16th-note snare too.

Now for the fill into the next section. Slice up the last bar of the second Pattern 04_16 at some transients and rearrange/copy the slices as you like. Since the source audio does not have things like toms in it, you need to create an interesting rhythmic phrase with just kick, snare and hi-hat – drummers often fill in this fashion.

Pattern 06_23: The introduction and first verse.

TIP
Whilst coming in directly on beat 1 is obvious and powerful, anticipating it with a little flourish or fill can add musical sophistication.

VERSE ONE

Repeat Pattern 04_16 three times to fill the 12 bars of the verse. Slice each of these into two-beat long slices, and then using shuffle-edit, rearrange the order of the slices to give an interesting improvised feel. Using a slice of this length will keep all the backbeats in place on beats 2 and 4, but just move the kicks around.

On another track, add the eight-bar Pattern 06_22. This was at 86bpm and so also needs to be time-stretched to fit. Now split and copy half of the region to fill up the required 12 bars. Feel free to choose which half you prefer; it does not really matter for this exercise.

We have also layered in a djembe percussion pattern, sourced from Stylus RMX, but rendered as audio. The RMX chaos function has been employed to change the pitch, pattern, and volumes of individual notes in a way that grooves along without ever really repeating exactly. There is another layer from RMX too – a sparse tambourine part with a sustained synthetic noise on every other downbeat, and the occasional synthetic kick. You can of course use any percussion loops that you have access to.

The edits in Pattern 04_16 for last two bars of the verse.

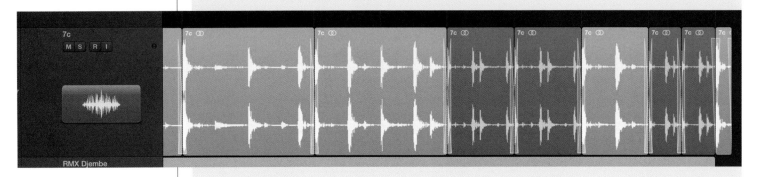

PATTERN 06_24: The 12 bars of first verse. For a fill at the end of this section, split the last bar of Pattern 04_16 into two-beat long regions and time-compress them by half, which gives a double time feel with a different sonic texture due to the shortened notes – you can copy or rearrange these new regions to your taste.

The overall effect is that of a real drummer improvising with a percussionist, with a layer of synthetic production in the background.

CHAPTER 6

WORKING WITH AUDIO

THE
DRUM
PROGRAMMING
HANDBOOK

165

LINK ONE

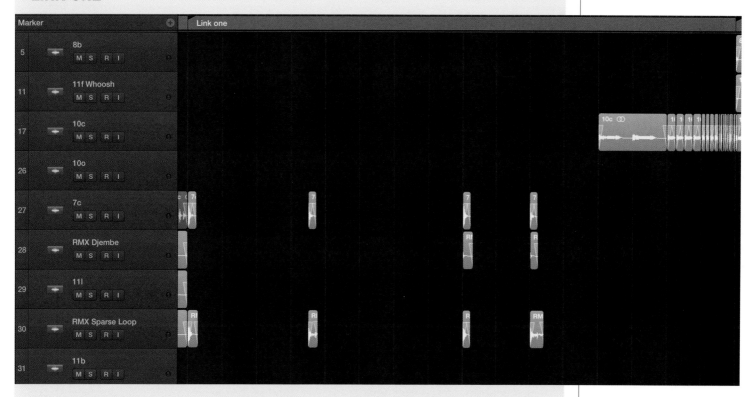

PATTERN 06_25: The four bars of the first link. This section requires some short hits on the designated notes – such hits might typically be joined in unison by the bass or perhaps a guitar chord and you might imagine other elements of the band playing between them too. You might wish to choose whether to borrow hits from the existing audio regions or import new and specific ones. Here, we have taken both kick drum and snare hits from Pattern 05_03 and Pattern 04_16 and also added the djembe, all layered together; just use your judgement when doing similar. Experiment with the actual length of region here, since you probably want to give the impression of a single strong hit each time, but also it might feel nice to allow a little of the rhythmic content to come through. You might also try mixing the order of kick and snare hits, which is much less prescribed than when playing a groove. It is just a question of taste. One-shots are often better than using slices of regions in a context such as this – they feel less 'chopped'.

The layout of Pattern 06_25. Notice the space between the specified hits.

Pattern 06_25

The layout of Pattern 06_26.

CHORUS ONE

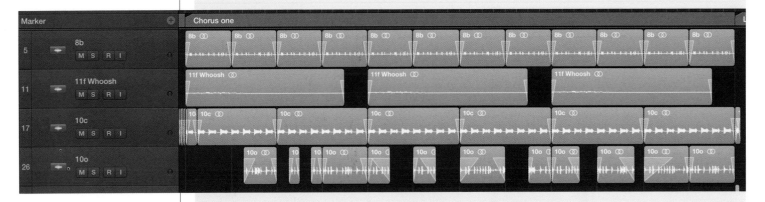

Pattern 06_26

PATTERN 06_26: The twelve bars of the first chorus. We have employed Pattern 05_03 and time-stretched it slightly to fit. It now has a slightly flabby feel due to the algorithm employed in the audio example, but arguably still has a certain charm to it; use a slicing algorithm if you require a more precise sound. Repeat it for the 16-bar duration of this section, and by adding Pattern 06_10 every four bars, the whoosh will give a useful cyclical feel.

Add another track with a two-bar bounce of Pattern Pattern 04_23. Time-stretch it to last only for one bar. That will give an interesting double time field, but turn the volume down to tuck it beneath the previous pattern; this will stop the double time being too dominant. Repeat it for the duration of the chorus. On another track still, use slices of Pattern 05_15 with fades to punctuate the phrasing – this will maintain interest. When doing this kind of thing in a real scenario, find natural gaps in the arrangement of the tune that you can accent and punctuate with such phrases.

TIP
It is often tempting to fill all the available space with grooves, but learning to punctuate particular notes of an arrangement is a skill that not only demonstrates musicality, but offers excitement and detail to the music as well. Always listen for moments were you can take this approach since it is a powerful weapon, and so often stopping (perhaps with a strong accent) and playing nothing for a tactical period is more powerful than filling it with many notes.

CHAPTER 6

WORKING WITH AUDIO

THE
DRUM
PROGRAMMING
HANDBOOK

167

LINK TWO

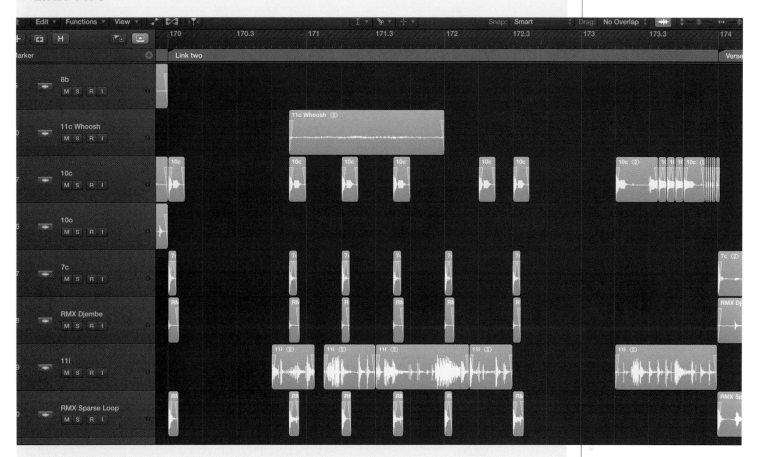

PATTERN 06_27: The four bars of the second link. The prescribed hits are slightly different here, but the same principle applies as for Link One. Superimpose Pattern 06_22, slice it up, and move it around the resulting regions in order to produce little buzzes that punctuate the principal hits, sounding both before and after, according to taste. The Pattern 06_06 whoosh could sound good, and here has been used on beat 4& of the first bar, in the manner of an acoustic crash. Create a fill by copying the end of Link One and then shuffle-editing it to provide variation. You might wish to layer some of 06_22 here as well for interest.

The layout of Pattern 06_27. Some of the space left in the previous link section has now been filled.

 Pattern 06_27

Pattern 06_28

VERSE TWO

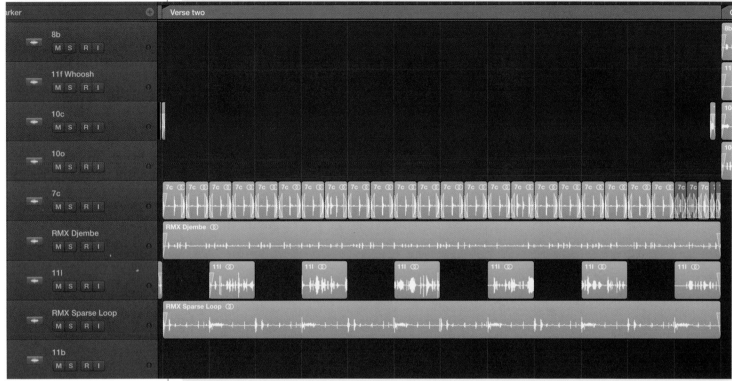

The layout of Pattern 06_28.

PATTERN 06_28: The 12 bars of the second verse. The brief requires that the acoustic part is a little more sparse in this verse. So selecting a single slice with a simple kick pattern and repeating it for the most part is a good approach when working in this way, although the result is more ostinato than actually minimal. Adding one of the other patterns every four bars can give a nice improvised feel. Once again you might scramble the order of the kit slices for variation. Try slicing up Pattern 06_13 into bar-long regions, and placing one every second bar of this section – with each slice being different, this gives the effect of a call and response against the main beat. On beat four of the last bar, anticipate the next chorus by adding one of the clap sounds from that section.

TIP

One limitation of audio is that you are committed to working with pre-constructed rhythmic phrases. If, as here, you need to change the nature of the performance (minimal was requested), then it might be better to take a different approach, for instance using a different set of audio or programming with MIDI. Of course, if you had originally created the audio regions with one-shots as we have done here, then you could go back to the MIDI sequence and edit it into an appropriate phrase for the situation.

WORKING WITH AUDIO

THE
DRUM
PROGRAMMING
HANDBOOK

169

CHORUS TWO

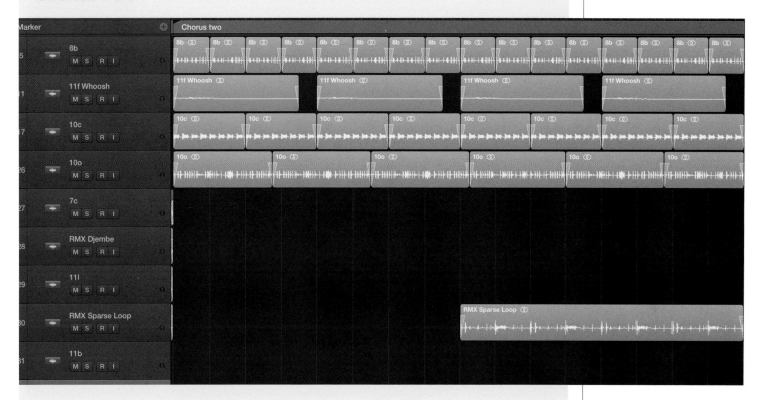

PATTERN 06_29: The 16 bars of the second chorus. This longer chorus is essentially the same as the first one except that you might wish to add another layer to come in partway through. Borrowing the RMX tambourine pattern works well for this in an unobtrusive fashion, just giving a subtle shift in texture. The double time pattern is rather louder. In the audio example, Pattern 05_15 was edited down to be 11 beats in length, and then repeated to give a polymetric and constantly varying feel.

The layout of Pattern 06_29: You can see how an extra layer comes in.

 **Pattern 06_29**

CHAPTER 6

170

THE
DRUM
PROGRAMMING
HANDBOOK

WORKING WITH AUDIO

LINK THREE

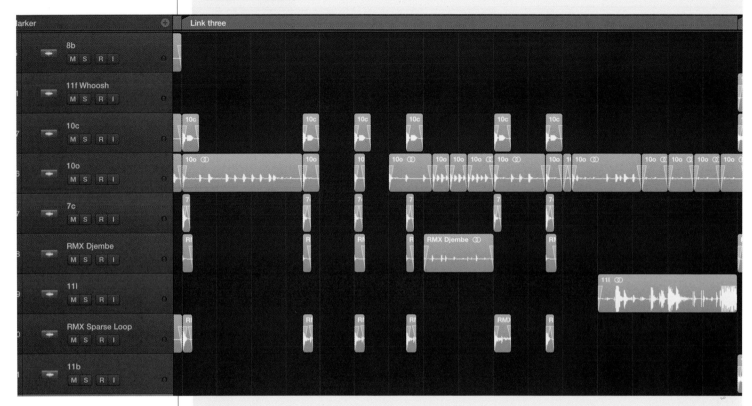

The more complex layout of Pattern 06_30.

  Pattern 06_30

PATTERN 06_30: The four bars of the third link. In this link section, phrase the specified hits as before, but this time we need to add some groove running through and between them. Slice up Pattern 06_15 and align it with the various hits. It can be very effective to take the crash cymbal notes from this pattern and align them with the specified hits, giving you the option to drag the region's start and finish out in either direction from this alignment to extend the phrasing. You will hear this for instance on the third bar, beat 2. In the second bar, program some stops so the groove drops out and that can give an exciting effect. Remember that the rest of our imaginary band is still playing through these stops.

In bar three of the audio example, there is a cymbal crash on beat 3, just before the prescribed hit on 3&. This could be thought of as a setup hit to add excitement. Also, in the transition from bar two to bar three, we have selected the cluster of four kick drum hits from

WORKING WITH AUDIO

THE
DRUM
PROGRAMMING
HANDBOOK

171

Pattern 05_15 and these are repeated. They are superimposed with the RMX Djembe, time-compressed to play at double time.

Create a fill for the last bar from a selected part of Pattern 06_22, layered with an ostinato from the jungle groove.

The layout of Pattern 06_31 showing the interplay of the different layers.

OUTRO

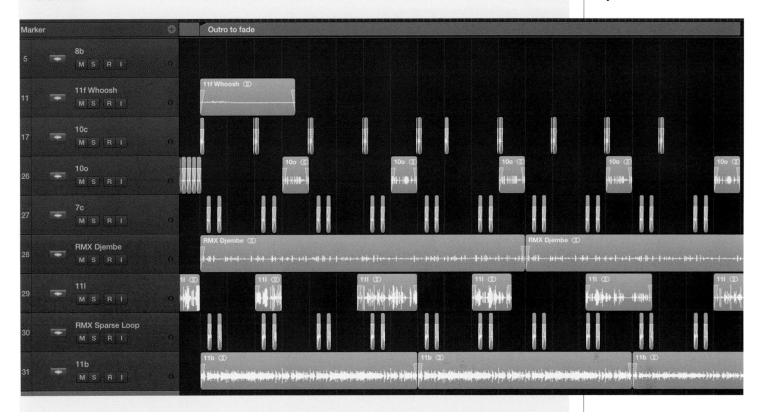

PATTERN 06_31: The 16 bars of the Outro, to fade. Start with the Whoosh sound to define the beginning of the section. For the main groove of this section, take Pattern 06_02 and time-stretch it to fit. Layer the Djembe on top of it, and then slice up Patterns 05_15 and 06_22 and place intermittently to provide flourishes and textures. The brief requires that the last two bars of the previous Link are repeated throughout this Outro, and so place the hits on beats 2 and 3&, every second bar. In the audio example the hits on beat 2 are masked by the

Pattern 06_31

172

THE
DRUM
PROGRAMMING
HANDBOOK

WORKING WITH AUDIO

snare backbeat, but it still feels like a powerful punctuation in the groove. The hit on 3& can be felt as a deep kick drum. Overall, these hits do not leap out of the (generally loud) groove, but if you imagine elements of the band playing simultaneously with them, they would provide a definite pattern.

In addition to this, an ostinato part using the kick from the chorus has been added: a two-bar pattern playing on beat 1 of the first bar, and the last 16th-note of the second bar. This simply grounds the overall feeling.

Obviously, this is a hypothetical scenario, but it demonstrates how you might typically use audio loops to create arrangements in a song structure. It is the principle that is of value here. You need to see past this specific example and practise applying this approach to whatever context/style you have. Of course, once you're comfortable with working in this fashion, there is no reason why you could not augment this approach with the various other techniques that we have discussed elsewhere.

PATTERN 06_32: The entire arrangement.

PATTERN 06_33: The entire arrangement with a click that helps you to keep track through the introduction and links.

Pattern 06_32

Pattern 06_33

Exercise One: Try writing your own short brief, just in text, making sure that you have at least one small section with some stops and starts in it; it does not have to be either one or complicated. Form an arrangement of audio regions that interprets the brief.

Exercise Two: Create a number of different interpretations of the start/stop section, experimenting with setup notes, elements of groove, and different drums performing the hits.

Exercise Three: Add a layer of MIDI one-shots to your audio arrangement: eg, cymbal crashes on the hits, or beginnings of sections, tom fills, or just phrases that run through and across the audio regions.

Things to experiment with
- Slice up several different-sounding audio regions at the kick and snare transients and re-sequence them on a single track.
- Time-stretch some whole regions by extreme factors – it does not matter if they are multiples of the original length. Then, slice at all the transients and re-sequence back into time in the order of your choice.

WORKING WITH AUDIO

THE
DRUM
PROGRAMMING
HANDBOOK

173

- Form a groove with several layers, all of which have slow fades, both in and out, in order to create a smooth, constantly moving effect.
- Create a polymetric sequence with multiple layers, and then bounce down the resulting one and two-bar phrases and keep them in your sample library.
- Utilise MIDI one-shots, rhythmic sample loops, and audio regions all in the same sequence. They do not all have to be playing at once!

CONCLUSION

Working with audio regions is a fast and gratifying way to create many types of music. There are an enormous number of approaches, but there are also limitations. The bottom line is that they are an essential part of programming, and although working with them in the most straightforward way is obvious, you should always try to develop interesting techniques that might define your own style as well.

In the next chapter we will develop our control of intricate timing to achieve a new level of musical expressivity.

Check that you can:
- Control the file formats that you bounce, record, and import.
- Control edit points relative to zero crossings.
- Edit audio regions at their transients.
- Apply fades and cross-fades.
- Comp multiple regions together.
- Time-stretch/compress whole regions to change their tempo.
- Time-stretch transients as a sound-design technique.
- Arrange multiple layers of regions creatively.

ADVANCED TIMING

CHAPTER 7

ADVANCED TIMING

So far, we have placed all of our notes at exact timing positions on the grid. Those notes are said to be quantised. We are now going to develop our palette of rhythmic feels by moving away from the grid, through consideration of swing and groove, as well as other aspects of advanced timing and rhythm.

SWING

The shuffle style (for instance Pattern 04_06 from Chapter Four) is sometimes described as a swing pattern. In their theoretical form, shuffle and swing use the first and third notes of the eighth-note triplet (quaver triplet). In contrast, a normal eighth-note (quaver) groove might be described as a straight pattern. Both patterns have a note on every beat, as well as one in between, but the in-between notes clearly do not align in time. Because of this, in drums, these two rhythms do not always sit comfortably whilst playing simultaneously, although this is not necessarily the case with pitched material.

Pattern 07_01: A kick drum playing straight eighth-notes, and a snare playing swung eighth-notes.

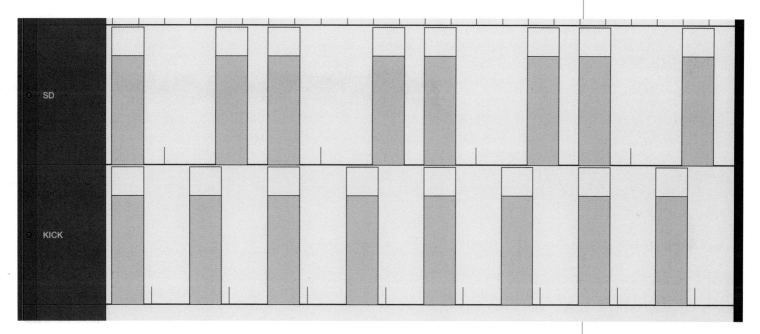

Pattern 07_01

CHAPTER 7

176

THE
DRUM
PROGRAMMING
HANDBOOK

ADVANCED TIMING

PATTERN 07_01: A kick drum playing straight eighth-notes, and a snare playing swung eighth-notes at 100bpm. Clearly, the patterns are related, and so we could actually talk about the eighth-notes being either straight or swung as a way of linking them. You can imagine taking all the in-between notes of the straight pattern and sliding them later in time until they aligned with the third eighth-note triplet of each beat. The straight groove would then have become a swung one. If you were to quantise a straight pattern to 8T, this is what would happen. In fact, you do not have to slide the straight offbeats all the way to the triplet position in order for them to start sounding swung. Even a tiny amount can make a massive difference to the feel of the groove, and many human drummers interpret the shuffle in this way, not to mention slightly swinging when ostensibly playing straight. Further, we could continue sliding offbeats beyond the triplet point, and this too can provide an interesting musical feel.

DAWs acknowledge this and generally provide ways to implement different amounts of swing. This might be termed swing strength, swing amount, or just be given a specific name or numerical value. The principle is always the same however, and basically offbeats are just time-shifted by a given amount. Purely for example, Logic Pro has a number of preset quantisation options labelled 'Swing A-E'. We will use these in our next audio examples, but whatever DAW you use will have a similar facility, with its own naming system. You will often also encounter some sort of slider that increments the time-shift by variable amounts, allowing you to gradually adjust the timing while listening.

In order to demonstrate the effect of varying degrees of swing, we will program a MIDI swing-jazz beat starting with straight eighth-notes using BFD3 sounds. You will notice the ostinato cymbal and hi-hat pattern that is punctuated with a number of offbeat and usually quiet snare hits and the occasional kick. It is not critical where these are placed at present since we are going for a very syncopated feel.

ADVANCED TIMING

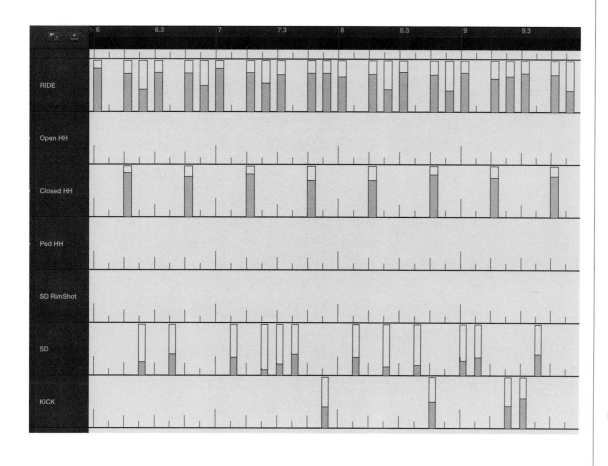

Pattern 07_02: Shown with straight eighth-notes.

PATTERN 07_02: Straight eighth-notes. Four bars at 170bpm, twice through.

PATTERN 07_03: Logic Pro eighth-note Swing A.

PATTERN 07_04: Logic Pro eighth-note Swing B.

PATTERN 07_05: Logic Pro eighth-note Swing C.

PATTERN 07_06: Logic Pro eighth-note Swing D.

Pattern 07_02

Pattern 07_03

Pattern 07_04

Pattern 07_05

Pattern 07_06

CHAPTER 7

Pattern 07_07: Logic Pro Swing E.

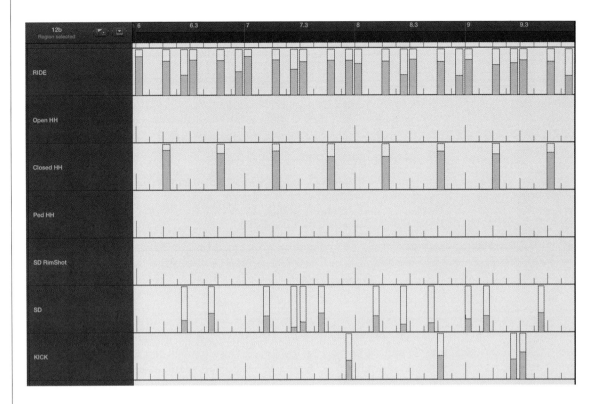

Pattern 07_07

Pattern 07_08

TIP

As always you need to study the manual of your DAW for its particular implementation of swing quantisation. Problems can still arise when importing swing-timing templates from third parties, of which there are many (of varying quality/authenticity) on the Internet. It is therefore useful to have some understanding of the various naming conventions. The famed Akai MPC60 and MPC 3000 hardware sequencers offered many different flavours of swing setting. These were typified by a percentage – 50 per cent means that the notes are evenly spaced and 66 per cent meant perfect triplets. Typically, the various in-between swings were listed as 51 per cent, 52 per cent, etc.

In Cubase and Nuendo, a swing value of 0% means that the notes are being played straight, whereas a swing of 100% equals perfect triplets. In Ableton Live, you will find both systems of nomenclature in the Groove Pool.

Pro Tools helpfully offers Cubase, Logic, MPC, and more groove settings, but although MPC percentages behave as expected, when working with straight quantise values the additional percentage slider requires 300 per cent to move by an entire grid position, but has a 200 per cent maximum value when working with grooves. Apparently, with control comes complexity, yet all that happens is a time delay of every second note. To the manual…

PATTERN 07_07: Logic Pro eighth-note **Swing E (exact triplet amount).** You can see how in Pattern 07_07 every in-between note has been moved closer to the following note when Swing E has been applied. The grid is still showing the original eighth-notes.

PATTERN 07_08: Logic Pro eighth-note **Swing F.**

ADVANCED TIMING

The principles of swing can also be applied to other note values, for instance 16th-notes (semiquavers). In this case, all the eighth-notes will remain on the grid, but the in-between 16th-notes will be time-shifted as before. These swing settings will typically be called something like '16th-note Swing A-E'. The relative amount of swing in the 16th-note case is the same; you might think of swing in a general sense as moving every second (offbeat) note relative to the grid of the prescribed note value.

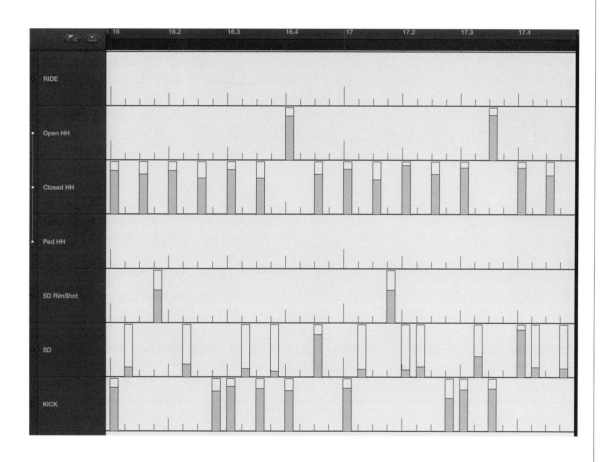

Pattern 07_09: A two-bar 16th-note-based funk pattern.

PATTERN 07_09: A two-bar 16th-note-based funk pattern, played four times at 116bpm.
It utilises ghost notes, anticipates the beat 4 snares by one 16th-note and displaces beat 4 of the first bar by an eighth-note.

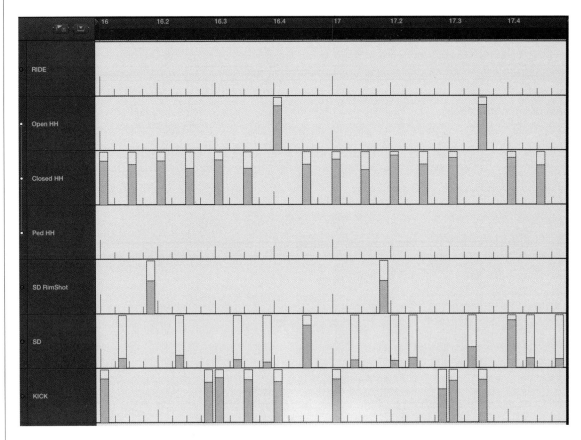

*Pattern 07_10: With Swing
16D quantisation.*

PATTERN 07_10: **Pattern 07_09 with Swing 16D quantisation, repeated four times at
116bpm.** With the grid still showing straight 16th-notes.

TIMING SWING

Unless your ears are very special, it will be quite hard to hear the difference of a single
percentage point of swing, and typically making jumps of a few per cent gives the most
discernible results. Delay values of less than exact triplets give a behind-the-beat feel or
'pulling', whereas values above exact triplets feel as if they are 'pushing' the beat, almost
rushing. Much is said about pushing and pulling rhythm, but depending on tempo, it is largely
the timing of the in-between notes that gives this impression.

ADVANCED TIMING

Exercise One: Practise applying different swing presets to some of your own beats. Also experiment with adjusting the various amounts of swing with a slider if you have such control available in your DAW.

Exercise Two: Take a couple of different beats that represent an imaginary verse and chorus of a song, and give the two sections different amounts of swing. Again, experiment to find some transitions that are musical and create different effects, both subtle and more dramatic. In general, subtle is better in such a context.

Exercise Three: As an ear-training exercise, spend some time listening to music that you like and try to identify some tunes that use a swing feel. Try to replicate this feel in your own beats.

GROOVE

Whereas swing is a rhythmic feel that is symmetrical over every given note value, the notion of groove is to replicate the micro timing of a longer passage of music and apply this timing to your own sequences. Typically, this longer passage might be either a MIDI performance or audio loop with a distinctive feel or a commercial track. If you want to use such a loop in an arrangement, keeping its feel and locking up the timing of your own programmed parts to match it, then this is the way forward. Similarly, if you hear a tune with a great feel then you can extract a rhythmic template from it and simply apply the timing to your own work.

As always, every DAW has its own particular way of doing this, but the principle is always the same. You need to identify the transients in the source audio, and then define their timing as a groove template – this template can then be applied as with any other quantisation. The source audio will typically be a small number of bars long and its timing will repeat in multiples of this length when you apply it.

Let's do a walk through of the process of applying a groove from a classic track to a MIDI beat.

Steps:
- Choose a source.
- Define an area of it to use.
- Identify the rhythmic content.
- Extract this content and generate a groove template.
- Apply the template to the chosen destination sequence.

We first need to select the track that we are interested in; we also have to consider the sound of the track. If for instance it has a great feeling that is being driven by the ghost notes of the snare, it might actually be hard to identify exactly when these notes happen, since there might be few obvious transients to detect in the waveform. Having said that, if a band has a great collective feel,

TIP

When using a MIDI source, everything is rather simplified, since the MIDI notes by definition already carry their own timing information. You will only need to define the appropriate region as being a groove template.

then the transients of the pitched instruments will serve you perfectly well. Here, we have used the disco classic 'Le Freak' by Chic and have imported it onto an audio track.

We must then define a section of the song, preferably a 'groove section' without a loud melodic part that could mask the transients. There is just such a passage in the middle of this tune. It is best to start with a length like one or two bars since any longer becomes hard to hear as a groove, and more like a randomisation of timing once taken into a new context. Without using a metronome, we have precisely edited the audio to define a region that plays exactly the two bars that we want.

We then need move this region to ensure that it starts on a downbeat in the timeline, and use a DAW function to adjust the tempo to match that of the excerpt – be careful not to do this the other way round since it is easy to inadvertently change the timing of the audio. The DAW metronome should now lock tightly with our excerpt (we did not use it previously since it would only have confused things). Crucially, the grid will also now be aligned to the timing of our audio, and therefore the precise position of the transients can be extracted relative to it.

Next, we need to detect all the transients – read your DAW manual if you do not know how to do this. This process will be automatic to some degree once triggered. You may well need to add some transient markers manually beyond those that are automatically detected. Since we are developing a quantisation template, if your source audio does not happen to have a note on one of the typical subdivisions, then you should take a best guess at adding a transient at that point. Placing this on the grid is likely to be the best strategy, but matching the swing of an adjacent transient by eye can also work well.

It is also possible that the automatic detection might guess wrongly, especially if there are two notes in the source audio that are very close together. Again, we might need to edit this, either by deleting unwanted transients or by moving existing ones. The end result should be that you have exactly the same number of transients per bar as the note value that best represents the feel of the excerpt. There is more on this process in Chapter Six.

PROPELLORHEAD RECYCLE

Propellerhead ReCycle is a dedicated piece of third party software that is specifically designed to make transient detection easy and intuitive. It has a couple of main advantages over some DAWs in that you can audition individual slices without starting the transport, as well as locking specific detections while changing the auto-detect sensitivity. Together they give a fast and flexible workflow. As well as the onset, you can hear the very end of a given slice; if there is a click then it is likely that the following transient is slightly too late and what you are hearing is part of that transient in the preceding slice. In such a case you might wish to manually adjust the transient to obtain a more precise lock, but be mindful of always using zero-crossings too, even if these slightly disagree with any such click or visual information.

TIP

If you have a function that can make the song position line jump between transients, with a key command to split the region at the desired transient, that can save time and increase accuracy.

ADVANCED TIMING

ReCycle can export a MIDI file that can be imported into your DAW to define the groove template. ReCycle defined a convention for beatslicing that many other manufacturers have followed, by incrementing successive note pitches in the MIDI file chromatically, the idea being that each pitch triggered a slice of audio on a different sampler keyzone. When creating templates however, it is only the timing of the notes that matters, and the pitches are irrelevant.

Transients of the two-bar loop in ReCycle

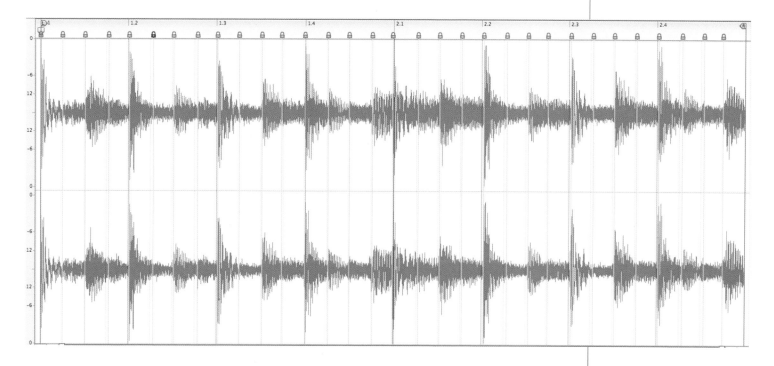

This shows all the transients of the two-bar loop in ReCycle: these are displayed as the vertical lines with padlocks above. At this magnification, it is quite hard to tell that they are not the same as a regular grid.

TIP

Once you have checked and assigned suitable transients, you will be able to apply regular quantisation to your audio as well. This works in exactly the same way as for MIDI, but the quality of the audio will deteriorate if it needs to be moved to far, so apply with care.

184

THE
DRUM
PROGRAMMING
HANDBOOK

ADVANCED TIMING

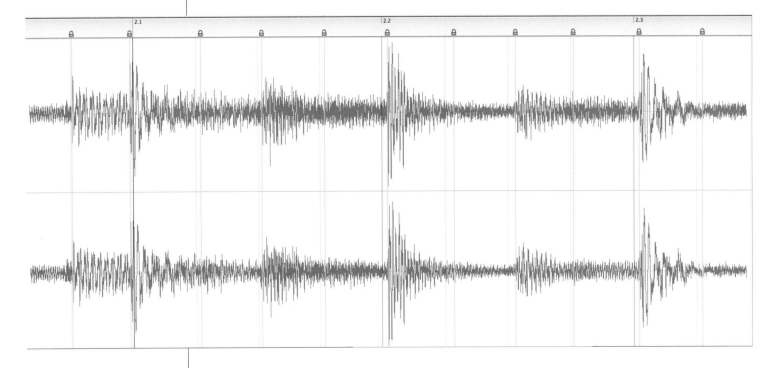

Transients of the two-bar loop, with greater magnification.

 Pattern 07_11

With greater magnification, it is quite apparent that this groove is not the same as the grid.

PATTERN 07_11: The two-bar groove extraction playing a single note, repeated another three times at 116bpm.

Once we have either properly aligned transient markers or an equivalent MIDI file, we can import the result into the DAW groove library (yes, read your manual), and use it just like any other quantisation setting. The end result will be the timing of the source audio imposed on whatever we quantise with it.

ADVANCED TIMING

THE
DRUM
PROGRAMMING
HANDBOOK

185

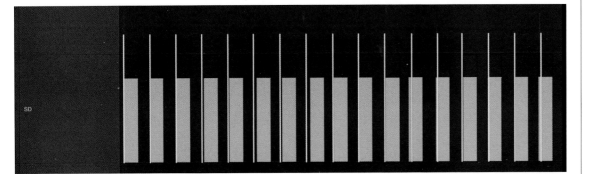

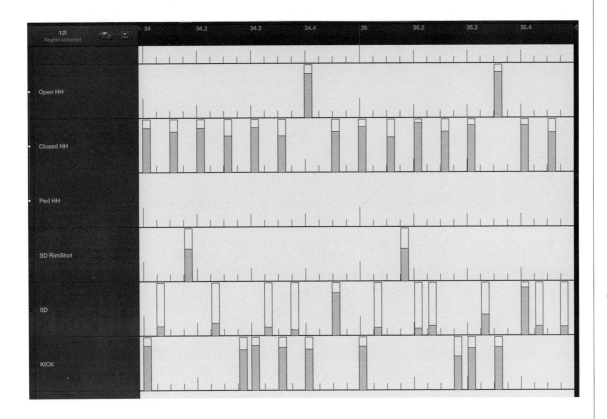

Pattern 07_12: Pattern 07_09 with 'Le Freak' groove quantisation. The first bar of the MIDI file that ReCycle generated. The white vertical lines emphasise the grid.

Pattern 07_12

PATTERN 07_12: Pattern 07_09 with 'Le Freak' groove quantisation, played four times at 116bpm. We now have a beat with a distinctly human feel to it. It pushes and pulls all within its own length, mostly feeling quite straight, but with just a few notes swung to different degrees.

186

THE
DRUM
PROGRAMMING
HANDBOOK

ADVANCED TIMING

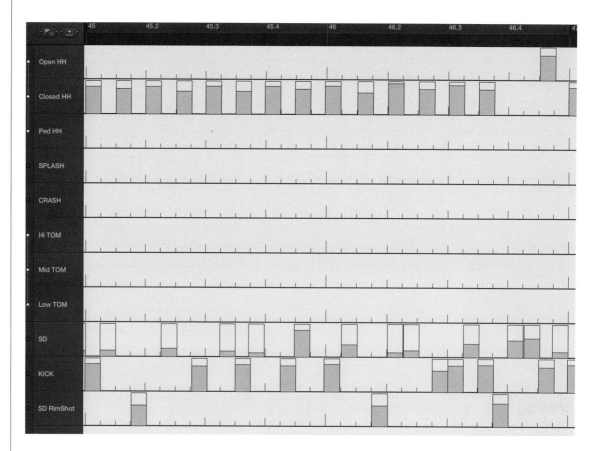

The third and fourth bars of Pattern 07_13.

PATTERN 07_13: An eight-bar long development of Pattern 07_09 with 'Le Freak' groove quantisation throughout, played twice at 116bpm.

ADVANCED TIMING

THE
DRUM
PROGRAMMING
HANDBOOK

187

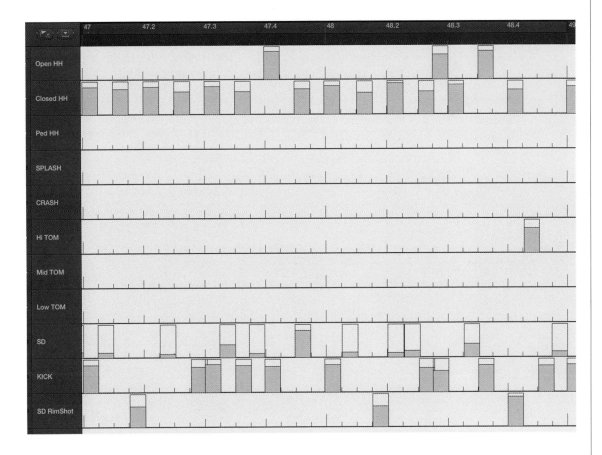

The fifth and sixth bars of Pattern 07_13.

In order to demonstrate the effect of groove quantisation on a longer passage, Pattern 07_09 has been copied three times and a number of variations edited into the beat. There are a number of snare drum beat displacements and velocity changes, a change in certain kick drum placements, the occasional tom tom hit, and a couple of splash cymbals. The two-bar groove template repeats throughout the eight-bar duration of this new sequence, however the changing accents and phrases disguise it to some degree, but still leaving a quite human effect.

TIP

Whatever kind of groove you are applying, you should think about using it for the other elements of your arrangement as well; you can apply all types of quantisation to audio elements too. The bass is particularly important, as indeed are the other elements of the rhythm section, typically percussion, guitar, and keyboards, etc. Having said that, it is worth trying different grooves on other instruments as well, to find if there is a particular combination of feels that you like. If the performances are generally good, then you might not wish to do anything to some, but simply anchoring the arrangement by tightening key elements can be useful. There are so many combinations and contexts that it is impossible to offer a definitive rule, but be prepared to experiment and take note of groove combinations that you like in case you forget them by the time you are working on another track at another time.

188
THE
DRUM
PROGRAMMING
HANDBOOK

ADVANCED TIMING

■ CHECK OUT

The track 'Kid Charlemagne' by Steely Dan. Played by Bernard Purdie, the drums have an infectious and slightly swingy groove to them, but some of the tom fills are played as much more rigid 16th-notes. Purdie also developed a famous approach to playing the shuffle.

The seventh and eighth bars of Pattern 07_13.

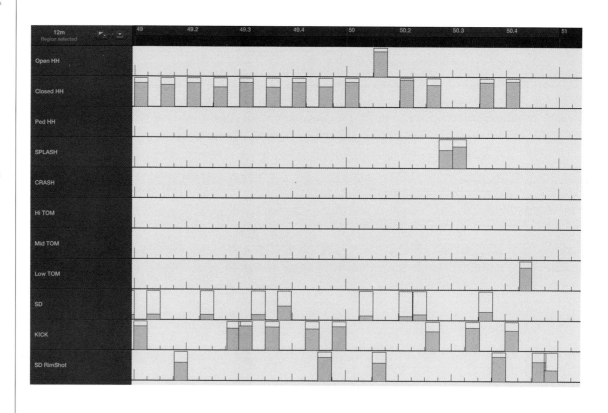

TIP

From time to time you will encounter a function called humanise; here we mean with respect to timing, although this is often also used on velocities. This generally offers a prescribed amount of random variation in the timing of the notes and is supposed to emulate the way a human plays the drums. You might enjoy the effect of this – or you might wish that your 'drummer' had not just been to the bar.

ADVANCED TIMING

THE
DRUM
PROGRAMMING
HANDBOOK

189

PARTIAL QUANTISATION

There are other types of quantisation that move notes towards a destination grid or swing position, but not all the way. Typically, this function will move each note by a proportion of its deviation from the ideal, perhaps specified by a percentage. This has the effect of tightening the original performance, but not to the point of imposing an absolute and consistent quantisation. Such a function might be named as Iterative Quantise or Q-strength.

There is also a function that does not quantise notes that are deemed to be close enough to the ideal already, and only operates on notes outside a prescribed range. Again, this has the effect of tightening without total quantisation. This function might be named something like Don't Quantise or Q-range.

Further still, various DAWs have more advanced and specialised quantisation functions, and it is worth reading about them in order to fully understand all the tools in your toolbox, since it might be one of these that is perfectly suited to making your music better with less effort.

Exercise One: Find a number of commercial releases that you think have a great feel, pick a couple of bars, bearing in mind the ease with which you might extract the timing information, and make groove templates. Apply these templates to a number of your preferred MIDI sequences and think about the effect.

Exercise Two: Generate a longer (starting at four bars) template and apply it to a one-bar ostinato MIDI sequence of your own. The longer template might work better with a shorter ostinato.

Exercise Three: Set up an imaginary verse/chorus arrangement using two different beats, and experiment with applying different grooves to each section.

ADDING DETAIL WITH SHORT NOTE VALUES

When programming so far, we have generally stuck to using set note values in a given passage. We will now experiment with decorating drumbeats with some shorter note clusters. The note values that we will use are 32nd-notes (demisemiquavers) and triplet 16th-notes (triplet semiquavers). These are typically denoted by quantise values of 32 and 24 respectively.

TIP

It is worth considering the technique that drummers often apply when playing short note values. It is common to use so-called double strokes that play the hands in an order such as RRLLRRLL. With practice, it is possible to perform this very rapidly, but often at low volume. Such a phrase might be preceded or ended with a single stroke that will often be greater in volume. Drummers often practise specific clusters of these combinations, for instance the five-stroke roll – RRLLR, or the six-stroke roll – RLLRRL, and these might also reverse the order of the hands. At speed, each double stroke will be on the same drum, although each hand might be on a different drum. Drummers also develop fast double-hits on the kick drum, although often these end up slightly quieter than regular kick drum hits.

190

THE
DRUM
PROGRAMMING
HANDBOOK

ADVANCED TIMING

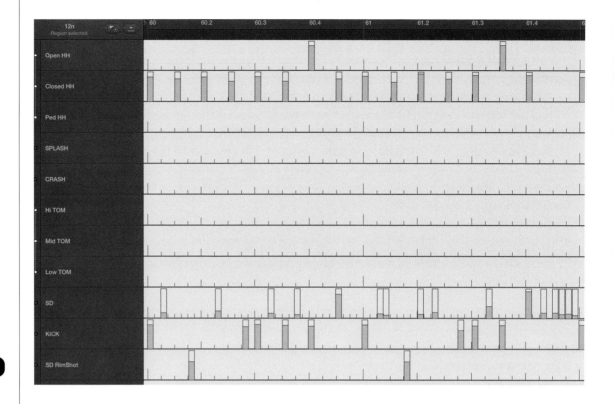

*The first and second bars
of Pattern 07_14.*

**PATTERN 07_14: An eight-bar long development of Pattern 07_13 with some ornaments,
played twice through at 116bpm.** The grid of the snare drum has been set to 32nd-notes, and we
have added an extra ghost note just after beat 1e in the second bar. Notice that the actual snare on
beat 1e still retains its groove-derived timing; in some cases you might wish to quantise this note
more rigidly. On beat 4&, we have emulated a five-stroke roll on the snare with the last note landing
on the hi-hat – note the velocities and think of how a drummer might play RRLLR.

ADVANCED TIMING

THE
DRUM
PROGRAMMING
HANDBOOK

191

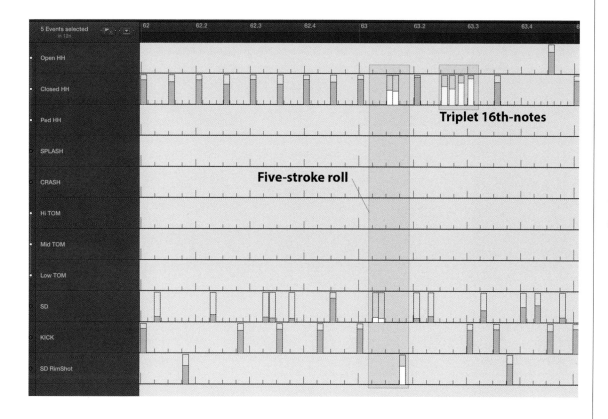

The third and fourth bars of Pattern 07_14.

The third and fourth bars of Pattern 07_14, highlighting a five-stroke roll, split between snare and hi-hat, with the grid for each of these set to 32. There is also a triplet 16th-note phrase, which was created with the grid set to 24.

There is another five-stroke roll in the second bar, starting on beat 1e, this time implied LLRRL since (for a right-handed player) the left hand often resides on the snare; this time the doubles are split between the snare drum and the hi-hat, landing on the anticipated backbeat on beat 1a. This gives a rather funky and fluttering feel. There is also a group of triplet 16th-notes on beat 1& of the second bar, on the hi-hat (its grid is set to triplet 16th-notes). The first and last notes of this cluster retain their original groove-based timing, but the two notes in between were placed on a grid set to 24. Again, depending on the groove template you are using, this might need some adjustment.

192

THE
DRUM
PROGRAMMING
HANDBOOK

ADVANCED TIMING

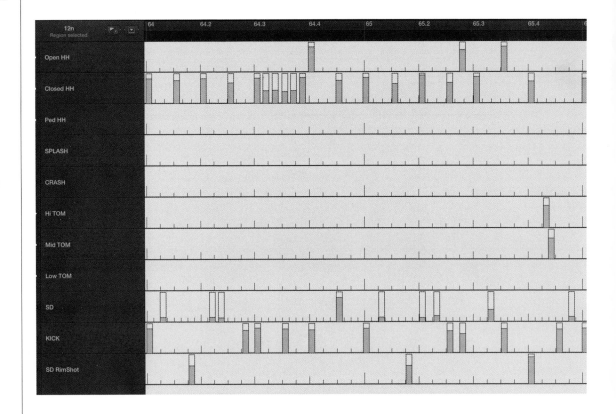

The fifth and sixth bars of Pattern 07_14.

On beat three of the first bar we have emulated a six-stroke roll on the hi-hat using triplet 16th-notes, again with velocities that imply a certain sticking. The kick drum is playing eighth-notes at the same time as this phrase, which align naturally with the middle note of the cluster. The last note of the roll is an open hi-hat. We have also added a second tom tom hit one 32nd-note after the existing one.

ADVANCED TIMING

THE
DRUM
PROGRAMMING
HANDBOOK

193

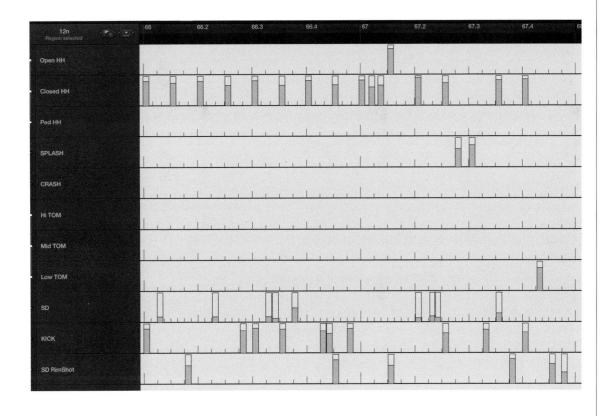

The seventh and eighth bars of Pattern 07_14.

In addition to another triplet 16th-note roll on the hi-hat and more ghost notes, there is a 32nd-note double hit on the kick in the first bar on beat 4e.

Adding ornaments such as these can give flamboyance and texture in almost any style. Although we have applied these to a groove here, the same note values can be used to great effect on all manner of fills.

Exercise One: Take one of your existing beats and spice it up using 32nd-notes and 16th-note triplets.

Exercise Two: Duplicate your groove a number of times, and change the ornaments in each repeat. The effect should be of an ostinato with subtly moving textures.

Exercise Three: Take some fills that you have already programmed and add some of these note values to add interest. Although snare ghosts can be most effective in this context, louder tom-tom and kick clusters will be more powerful. Try both.

TIP
It is worth mentioning how these ornaments fit into the greater workflow. You really need to have established whatever rhythmic feel you are going for before adding them. Imagine you have a tightly quantised 16th-note part and you add some 32nd-note decorations; if you then try to apply a swung 16th-note feel, all the 32nd notes will be pushed to the nearest swung 16th-note, likely ending up superimposed on their previous neighbours.

CHAPTER 7

LAYERING DIFFERENT GROOVES

When you layer beats that feature different grooves, there are a number of issues to consider in order to get a good feel, since the in-between notes will happen at slightly different times and this can feel lumpy. There are two main issues to consider, the sounds you are using and their relative volumes.

If you attempt to layer to beats with strong sharp sounds at similar volumes you might indeed be dissatisfied with the result.

PATTERN 07_15: Pattern 07_09 with straight 16th-note quantisation played four times at 116bpm, layered with a loud shuffled beat from Stylus RMX. You can clearly hear that the patterns do not sit comfortably together; however, if you reduce the volume of one and tuck it underneath, you can create some nice feels. This happens because the ear is very sensitive to loud transients happening at very slightly different times, but if the transients of a second beat layer are quieter, the ear is more forgiving and locks onto the main beat, and you feel the groove in a more pleasing way. Of course, you may just prefer the first version.

PATTERN 07_16: Pattern 07_09 with straight 16th-note quantisation played four times at 116bpm, layered with the same shuffled RMX beat, but quieter. This composite beat is now much more agreeable and has a nicer feel. In terms of the sounds themselves, layering different tones can be quite forgiving in this context. Only having one drum kit part supplemented by percussive instruments such as shakers and congas can blend very effectively. With care, you can layer several different grooves on top of each other. This tends to give a very dense sound to the composite beat, and is a common technique in popular music styles. Exactly the same applies when considering the pitched instruments in an arrangement, which can be grooving differently, although keeping the bass (guitar) and the kick drum locked tightly is often beneficial.

Exercise One: Combine some drum and percussion parts with a slight swing on one and the other more rigidly quantised. Change the amount of swing, and adjust volumes as required, listening for what you like and what you do not.

Exercise Two: Repeat Exercise One, but with both parts swinging by different amounts.

Exercise Three: Build up a number of layers with different timing inflections on each layer. You man feel that something clashes. To pull it in line, just copy the groove from another track and apply it to that part.

TIP

When drummers deliberately play two notes almost simultaneously, but very slightly apart, this is termed a flam. When programming, any notes that are almost, but not quite in time with each other are often referred to as flamming.

CHAPTER 7

ADVANCED TIMING

THE
DRUM
PROGRAMMING
HANDBOOK

195

CONSTRUCTING A PROGRAMMED PERFORMANCE TO FREE-TIME AUDIO

Everything we have done up to this point has been based around a fixed tempo. It is possible to set up tempo variations in your DAW, and these can be very useful when constructing an arrangement, for instance making the chorus of a song one or two bpm faster than the verse in order to raise its intensity, or perhaps gradually getting slower at the end of a tune. Read the manual for your DAW and find out how to control its tempo.

Sometimes, you might want to program drums along with a pre-recorded piece of music that has not been played to a fixed click and therefore has natural human tempo variations within it. These variations make it impossible to use the grid for programming, and although it is possible to ignore visual references and program by ear, it is a long winded and cumbersome process with much guesswork involved; generally, playing live with a MIDI keyboard is the best approach to this, but you are at the mercy of your performance skills on the keyboard. In this workshop however, we will look at a much more sophisticated approach to tackling this problem, that of beat mapping.

This process goes by a number of names in different systems, but the principle is always the same. Again, read the manual in order to understand how your DAW facilitates this. We need to identify important transients in the audio and specify their intended position in a given bar along the timeline of the DAW. Once the transients are mapped in this fashion, the DAW can automatically produce a tempo map that causes its internal timing to adjust in order that the grid maintains alignment with the audio, thus allowing us to program in the familiar manner, but constantly maintaining synchronisation. Remember that although MIDI notes are generally tied to the grid, audio (including sampled loops) will play back exactly as it was recorded, independently of any tempo changes, unless you have set up automatic time stretching.

To explore this we will take a recording of a loose, but 'feeling good' rock band and program a drum part with the FXpansion BFD3 plug-in.

PATTERN 07_17: a 16-bar tune with no drums.

This track is at about 116 bpm, and was played without a click. It features both rhythm and lead guitars, Hammond organ, and a MIDI bass-guitar part played live on a keyboard with Spectrasonics Trilian, a software instrument that can replicate many of the performance nuances of a real player such as slides and muted notes.

First, you must edit the source audio so that its first note (which we will assume to be on

TIP
If you are having difficulty hearing what is described as a problem here, then set the pattern to loop and listen to it over and over until you start to perceive the double hits. This style of listening is a powerful technique that helps to really understand what is going on with a piece of music in any context.

■ CHECK OUT
'Gust Of Wind' from *GIRL* by Pharrell Williams, which has a number of different grooves playing simultaneously that are quite easy to hear in the arrangement. You will hear a swinging bass guitar, loose-feeling electronic percussion and 16th-note-sounding strings. The 16th-note hi-hat has an interesting feel.

 Pattern 07_17

TIP

If you need to work with a multi-instrument file where it is hard to identify clear transients, then a good option is to perform a manual metronome-type part playing quarter-notes along with it via MIDI. Edit this until it feels tight, and then use this as the reference for beat mapping. Even if you then have all the quarter-notes, do not be tempted to add too many markers.

 Pattern 07_18

 Pattern 07_19

beat one) aligns precisely with beat one of your DAW grid. This might typically involve deleting some unwanted audio at the beginning of the tune and sliding the regions until they are aligned as required. If you are working with multitrack audio, then make sure that you treat all the tracks as one as you edit in order to maintain coherence between them, since even tiny differences can have a big impact on both the feel and the sound.

Next, set an approximate starting tempo in your DAW on beat one. There will likely be tools to help you discover this by selecting the first couple of bars and asking the DAW to compute the tempo, but you can also do it by manually adjusting the tempo through trial and error.

Now, you must identify the transients in the source. If multiple instruments are playing together with human timing, then it can be very hard to determine exactly where the beat is since several different instruments might be flamming. If the band is very tight, then this will be okay, but if not and you have access to the multitracks, it is a good idea to select a single instrument and use only this as a reference, although some DAWs actually allow selection of transients from a range of audio tracks. We will use just a rhythm guitar part as our timing reference here. First, program a simple, but tightly quantised one-bar pattern that is repeated over the duration of the tune.

PATTERN 07_18: rhythm guitar and a one-bar drum loop.

PATTERN 07_19: just the rhythm guitar.

You can hear that in this pattern things start out quite well, but a clash soon develops between man and machine. It is clear that we need a more flexible strategy.

Next, use your transient-detection function on this guitar part, and adjust the sensitivity (which will add more or less transient markers) until you capture most of the key transients. On a distorted guitar such as this, it can be hard to see where these should be if the chords are rolling into each other, but try to get as many obvious clean detections as possible with that worrying about capturing everything. You can add further transient markers manually if you feel the need.

It is a good idea to audition the file precisely between each pair of transients since you can often hear small errors in the detection points; we need to adjust these manually. Work through the entire guitar part in this fashion, since if any of the transient markers are a little bit off the mapping will not work so well. You can lose a lot of time if you map the whole thing only to realise that there was an error earlier, since this error will cascade through all subsequent tempo operations.

ADVANCED TIMING

THE
DRUM
PROGRAMMING
HANDBOOK

197

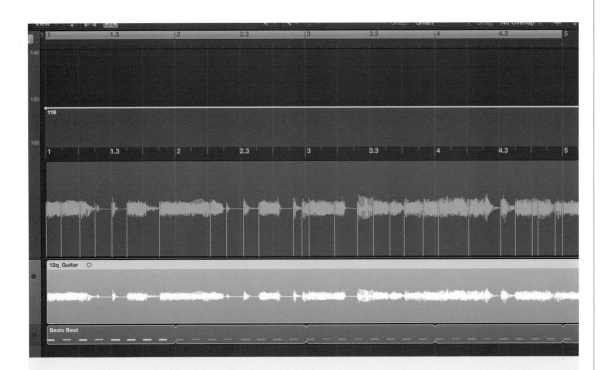

*The first four bars of
transient markers.*

At the bottom of the diagram is the basic one-bar drumbeat, next up is the rhythm-guitar audio, and above that the vertical transient markers can be seen superimposed upon this same audio. Next up is the grid of bar numbers with a resolution of eighth-notes (chosen to match the general feel of the guitar), and at the top is the tempo map, with a starting tempo of 116bpm.

Now for the tricky bit. Study the guitar part in two different ways: use your eyes to spot where the audio obviously drifts from the grid, and also use your ears and count along in order to understand which beats (and subdivisions) particular transients fall on. Solo the guitar whilst you do this so that you only have its own internal timing as a reference point. It might take a bit of practice to get comfortable and accurate doing this, but it is very important. Keep the click turned off to avoid mixed messages about the timing.

You now need to associate certain transient markers with the appropriate places on the grid. It can be tempting to make many alignments, but doing so too frequently will give a very lumpy and awkward-sounding result. In general, try to do as few as you can get away with and pick musically important points. If your music is based around a strong beat one, then that is an obvious place to focus. But if, as in this case, the music is syncopated with many offbeats, you will have to work a little harder. This tune has many accents on beat 4&, so in bar three, link the transient marker that you can hear as happening on this beat with the corresponding point on the grid.

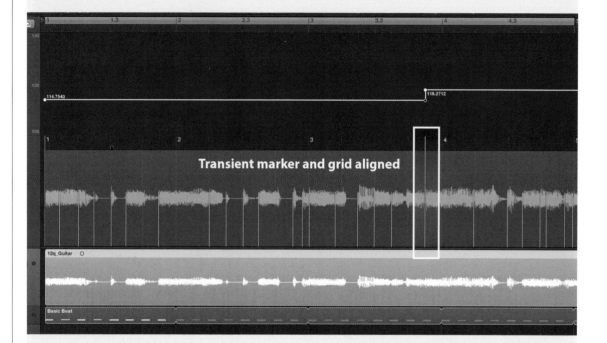

Pattern 07_20: The vertical line represents a transient marker linked to the grid. Bar numbers are indicated.

Pattern 07_20

PATTERN 07_20: The first four bars of the tune – guitar and drums after linking beat 4& of bar three. You will notice that a single tempo of 118.2712bpm has been inserted at the linked transient, and the map has also calculated backwards and started the piece at 114.754bpm in order that the correct amount of time elapses to align our marker with the grid. This precision of tempo is necessary in these circumstances, but if your own readings do not match exactly then do not worry. This is simply because of tiny differences in where the transients have been detected.

ADVANCED TIMING

THE
DRUM
PROGRAMMING
HANDBOOK

199

 Pattern 07_21

PATTERN 07_21: The first four bars again, guitar and drums, after curving the tempo shift.

A sudden change of 4bpm can feel a little jarring, and in fact was not what happened in the original performance. Because the performance got slightly faster over a period of time, it is a good idea to substitute the step tempo-change with one that gradually changes – a tempo curve. Experiment with different shapes of curve, using your ears to determine the best fit. The problem now is that such a curve takes a different amount of time from a steady tempo to reach the link point, and so the link point might typically slip while trying to compensate. You can hear that things are holding together better until the end, at which point we lose synchronisation.

Correct the link point visually by selecting a tempo of 117.6bpm or so to realign the link point after the ramp. The synchronisation at the end is still slightly off, but the next adjustment will feed back into this area. You will notice that many of the transient markers are now fairly aligned with the grid as a consequence of what we have done.

PATTERN 07_22: The first four bars, guitar and drums after curving with the link point now corrected.

TIP
On some systems, the tempo map calculates backwards by one step to the previous change. This is because a change of tempo by definition causes a different amount of time to elapse up until a given point. For this reason, it is good practice to work methodically in a forward direction, always starting from the beginning.

 Pattern 07_22

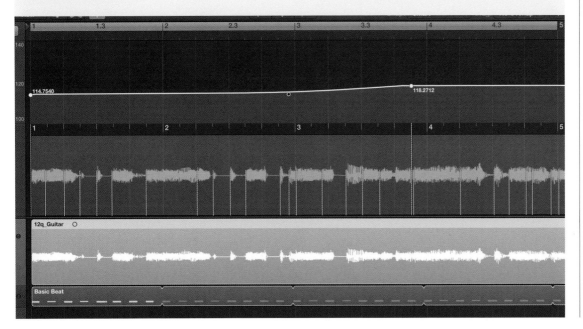

Pattern 07_22: The first four bars: the tempo curve with the corrected link point.

Pattern 07_23

The next four bars sound and look fairly steady at this tempo and so we do not really need to do anything here.

PATTERN 07_23: Guitar and drums over bars nine to 13. They are drifting out of time and so need correction. Place another link point at beat one of bar nine there so that any further tempo adjustments do not cascade backwards past this point.

After locking at both that point and the push (a term sometimes given to a chord change that anticipates that downbeat) on beat 4& of bar 11, the audio is misaligned once more, but this can be corrected by adding a link point at beat 3& of bar 10. After applying a tempo curve to smooth the transition, correct this link point to around 117.8bpm, which will help it regain its alignment. This value is a minimal difference from the following tempo change, but importantly this point separates the tempo curve from a section of steady tempo, thus controlling the greater alignment.

PATTERN 07_24: Guitar and drums over bars nine to 13 – after correction.

Pattern 07_24

Pattern 07_24: The tempo map over bars nine to 13.

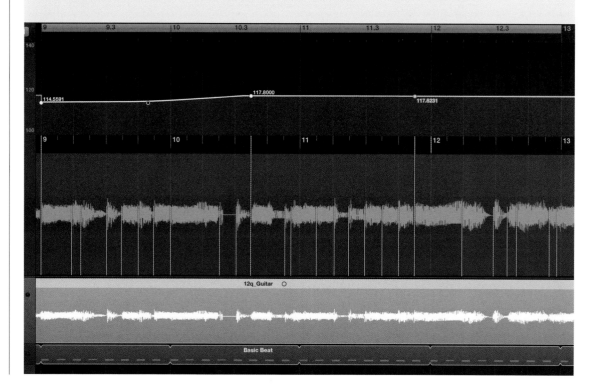

ADVANCED TIMING

THE
DRUM
PROGRAMMING
HANDBOOK

201

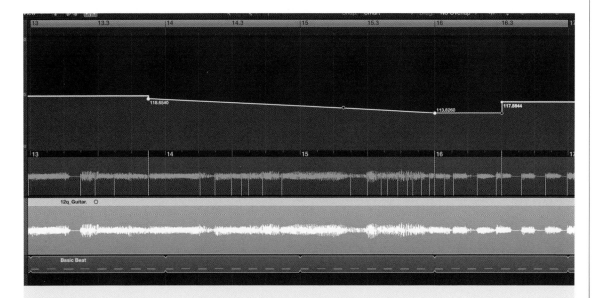

Pattern 07_25: Guitar and drums over bars 13 to 17.

PATTERN 07_25: Guitar and drums over bars 13 to 17 – after adding only a curve.
Another tempo curve has been added, but the 16th-notes in bar 16 have now been displaced out of time. There is a more dramatic looking tempo shift here, but this was just the phrasing of the band. Smooth out this section by ear with curves and necessary compensation.

CHAPTER 7

202

THE
DRUM
PROGRAMMING
HANDBOOK

ADVANCED TIMING

Pattern 07_25: Bars 13 to 17 after final adjustments.

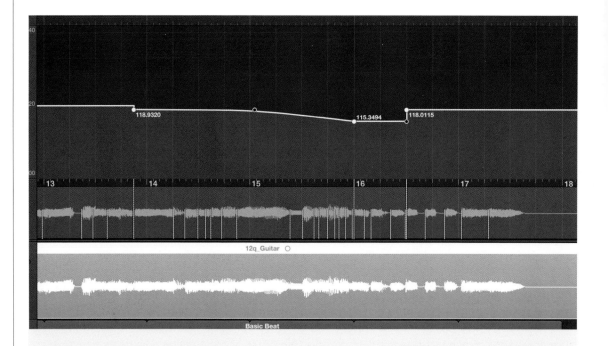

Bars 13 to 17: final adjustments to bring the end 16th-note phrase back into time, although not all the way, since that felt slightly unnatural.

ADVANCED TIMING

THE
DRUM
PROGRAMMING
HANDBOOK

203

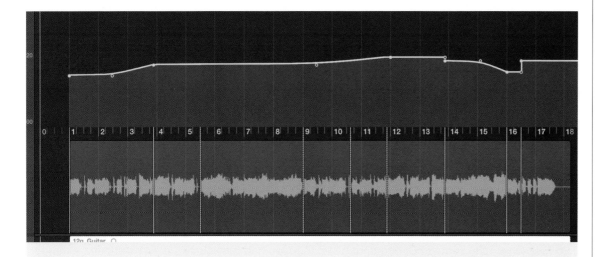

Pattern 07_26: The 16-bar tempo map.

Pattern 07_26

PATTERN 07_26: Guitar and drums – the whole 16 bars after mapping. The drums now track the guitar for the entire duration of the passage. Although not perfect, it perhaps holds together well enough to program a more meaningful and musical drum part to accompany it, with the aim of sounding like a rock'n'roll band. Mute the guitar part and instead now play the full backing track.

PATTERN 07_27: A 16-bar drum part that is more in keeping with the phrasing of the tune, using the tempo map.

Pattern 07_27

PATTERN 07_28: The 16-bar drum part along with the full backing track (Pattern 07_17).

Pattern 07_28

The concept here has been to keep a classic rock feel through using a consistent backbeat, an open hi-hat groove, a driving kick drum pattern that phrases with the bass sometimes, crash cymbals on certain chord changes in order to accentuate them, and a couple of fills. Everything is absolutely quantised, although considerable human feel is given by the tempo fluctuations. Program your own version on the grid.

There are a number of embellishments in Pattern 07_27 that are worth mentioning, although none of these are essential to the spirit of the tune. There is a short fill before the tune begins, using a cluster of four triplet 16th-notes starting on beat 3& and finishing with a snare on beat four. You might have to create an empty bar to make space for such a thing, taking care that your tempo map maintains its alignment with the audio.

CHAPTER 7

There are some ghost notes, which as always add feeling to the groove without necessarily being heard. In bar 13 there is a snare fill that uses the six-stroke roll approach; this fill is used to build excitement before the following section of the music. Leading onto beat 2 of the following bar are two 32nd-notes on the kick drum. In bar 15, the snare plays on quarter-notes, and the ride bell replaces the hi-hat to highlight a change of section and to set up the final phrase. In bar 16, the drums follow the syncopated 16th-note hits of the band, alternating between open hi-hat and crash, each backed up with either kick or snare. Just after beat 3 there is a short flurry of 32nd-notes on the toms, and finally in bar 17 a fill that uses a mixture of 32nd-notes and 16th-notes, finishing together with the guitar on beat 3.

Exercise One: Take some MIDI one-shot beats that you had previously created and build a tempo map to control them. Try speeding up and slowing down by both small and large amounts and consider how you might use these effects.

Exercise Two: Take a short section of a commercial track that does not have a metronomic feel, and program some drums to it via a tempo map. Even a very simple programmed part would do, but do aim to get tight synchronisation. Tracks from the 1960s or early 70s are pretty much guaranteed not to have used a click – most more modern tunes do. Tunes by The Beatles often had radical splitting of the instruments between the left and right channels, and these can offer good opportunities for transient detection.

Exercise Three: If you have access to any non-click-based recordings of musicians that you know, for instance if you are in a band, then map them out and program along with them.

Things to experiment with

- Apply swing to only one component of a MIDI drumbeat, for instance the hi-hat.
- Find some old tunes with break beats (where the drummer plays a groove on his or her own for a little while) and extract groove templates from them to try on your own music.
- Starting with a precisely quantised MIDI part, say just hi-hat, apply tiny edits in order to turn it into a pleasing groove, and then use this as a template on other beats.
- Try recording yourself playing a groove, even just tapping on your laptop microphone and use this as a template.
- Investigate how your sampler might support loop playback when wishing to apply swing or a groove.
- Apply both swing and groove templates as audio quantisation.
- Work back through old MIDI beats that you have made and decorate them with short note values.

CHAPTER 7

ADVANCED TIMING

THE
DRUM
PROGRAMMING
HANDBOOK

205

- Create some MIDI fills using only short note values.
- Try using groove templates in combination with tempo maps.
- With your conductor's cap on, program a quarter-note MIDI part by tapping a keyboard whilst thinking in four or eight-bar phrases, and use this as the basis for a tempo map to apply elsewhere.
- Learn how to make your audio tracks follow tempo maps.

CONCLUSION

We have now strayed from the grid and learnt a number of subtle yet exciting techniques based purely on timing – techniques that are sure to enliven your programming. We have also looked at more intricate clusters of notes that can add excitement and sophistication to your work. Lastly, you have now seen that the DAW is not a slave to a steady click and is not the sterile beast that many people perceive. In many genres, this will offer you great flexibility. In the next chapter, we will learn how to create our own unique drum sounds, using the process known as synthesis.

Check that you can:
- Apply different degrees of swing on different note values.
- Capture and apply groove templates.
- Program decorations using shorter note values for both beats and fills.
- Create and control a tempo map.
- Beat-map to a target piece of audio or MIDI.

CHAPTER 7

DRUM SYNTHESIS

CHAPTER 8

DRUM SYNTHESIS

THE
DRUM
PROGRAMMING
HANDBOOK

207

When we think of a synthesizer we typically imagine a keyboard-based instrument. While it is true that the majority of synthesizers play back pitched sounds, it is also quite possible to synthesize electronic drum sounds. These sounds are popular in electronic dance music, but their relevance extends far beyond that genre. The theory involved in creating such sounds is also applied in almost every piece of specialist drum software; understanding it will help you shape your sounds, whatever context you work in. Furthermore, this knowledge will also underpin any production and mixing that you undertake, since the terminology overlaps considerably.

In this chapter we will first consider some necessary physics of sound, then investigate the building blocks of synthesis, and finally create our own custom sounds from scratch.

THE PHYSICS OF SOUND
This title might appear a little frightening, but we are only going to cover this in an elementary fashion in order to learn the language of synthesis.

SOUND
Sound can loosely be defined as our perception of vibrations in the air. These vibrations are generated by something that releases energy into the surrounding air. If you stretch a rubber band with one hand and give it energy by plucking it with the other, it vibrates back and forward. When it does so, it also makes the surrounding air vibrate. Vibrations in air are actually pressure variations: alternating compression and stretching of the air, as it is first pushed and then pulled by the rubber band. Adjacent air particles cascade this effect in all directions, and so the air can transmit the energy of the band's vibrations to your ears.

The sound that you perceive has a number of qualities, for instance its volume, its tone, and its pitch. Anything else that releases energy into the air might also be heard by the same mechanism, be that a handclap, a guitar string, a waterfall, or dropping a saucepan. These, and indeed every other sound, can all be described in terms of volume, tone, and pitch, but note that of these examples there is only one that you could copy by singing a steady note.

SPEED (VELOCITY)
We are used to the idea of water waves, for instance when you drop a stone into a pond. The water itself does not travel, but rather the energy of each wave moves across its surface. Air behaves similarly in that it does not actually travel: the cascading pressure variations take the form of sound waves. The velocity that the variations travel at is the 'speed of sound': about 768 mph.

208
THE
DRUM
PROGRAMMING
HANDBOOK

DRUM SYNTHESIS

FREQUENCY

Imagine steadily pulling the rubber band tighter whilst plucking it repeatedly. You might expect to hear the pitch going up as it gets tighter. This is caused by the fact that the band vibrates faster when tighter. The number of vibrations every second is termed frequency (f), and frequency is measured in Hertz (Hz): eg, 500Hz is 500 vibrations per second. Frequency is often related to musical pitch.

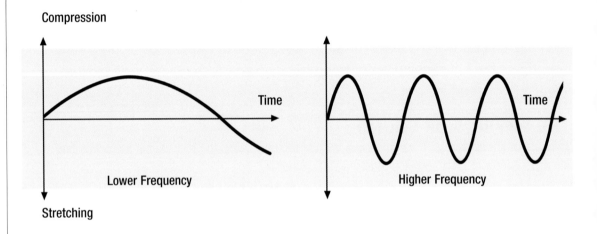

The alternation of compression and stretching for two different frequencies. Because we are representing vibrations per second, we have used time on the horizontal axis – this is called the time domain.

AMPLITUDE

If you pluck the rubber band very gently, it would not move back and forward by very much since it does not carry much energy, and we would perceive this as being quieter than if we were plucking harder and making it move more. The amount that it moves is termed the amplitude. A greater amplitude causes larger compressions and stretches in the air, and we perceive this as being greater in volume.

DRUM SYNTHESIS

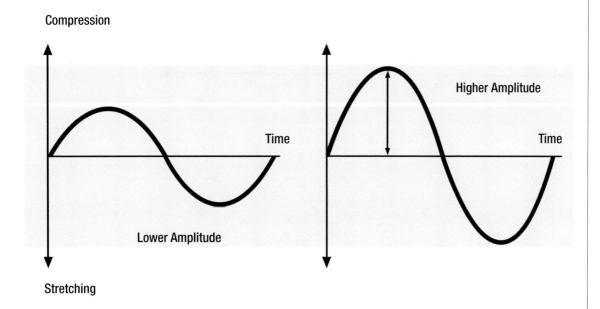

Two different amplitudes at the same frequency.

TONE (TIMBRE)

In the world of physics, the above shapes are called sine waves, regardless of their amplitude or frequency. A sine wave is a representation of a single frequency, for example 500Hz, but such a thing will rarely occur in nature. Real-world sounds are composed of a great many individual frequencies at different amplitudes, quite probably changing over time. It is the mixture of these frequencies that defines the tone, or timbre, of a given sound. It is why a note played on a trumpet sounds different from the same note played on a violin.

CHAPTER 8

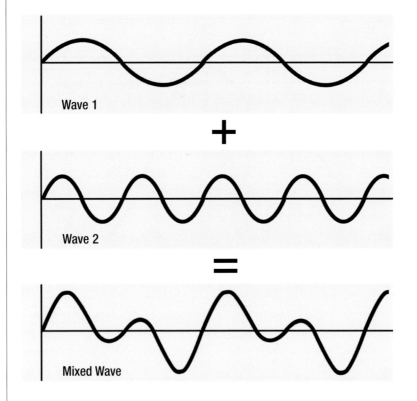

Combining two sine waves.

PATTERN 08_01: A sine wave at 500Hz. If more than one frequency is present at the same time, they combine to form a new waveform that looks rather more complicated. Here you can see just two sine waves at different frequencies being added together, and the mixed result. Any such mixture will usually be perceived as having a notably different tone to either of the original sine waves.

You could say that Wave 1 has a frequency of f, and that Wave 2 has a frequency of 2f: twice the frequency. This means that there will be two cycles of Wave 2 in the same amount of time as a single cycle of Wave 1. In a real musical sound, there are likely to be hundreds of such frequencies all happening simultaneously, and the summed result will look like the familiar complex waveforms in the audio editor of your DAW.

PITCHED SOUNDS

A typical pitched sound has many individual frequencies, and these will generally be multiples of the lowest frequency, so for instance a sound might contain frequencies at 500Hz, 1000Hz, 1500Hz, 2000Hz, etc. In a more general sense, this could be written as f, 2f, 3f, 4f etc.

DRUM SYNTHESIS

THE
DRUM
PROGRAMMING
HANDBOOK

211

TIME DOMAIN VERSUS FREQUENCY DOMAIN

When dealing with large numbers of sine waves, the complex shapes that they create when added together can quickly become confusing. However, if we represent them in a graph with frequency on the horizontal axis (which is called the frequency domain), then each single frequency simply appears as a vertical line. Thus, when we add together two sine waves of frequencies f and 2f we can clearly see two vertical lines in the frequency domain. Although this seems like a complicated way of representing these two waves, you can imagine that, when dealing with dozens of waves, the frequency domain is much easier to understand.

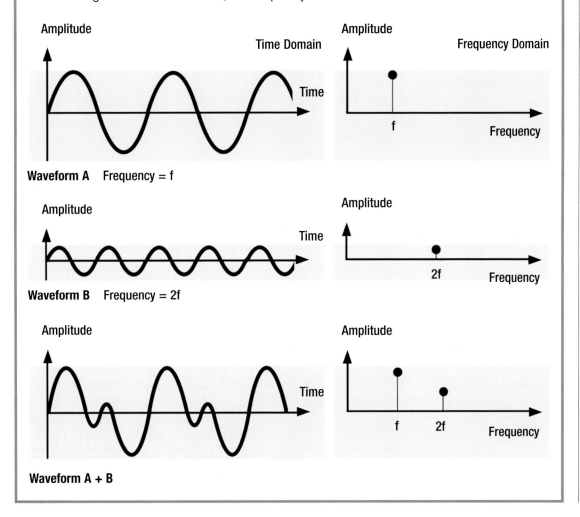

Waveform A   Frequency = f

Waveform B   Frequency = 2f

Waveform A + B

It is normal for the lowest frequency to have the highest amplitude, and common for the other frequencies to steadily decrease in amplitude as they get higher. The lowest frequency is termed the fundamental, and this is what gives us our perception of musical pitch. The higher frequency multiples are called harmonics, and it is the number and relative amplitudes of these that define timbre. That explains the difference between the trumpet and violin as above. They have different harmonic content, but the fundamentals would still be the same for a given note.

UN-PITCHED SOUNDS

Drum and percussion sounds do not typically feature a note that you can whistle. This is because they do not have a tidy relationship between the fundamental and its harmonics. All the component frequencies might instead be arranged in haphazard clusters with unpredictable amplitudes. Such sounds might be termed as being 'unpitched' or 'inharmonic'.

BASIC WAVEFORMS

The sine wave could be considered as a basic waveform. There are however a number of others in common usage in synthesizers, and each has a characteristic harmonic content and hence timbre. Whereas a sine wave has the purest tone from its single frequency, the triangle wave has a little more presence to it. The square wave has a characteristic hollow sound, and the sawtooth wave has a bright and buzzy quality.

The most common basic waveforms and their harmonic content. As can be heard in the audio examples, the presence of greater numbers of harmonics also contributes to volume.

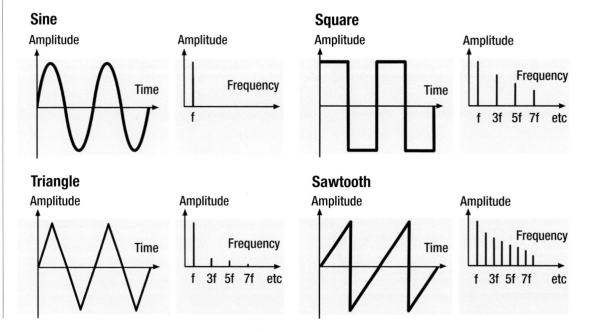

CHAPTER 8

DRUM SYNTHESIS

THE
DRUM
PROGRAMMING
HANDBOOK

213

PATTERN 08_02: A triangle waveform, playing note C2.

 Pattern 08_02

PATTERN 08_03: A square waveform, playing note C2.

 Pattern 08_03

PATTERN 08_04: A sawtooth waveform, playing note C2.

 Pattern 08_04

Such waveforms are the classic sonic starting points in synthesis. As you can see in the time-domain pictures, these waveforms all have a repeating form. They are said to be 'periodic', which indicates that they all produce a pitched sound. In the synthesis of drum sounds, however, we will more often use something called noise as a starting point. Noise is a random mixture of many frequencies, not tidy multiples of a fundamental as we have seen before, and these frequencies have random amplitudes. As such, noise has no pitch. The sound of noise is a bit like standing beside a large waterfall.

PATTERN 08_05: Noise. There are a number of different kinds of noise, and this particular variant is called pink noise.

 Pattern 08_05

Exercise One: Review all of the key concepts listed above. This might mean reading and re-reading a number of times, and possibly referring to other texts online, where this kind of thing is widely documented.

Exercise Two: Try to understand the actual connection between the various concepts and how they work as different aspects of the same thing: describing sound.

Exercise Three: Seek out some other sources that deal with the physics of sound, and try to develop your understanding even further than has been described here.

THE BUILDING BLOCKS OF SYNTHESIS

There are a number of different forms of synthesis, all of which make different types of sound. We are going to consider the classic form: subtractive synthesis. In order to implement this we need to understand three key building blocks: oscillators, filters, and amplifiers. All three can have their behaviour controlled. Many synthesizers feature more complicated elements, but try to focus on just these as you start to learn this art; you will be able to generate interesting sounds using only these three. Once you master the key elements, you can add features specific to the particular instruments that you might have.

In the following examples, we are going to use the free NoiseMaker synthesizer, by TAL. The audio examples and screen grabs are taken from that.

OSCILLATOR

An oscillator is the sound-generating component found in all synthesizers; it can typically produce one of the basic waveforms as audio. It will often feature a switch to select which waveform that you would like it to output. In addition, it will also have some means of manually altering the tuning, perhaps both 'coarse' in musical intervals, or 'fine' by much smaller amounts, in the same way you can tune a guitar. The tuning is also typically influenced by receipt of a MIDI note, so that the oscillator can play tunes from a keyboard or DAW. Sometimes you will see further controls, but these are beyond the scope of this book.

Basically, we use an oscillator to define a starting point for our sound, and we will then be able to process it in order to make it sound more interesting.

FILTER

The output from an oscillator will be fed through a device called a filter. Whereas an oscillator might typically output harmonically rich sounds, it is the filter's job to remove some of these harmonics in a specific fashion, thus shaping the sound. It is this removal that gives rise to the name – subtractive synthesis.

There are several different types of filter, but the one in which we are initially interested is called a low pass filter (LPF). Such a device allows low frequencies to pass through it, but will filter out high frequencies, hence its name. Its most important control is called the cut-off frequency, and this defines the boundary between the arbitrary low and high.

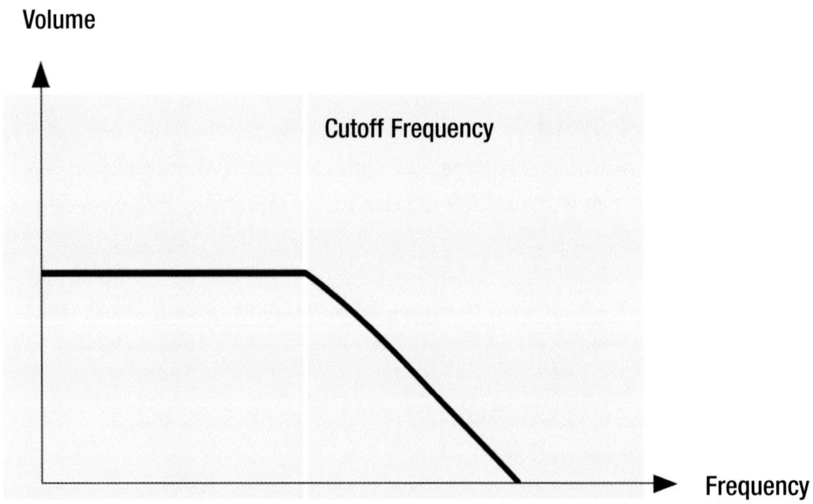

The frequency response of a low pass filter.

DRUM SYNTHESIS

The 'frequency response' of a low pass filter shows us how the volume of sound passing through the filter changes relative to frequency. At low frequencies the volume is 'up' so that these frequencies pass through unchanged, up until the cut-off frequency (f_c). At frequencies higher than this, the volume drops, although not immediately, as indicated by the slope. Often you will see the volume instead referred to as gain, and this might be specified in decibels (dB).

If we imagine a waveform with multiple harmonics passing through the filter, we can see which harmonics will be removed by looking at the response and the harmonics simultaneously.

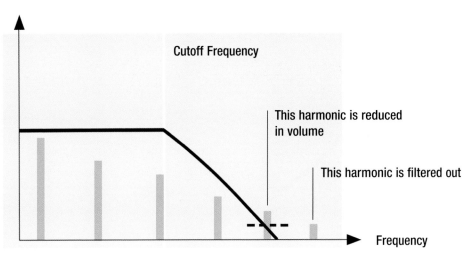

The effect of the cut-off slope on individual harmonics.

The harmonics to the right of the cut-off curve will be removed completely. The single harmonic that is sliced by the cut-off curve will be reduced in volume, but not completely removed. Technically, the harmonic to the left of this one will also be quieter too in response to the slope of the filter.

PATTERN 08_06: This is a sawtooth wave with the filter being activated after a short time. You can hear how the sound is dulled as the filter removes the high harmonics.

216

THE
DRUM
PROGRAMMING
HANDBOOK

DRUM SYNTHESIS

Another control that is commonly found on a filter is called resonance, sometimes given the letter Q. The resonance actually increases the volume around the cut-off, and also slightly decreases the volume of the lowest frequencies as well. The more this control is increased, the more the frequencies around the cut-off are boosted, and the more the lowest frequencies are reduced.

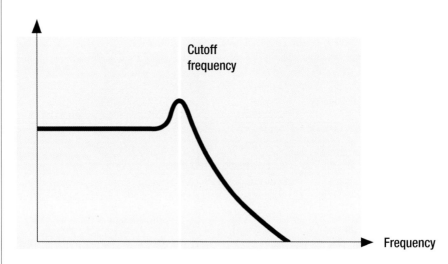

Resonant low pass filter frequency response.

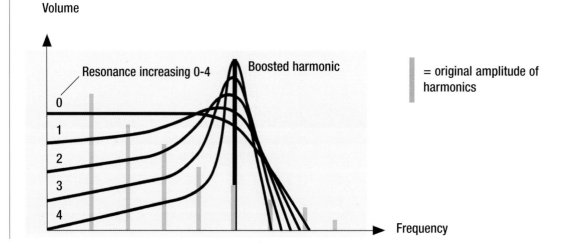

How increasing resonance affects the amplitude of a single harmonic.

DRUM SYNTHESIS

Here you can see the frequency response for different values of the resonance control, ranging from zero, with no resonance, to four, where it is quite high. The original harmonics of the waveform are indicated, but notice how the harmonic at the cut-off point is boosted. The effect on the other harmonics has not been indicated for clarity.

With resonance turned to its maximum, the filter is forced into a state called self-oscillation where only a narrow range of frequencies around the cut-off frequency can be heard. In its basic form, this produces a rather unpleasant howling sound, but this phenomenon is at the heart of many great synthesized-drum sounds.

One of the most common techniques used with filters is to change the cut-off frequency (termed 'sweeping') with a prominent amount of resonance. This has the effect of scrolling through the various harmonics in the source waveform and accentuating them all in turn. Doing so produces a characteristic squelching sound.

PATTERN 08_07: This excerpt starts with a sawtooth wave and the resonance set to zero, and the filter then sweeps downwards. Without changing the cut-off, the resonance is then increased, which in this context just produces a slight background ringing sound. With the resonance maintained at that level, the filter is then swept back up, and the classic filter-sweep sound can be heard. If you listen carefully, you can even hear the individual harmonics being accentuated in turn at the beginning of this sweep.

It is worth noting that you will often encounter a control to make the cut-off frequency track MIDI notes, which is most useful when synthesizing pitched sounds that you want to behave consistently across the range of the keyboard.

 **Pattern 08_07**

AMPLIFIER

The notion of an amplifier is traditional in discussions of subtractive synthesis. We will sidestep this slightly in order to simplify the bigger picture.

An essential element of synthesis is modulation. Modulation is where one control (generally termed the modulator) influences another destination parameter, eg, the volume or the cut-off frequency. One of the most-used modulators is the envelope. An envelope is triggered by a MIDI note (from either the keyboard or the DAW), and causes the destination parameter to automatically change over the duration of that note until it is released, and perhaps even beyond.

In fact, there will be an envelope at work every time you press a key on any synthesizer. This envelope will be routed to volume and the fact that it controls the volume means that we could describe it in this context as being an amplifier. An oscillator actually outputs a steady tone continuously, but you only want to hear it when you press a key. It is the envelope that allows you to hear it in response to that key press.

There are a number of different kinds of envelope, but the most common is called the ADSR:

218

THE
DRUM
PROGRAMMING
HANDBOOK

DRUM SYNTHESIS

Attack, Decay, Sustain, and Release. Each of these terms refers to a period of change in response to a MIDI-note key press. When the key is first pressed, the envelope increases in amplitude over a period of time to a maximum; this is the attack segment of the envelope. After this time, the envelope will then reduce over a period determined by the decay time until it reaches the sustain level. As you hold the key down, the envelope amplitude will remain at that steady level. When you release your finger from the key, the envelope amplitude will reduce to zero over the release time. Each of these parameters can typically be set by the user, making them faster or slower, or in the case of sustain, louder or quieter. Thus, changing the ADSR parameters will shape the volume and give different sonic effects to your sound.

An ADSR envelope.

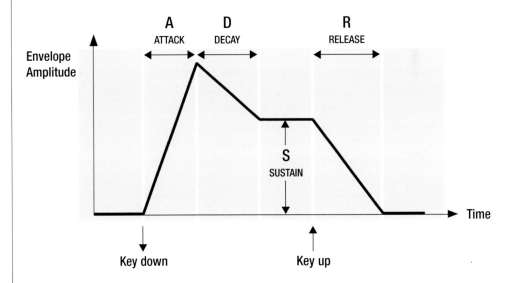

TIP

Many envelopes also feature a control called 'envelope amount' or similar. This dictates the degree of effect that the envelope has on its destinationIn. In general it is a good idea to have envelope amount set to maximum at first so that you can really hear what it is doing. Later you might wish to reduce this in order to further refine your sound. You might also see a control that inverts the envelope, meaning that the attack goes from high to low, and the decay and release from low to high. Such a feature offers extended sonic possibilities.

CHAPTER 8

DRUM SYNTHESIS

THE
DRUM
PROGRAMMING
HANDBOOK

219

PATTERN 08_08: A sequence of three pitched notes played with different ADSR settings as described below.

The envelope settings for the first three notes of the sequence.

ENVELOPE SETTINGS

The vertical position of the faders relates to the time settings; low is fast and high is slow. For the sustain fader, vertical position equates to volume. Here we have a very fast attack and decay with sustain at its maximum level, which together mean that the note appears to play at full volume instantaneously. The release is at its fastest, and so the notes die away immediately the keys are lifted. Only the vertical faders are relevant in these images.

Pattern 08_08

The second three notes. The attack is now set to be slower, and so the notes have a much softer start.

The third three notes. The sustain level is now lower, and so the note is quieter, but with a fast attack and a longer decay, a bleep can be heard at the beginning of each note.

CHAPTER 8

220
THE
DRUM
PROGRAMMING
HANDBOOK

DRUM SYNTHESIS

The last three notes. A longer release time means that the notes take a while to die away after the key has been released.

There are many other combinations that will produce different sounds, some of which are suited to playing long notes, and others only to short ones.

An envelope can also be used to modulate the cut-off frequency, and doing so is where the sounds will start to become rather more interesting. Many synthesizers have a dedicated envelope for this purpose, but on others you might have to manually route the output of a general-purpose envelope, or perhaps even the main volume envelope, to the filter in addition to volume. It is common to have to set the cut-off control to a minimum value, since the envelope will likely increase from this and then reduce back down to it. If you do not do this, then the envelope will probably not seem to have any effect. Read the manual for whichever synthesizer you are using.

ENVELOPES AND AMPLIFIERS

Even when an envelope is operating with the cut-off frequency, it is still technically an amplifier since it is affecting the amplitude of the destination parameter. In very early synthesizers, the envelope and the amplifier were actually separate things, but nowadays they tend to be integrated and so the terminology is blurred.

CHAPTER 8

DRUM SYNTHESIS

Assuming that we have a separate envelope for volume and cut-off frequency, we will now investigate to what degree modulating the cut-off can assist with producing a drum-like sound. With the volume envelope as in the first example above, we will set the static cut-off frequency fairly low, and the resonance fairly high.

PATTERN 08_09: A sequence of three sawtooth-wave based pitched notes played with different ADSR settings as described below and over the page.

A slow attack on the filter envelope allows us to hear the filter opening up as each note plays.

The attack is now set to be faster and there is also a rapid decay on the cut-off. This gives a filter-driven blip at the beginning of each note, with a slightly science-fiction quality.

Pattern 08_09

CHAPTER 8

The decay is now even shorter and this forces what we hear to be only a blip, although there is still a pitched element to the note.

With the filter envelope the same, we have now reduced the sustain level on the volume envelope to zero, and added a short decay to this envelope, in an attempt to make the sound more percussive. As can be heard in the audio example, this has little effect on the sound in this context.

Pattern 08_10

PATTERN 08_10: With all the envelope settings as above, we have changed the oscillator waveform to noise. Although the different pitches are still playing, the nature of noise is that it sounds the same regardless. While the earlier examples in this excerpt are interesting, there is a synthetic percussion noise emerging as the filter envelopes tighten.

DRUM SYNTHESIS

THE
DRUM
PROGRAMMING
HANDBOOK

223

LFO

The LFO (low-frequency oscillator) is another modulator, but it will operate at very much lower frequencies. Humans can only hear over a frequency range known as the audio spectrum. The audio spectrum has a range of 20Hz to 20kHz, although these figures are very generalised and many of us do not hear this full range at all. If an oscillator is tuned to operate some way below 20Hz then it might be termed as being a LFO, and although it is too low to function as the source of a pitched note, it can still be very useful for modulation. It will have a parameter called rate to precisely control its frequency, and the familiar basic wave shapes. Using such a device to modulate the pitch of a sustained note can provide an effect known as vibrato. If it were to modulate the volume of a sustained note, then it would produce the effect known as tremolo. The parameters found on an LFO are very similar to those of a regular audio oscillator, but often it will have a destination field so that you can direct it towards whatever you would like it to modulate.

So, in summary, we have now explored some of the principal elements of a subtractive synthesizer, and investigated the effect of changing various parameters. We have yet to create any meaningful electronic drum sounds, but we will now apply this knowledge towards that end.

Exercise One: Review the synthesizer architecture in this text, and make sure that you understand the interaction between the various elements.

Exercise Two: With pen and paper, draw the harmonic content of a basic waveform and try to redraw it a number of times, as if it has passed through an imaginary filter set to different degrees of cut-off frequency and resonance.

Exercise Three: Find some further discussions of synthesizer architecture on the Internet, and develop your knowledge from this. Be careful to stick to what is being discussed in this chapter and not step too far beyond; many sources will quickly proceed into more specialised territory, often relevant only to the creation of pitched sounds.

CHAPTER 8

224

THE
DRUM
PROGRAMMING
HANDBOOK

DRUM SYNTHESIS

Pattern 08_11

CREATING A SYNTHESIZED DRUM KIT

Drum sounds based on subtractive synthesis will never sound like an acoustic kit. Having said that, we can create some pure electronic sounds with a classic quality to them, reminiscent of the 'analogue kits' popularised by the Roland TR-808. The great advantage of working in this way, rather than using samples, is the countless sonic variations that you will be able to create.

First, set up a number of instrument tracks in your DAW, one for each part of the drum kit, with a different instance of the subtractive synthesizer of your choice on each; be aware that not all synthesizers are equally good at generating drum sounds, so perhaps have a listen to the factory presets in advance of making your choice. If there are some convincing electronic drums, then the chances are that this synthesizer can do the job, but be careful in case what you are hearing has been generated by using samples, which is not necessarily appropriate here. Name the tracks: closed hi-hat, open hi-hat, crash, tom tom, kick, snare, and clap.

CLOSED HI-HAT

Real cymbals have a metallic quality, but contain a high proportion of noise-like tone in their sound. Because of this, we can use a noise waveform as a starting point for cymbal-based sounds, so select noise as the source in an oscillator on your 'closed hi-hat' synthesizer. A closed hi-hat sound is really just like a short burst of noise. Using the volume envelope, set all the ADSR controls to their minimum value. Whilst listening to the sound, slowly slide up the decay. You will hear the sound moving from a very short click through to a longer burst of decaying noise. Back off the control until you get a tight click that is reminiscent of a closed hi-hat. The sound that you have just created is likely reminiscent of a classic drum machine hi-hat, but notice all the variations that you moved through as you adjusted the decay control. It might be a good idea to save the sound that you have just created as a user preset in your software instrument. Always do this in the future, perhaps even before you have finished synthesizing sounds in case you subsequently take things in the wrong direction and need to revert back.

PATTERN 08_11: A simple hi-hat sound made from a short burst of noise.

In order to offer a different approach, we will now apply some filtering to give a slightly more metallic quality. First, turn the main volume of your synthesizer down a bit! We are about to crank up the resonance control; things can get very loud as you do this, and you do not wish to damage either your speakers or your ears. Keeping an eye on your meters to be sure that

DRUM SYNTHESIS

THE
DRUM
PROGRAMMING
HANDBOOK

225

you are not overloading the DAW, turn the resonance up to about three-quarters, and start sweeping the cut-off downwards. Listen to the various tones that you are getting and tweak the resonance as you go. Now apply some filter envelope in the form of attack and decay to further shape the sound. Compensate with the volume as required.

PATTERN 08_12: A hi-hat sound made from short burst of noise with band pass filtering.

ADSR settings for the hi-hat. There is nothing definitive about these particular settings; do it by ear and save any combinations that you like.

OPEN HI-HAT

We now need a sound that sustains for rather longer. There are two options here, the first being to use decay and/or release on the volume envelope to make the sound longer, or alternatively to increase the sustain and program longer MIDI notes when you would like the sound to be longer.

Starting with your closed hi-hat sound, save it under a different name, as it will become your open sound. Simply adjust the volume envelope's decay and release until you get an appropriate length of note but be aware that this approach will always give a sound that dies away, as opposed to having an abrupt finish. That does not mean that it is bad, however.

TIP
There are a number of other filter types as well as the low pass filter. Whilst a low pass filter will be very effective in many situations, it is worth exploring both the high pass (HPF) and band pass (BPF) filters too. The high pass only allows high frequencies through, and the band pass allows through only a range of frequencies around the cut-off.

Alternatively, edit your MIDI notes to actually last for longer: an eighth-note is a good starting point here. Next, pull the decay and release back down to zero, and increase the sustain level. The effect of it should be that the sound will last as long as the duration of the MIDI note. If you tweak the release, then you might get something slightly longer that could be useful too. You might also care to change the other settings away from those of your closed hi-hat if you find that pleasing.

PATTERN 08_13: An open hi-hat sound made from short burst of noise with band pass filtering.

Example ADSR settings for the open hi-hat.

These settings actually use a combination of the methods described above, with a little release present, but with the ability to change the length of MIDI note as well. The latter is facilitated through use of the decay parameter rather than sustain, which gives a slight motion to the sound over its sustained period.

DRUM SYNTHESIS

THE
DRUM
PROGRAMMING
HANDBOOK

227

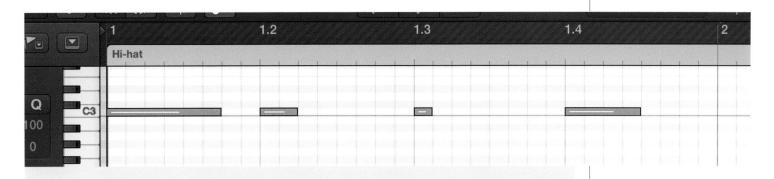

The piano-roll editor shows the lengths of note that are triggering the sounds heard in Pattern 08_13.

CRASH CYMBAL

Once you have made an open hi-hat it is fairly straightforward to simply lengthen the envelope so that it sounds like a crash. It is worth making an explicit distinction between decay and release here; the decay is always a function of the actual length of the MIDI note, whereas the release will run its own course after the note has been let go, much like a real cymbal.

The main decisions when creating a crash are: how long to make the release, where to set the cut-off, and what sort of filter to use. Set up an auto-playback MIDI pattern that has a single short note at the beginning and a two-bar cycle. Starting with your open hi-hat sound, increase the sustain and adjust the release until you feel it appropriate, and do the same with the cut-off frequency. Experiment with the attack and decay of the cut-off envelope to try to generate a chirp at the onset of the note, which will have a similar effect, albeit highly synthetic, to the stick striking the cymbal. If you are happy with the sound that you have created, remember to save it. Once you have done that, try selecting different filter types; this will likely lead you to change the cut-off frequency as well. You might wish to save some of these alternative cymbals too.

228

THE
DRUM
PROGRAMMING
HANDBOOK

DRUM SYNTHESIS

PATTERN 08_14: Crash cymbal sound using high pass filtering.

Pattern 08_14

Example envelope settings for the crash.

Just to spice things up, let's add another modulator here – an LFO. Route this to the filter cut-off frequency; this will work in addition to the envelope that you have already set up. You will notice that with a high modulation amount you will have a very science-fiction sort of sound, but what can be more interesting is if you choose a very low modulation amount to just give a subtle shimmering effect to the cymbal.

Pattern 08_15

Pattern 08_16

PATTERN 08_15: This is Pattern 08_14 with an LFO slightly modulating the cut-off frequency.

PATTERN 08_16: This is Pattern 08_15 with a low pass filter instead.

DRUM SYNTHESIS

THE
DRUM
PROGRAMMING
HANDBOOK

229

TOM TOM

One of the problems in trying to synthesize a tom tom sound is to simulate the (natural) resonance of the shell without playing obvious pitches. One solution that people have applied to this is to use an additional envelope routed to the pitch of the oscillators in order to make the drum sound dive downwards very quickly to avoid sitting on a recognisable pitch, potentially out of key with the surrounding music. Actually, it is possible to tune acoustic drums to give something of a pitch dive as well, although this of course does not come from the shell.

First, set up a backing sequence that plays three notes consecutively, each on a different pitch (you should experiment with a number of different intervals here). With an oscillator set to a square wave, configure the volume envelope so that it plays a very short burst of tone. On the filter, turn the resonance up quite high so that it howls, and then tune it to a lower pitch with the cut-off. Again, be careful of volume here. The reason we are doing this is to generate a strong fundamental from the filter, which can then be modulated by an additional envelope. You need an envelope that is capable of a very fast decay. Although not an ADSR, the powerful Envelope Editor on NoiseMaker is suitable for this and can also be routed to cut-off. If you are using this device, assign this routing then set its speed to be x32 to get a really fast pitch dive, and adjust its shape to do this. If using a different system, then find an equivalent suitable envelope.

PATTERN 08_17: Tom toms created with square wave and a pitch modulated envelope.

Pattern 08_17

Example envelope and filter settings for the toms.

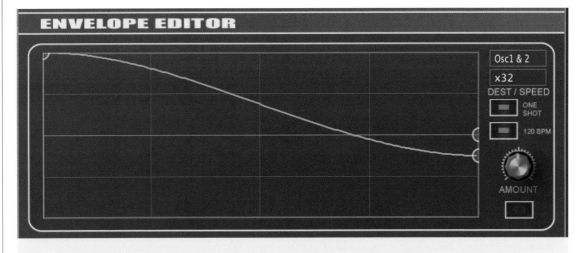

The Envelope Editor that is modulating the pitch – the pitch just follows the contours downwards.

Pattern 08_18

You can now enhance your sound further by employing another oscillator that generates noise. Set this up, mixing the two oscillators' outputs together, and adjust their relative balance to your liking. Be aware that both the pulse wave and the noise are being fed through the same enveloping, although the Envelope Editor has little effect on the pitch of the noise component since it has no pitched content.

PATTERN 08_18: Tom toms created with pulse wave and noise, and a pitch modulated envelope.

KICK

A real kick drum has a sonic contour that is quite hard to hear because it is so fast. What actually happens is that the pitch descends very rapidly with every hit, and trying to emulate that to some degree is a useful strategy when synthesizing kick sounds. There is often also a clicking quality to the sound that is caused by the beater slapping the head of the drum.

It has long been common in electronic dance music to use kick drums with a sustained deeply pitched quality to them. This comes from the classic Roland TR-808 drum machine (and indeed the machines from before and after), which was itself actually a synthesizer. The classic mistake that all beginners make is to use a short envelope on a pitched oscillator and tune the oscillator down in order to get a kick-like quality. Whilst this is easy, it will not produce a powerful kick.

DRUM SYNTHESIS

THE
DRUM
PROGRAMMING
HANDBOOK

231

PATTERN 08_19: Creating a kick with an oscillator, simply pitched low, does not give a gratifying sound.

We have already used resonance to create a howl, but now, create a new sound with noise in the oscillator, but leave the output volume of the oscillator down. Give your volume envelope a short decay keeping all the other controls at zero. Being careful of your monitoring volume, turn the resonance up full. You have just forced the filter into self-oscillation, where it is tends to become an oscillator and just sing forever – it does not even need its input to be at a significant volume because it now has an internal feedback loop and indeed its output is similar to a PA system that is feeding back. This oscillator can be tuned with the cut-off frequency, so now turn the cut-off down until you get a deep boom.

Now start turning up the decay control on the filter envelope, which of course will affect the cut-off. The booming sound should start to change to a familiar 'dive' on the end of the sound. Balance this against the volume decay, and you have just created your first kick drum sound. Just to add a little grit to it, turn the volume of the noise oscillator up very slightly, and leave it just present for a subtle effect.

Example envelope and filter settings for the kick.

Pattern 08_20

Pattern 08_21

Pattern 08_22

PATTERN 08_20: A kick drum created with a self-oscillating filter.

PATTERN 08_21: The previous kick drum with a little noise added.

We can emulate the beater hit of a real drum by adding a noise-based click (a bit like the closed hi-hat from earlier, but with a lower-frequency quality) at the beginning of each hit. If you play this simultaneously with one of the Pattern 08_19 to 08_22 sounds, then your ear will join the two together. Be subtle with this though: you do not want an obvious smack, but simply to give the illusion of a more pronounced single note.

PATTERN 08_22: The previous kick drum with an added (quite loud) click.

SNARE

A snare drum sound can be broken down into three characteristic components: the slap of the stick hitting the head of the drum, the natural resonance of the shell, and the buzz of the snare wires underneath the drum. Each of these will require a different synthesized element: the slap will be a short click, the resonance will be a self-oscillating filter, and the buzz will be a burst of noise. It is possible that you will need to use a different synthesizer for each of these components, and then make a MIDI connection to trigger them all from a single key.

For the click, use a noise source with a very short volume envelope, as for the kick. For this click, adding quite a bit of resonance and then tuning with the cut-off can give a sharp sound, and it is worth experimenting with different types of filter. A band pass filter can offer a nice neutral sound here, but there are no rules. You might wish to change the sound of the click once the other components are in place.

TIP

When you need two or more MIDI instruments to play simultaneously from a single MIDI note, there are a number of strategies particular to each DAW to make this happen: Ableton Live has the drum rack, Cubase/Nuendo has the drum map, Logic Pro has either its mapped instrument or track stack, and Sonar has the drum-map manager, etc. It can be very useful to know how to do this; as ever, check the manual for your own DAW. Even if you cannot do this, an alternative is to program a complete part on one instrument using only its sonic component. Then, when you have finished programming the MIDI notes, duplicate the regions onto another track that in addition plays the other component of the sound.

Of course, this approach can also be used to build a single kit that plays all of the various instruments from a single MIDI track.

DRUM SYNTHESIS

THE
DRUM
PROGRAMMING
HANDBOOK

233

*Example envelope settings
for the click of the snare.*

 Pattern 08_23

PATTERN 08_23: This is just a quick component for the click of the snare drum.

To synthesize sounds for the shell, again use a self-oscillating filter, but tuned quite a bit higher than for the kick drum. Again, as with the kick, a slight pitch dive can be effective here, but it is purely personal preference.

PATTERN 08_24: This is just a quick component for the shell of the snare drum.

 Pattern 08_24

*Example envelope settings
for the shell of the snare.*

CHAPTER 8

Lastly, the snare wires. Use filtered noise for this. There are many combinations of both volume and filter envelope, not to mention filter type, that will work well here just to different effect. Start with a volume envelope that is just longer than your shell sound and a simple low pass filter, tuned to your preference. If the sound is too deep, then switch to a band pass filter and retune. It is best to shape this sound whilst listening on its own, but once you have three usable components, combine them together and balance their relative volumes. The shell sound can often be surprisingly quiet for the best effect.

Pattern 08_25

Example envelope settings for the wires of the snare.

PATTERN 08_25: This is just the wire component for the final snare drum.

Pattern 08_26

PATTERN 08_26: When the three components are mixed together this is the composite result.

DRUM SYNTHESIS

THE
DRUM
PROGRAMMING
HANDBOOK

235

CLAP

If you imagine the sound of many hands clapping simultaneously, actually what you are hearing is a number of clicks all happening slightly apart in time. One approach that has been traditionally used to synthesize this was to use an LFO to modulate volume on an oscillator that was outputting noise, with the effect that turning the volume up and down rapidly sounds like a burst of clicks, hence a clap.

   NoiseMaker does not perform to good effect when programmed like this, but its Envelope Editor has a highly controllable envelope contour and it is possible to program many changes of direction by inserting break points and setting the speed to x32; getting the speed approximately correct is crucial for the simulation you are after. If this envelope is routed to modulate the filter, then a useful clap-like effect can be achieved, although it is not wholly authentic.

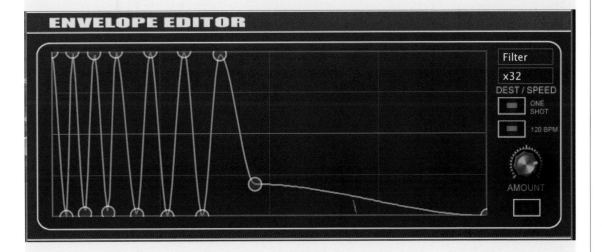

A complex envelope that emulates an LFO.

*The envelope settings for
the clap sound.*

 Pattern 08_27

 Pattern 08_28

PATTERN 08_27: The clap emulation.

PATTERN 08_28: A two bar sequence using all of the synthesized sounds, repeated
twice at 105bpm.

Exercise One: Take the drum kit that you have created and tweak each of the component parts to
make a new set of sounds, and save these as an alternative kit. Where different approaches
have been suggested above, try to embrace these before trying your own.

Exercise Two: Synthesize a drum kit that sounds radically different from that of the workshop,
where the sounds are only a creative response to the names of the kit. But try to ensure that
each sound will function with its designated name, eg, the kick drum sound can work as a kick.

Exercise Three: Try out, at a variety of tempos, the earlier MIDI one-shot beats that you previously
created with your new drum kits. When a given beat does not work optimally with your kit,
instead of changing the beat, try changing the sounds to make them respond in an interesting
fashion.

CHAPTER 8

DRUM SYNTHESIS

THE
DRUM
PROGRAMMING
HANDBOOK

237

Things to experiment with
- Try all your own sound-design ideas, and do not be afraid to explore parameters that your instrument might feature, even if not listed here. You might need to consult the manual since some functions do not appear to do very much unless used in the correct context.
- Build a drum kit that functions using some sort of mapping so you can play the entire kit from a single keyboard. Assign the drums to GM keys.
- Experiment with the principles of synthesis in your own more sophisticated (or just different) instruments if you have them; you will likely be able to create higher quality sounds with practice.
- Do some research on how to develop drum synthesis beyond where it has been presented in this introduction. There is an exciting world out there. Ring modulation and frequency modulation offer an immediately different palette of drum sounds.

CONCLUSION
We have now discussed many key technical terms associated with the physics of sound. We have also learnt about synthesizer architecture, and how to control some typical parameters to create analogue-sounding drum kits through subtractive synthesis. Although the sounds that we have created are quite basic, the principles that we have applied are fundamental. You can now continue to develop those in order to create your own unique sounds, not just through pure synthesis, but also by applying these principles in other contexts, as will be done later in this book. In the next chapter, we will develop our sonic palette even further by exploring the world of special effects and production, in order to add further polish and professionalism to the end results of your programming.

Check that you can:
- Understand the technical terms associated with the physics of sound.
- Understand the theory and function of the building blocks of subtractive synthesis: oscillators, filters, envelopes, and LFOs, and also their parameters.
- Create each of the principal parts of a synthetic drum kit using subtractive synthesis techniques.

CHAPTER 8

PRODUCTION AND EFFECTS 1

CHAPTER 9

PRODUCTION AND EFFECTS 1

THE
DRUM
PROGRAMMING
HANDBOOK

239

This chapter will deal with the use of DAW production processes to sonically enhance or modify things that you have already created. Such processes include equalisation (EQ) and dynamics processing; applying these is standard practice in the creation of professional tracks. Production is an entire subject in itself and there are many books on this alone. Here, we will focus on some applications that are immediately useful for creating a great-sounding programmed drum part that will really polish your tracks.

MIXERS

In order to best apply our various processes, it is useful to consider the architecture of a typical mixer in a DAW. So far, we have been assuming that you have been inserting your software instruments into a channel strip and simply sending their output out of your computer as audio. We will now consider the possible routing of signals inside the DAW.

CHANNEL TYPES

We will refer to channel strips with MIDI-controlled instruments on them as instrument channels, and strips that carry audio recordings as audio channels. In addition, there are also buss channels, which receive their input from a buss. A buss is a group of connectors that typically has lots of inputs leading to a single designated output, although multiple outputs are possible too. Lastly, there are master channels, which receive many signals and sum them together before sending them out of your computer so that you can hear them. Both channels and busses can be either mono or stereo. Your DAW will probably offer a degree of compatibility between these two, but this can be slightly confusing, so check your manual for the way it behaves in these situations.

INPUTS AND OUTPUTS

One difference between instrument and audio channels is that on an instrument channel the instrument that resides within the channel is generating audio; for an audio channel, the audio is playing from a track in the arrangement and being sent to the channel for mixing. The channel must be assigned to receive its input from a given track, although this is most often done automatically by your DAW. A buss channel will receive its input from a designated buss. The master channel will receive its input from the master buss, likely to be named something like 'stereo output' or 'main output'.

Every channel strip will feature an output destination, to which its audio is routed via a buss. Output destinations could be the main output or a buss channel, although you will typically select the buss that leads to these destinations in the output field, not the actual destination. If your

240

THE
DRUM
PROGRAMMING
HANDBOOK

PRODUCTION AND EFFECTS 1

interface has multiple physical outputs, these will all be available as possible destinations too. It is common to imagine the audio arriving at an input at the top of the channel strip, passing through the channel strip downwards through each of its component parts, and then exiting via an output at the bottom. It is unlikely that your DAW will have its channel in exactly this visual configuration, but it is still helpful to perceive it like this.

INSERTS

As the signal travels down through the strip, it will go through a number of insert slots in succession. Various types of audio effect can be placed in these so-called inserts, and the signal will pass through the effect unit and be completely processed by it, before entering the next slot. Some DAWs require EQ (which will be discussed shortly) to be placed in these slots, but others have dedicated slots for this purpose.

SENDS

Each channel strip features a number of controls called sends. A send takes some of the signal that was passing through the channel strip and sends it to another destination via a buss, with the amount actually sent controlled by a knob or fader. The buss will usually feed a buss channel (we could now refer to it as a send channel in this context) that has an effect on its insert. Using a send allows the main signal to be heard alongside an element of processing from the send channel.

PRODUCTION AND EFFECTS 1

THE
DRUM
PROGRAMMING
HANDBOOK

241

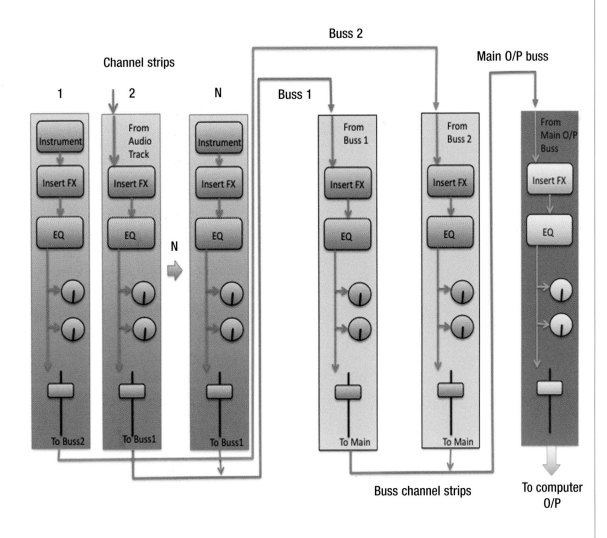

Different types of channel strip and busses.

Above we can see any number (N) of channel strips whose outputs are being routed to busses. Channel strip number one is being routed to buss two, and channel strip numbers two and N are both being routed to buss one. Both busses in turn are being routed to the main output. In effect, strips two and N are being summed and could therefore share some processing on the buss-channel insert or EQ. Channel strips one and N are hosting instruments, whereas channel strip two is receiving audio from a track in the arrangement. Note that the order of the inserts and EQ is somewhat arbitrary in terms of the signal flow.

Send effect routing.

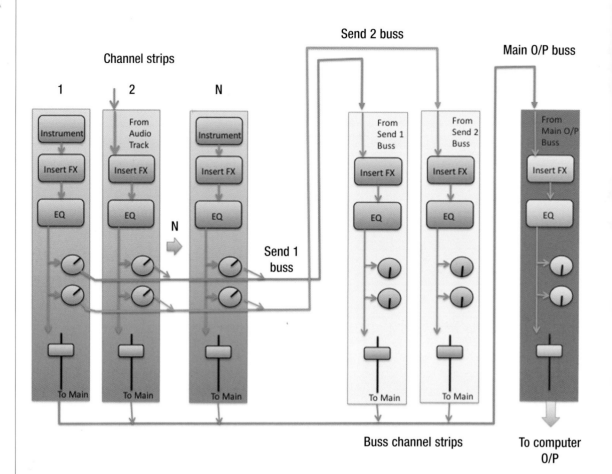

Channel strips one, two and N are all being routed to the main output. Their send controls have all been turned up by the same amount and are tapping off some of their audio, and bussing it to a pair of buss channel strips. These strips would have effects in their insert slots, and the strips are in turn feeding their output to the main output buss. Lastly, the main output channel is summing the various signals.

PRODUCTION AND EFFECTS 1

THE
DRUM
PROGRAMMING
HANDBOOK

243

MULTICHANNEL INSTRUMENTS

Some instruments are capable of sending elements of their output to a number of different channels: for instance, the kick to one channel and the snare to another. If you use a multichannel version of your instrument, then you will need to assign particular elements to specific busses. This is done within the instrument. You will often find that the names of the multiple outputs of the instrument do not match the names of your available busses, but if you apply some logic, you can usually figure it out.

It is worth briefly considering how an acoustic drum kit is recorded. Each drum will have its own dedicated microphone, placed close to it, as will the hi-hat. There is sometimes a second microphone for the kick drum, or another underneath the snare drum, which gives a more rattling sound. The tom mics will often be mixed into a single stereo channel. There will generally be two microphones above the drum kit, which are referred to as overheads, and these are generally responsible for capturing a stereo image of the cymbals. There will often be other pairs of microphones further away from the drum kit, and these will capture a more spacious sound of the room, which is a very important component of a realistic recording. These are often referred to as room mics, or ambient mics. Understanding this offers some logic for the mixture of mono and stereo channels that might typically be offered by a multichannel instrument that emulates real drums.

On the right we can see a number of individual outputs from the instrument, numbered 1 to M, which are routed to buss channels for individual processing. In these channels, you might wish to apply inserts or sends to individual drums. The instrument channel is routed to the main output. Any elements of the instrument that you do not specifically assign to individual outputs will still appear here.

Multiple audio outputs from a single instrument.

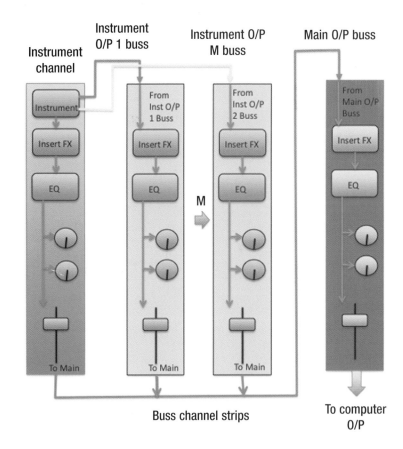

244

THE
DRUM
PROGRAMMING
HANDBOOK

PRODUCTION AND EFFECTS 1

EQUALISATION (EQ)

EQ is the mechanism for shaping the tonal colour of an audio signal – an extended version of the bass and treble controls commonly found on home audio equipment, which in EQ terms are actually called shelving filters. Technically, what these do is offer the ability to either boost or cut all frequencies above a certain point (treble) or below a certain point (bass). On the home audio system above, that point will be fixed, but in a studio unit there will likely be a parameter to sweep it.

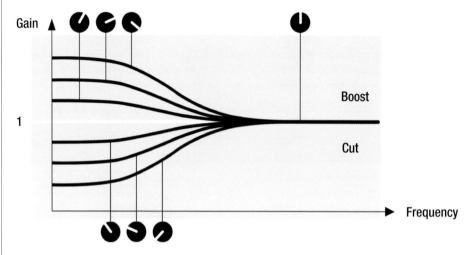

The frequency responses of both high and low shelving filters.

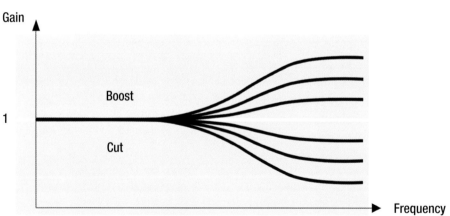

The diagram shows a low shelf filter on the top and a high shelf below. Different degrees of cut and boost are indicated, and on the low shelf diagram the corresponding control-knob positions are indicated.

CHAPTER 9

PRODUCTION AND EFFECTS 1

THE
DRUM
PROGRAMMING
HANDBOOK

245

Another type of EQ uses filters, of which there are both high pass and low pass varieties. These operate just like the filters that we saw in Chapter Eight. They tend not to have an assignable frequency, and might also offer different degrees of gain reduction, which means the extent to which they reduce the volume. They will not be capable of boosting. Rather confusingly, the high pass filter is generally used to cut low frequencies, and the low pass to cut high ones.

Arguably, the most important type of EQ is called parametric EQ. This has an adjustable centre frequency and a gain control that can cut or boost a range of frequencies around the centre. There will also be another control called Q (which stands for quality), which defines the range of frequencies to either side of the centre frequency that are affected by any cut or boost.

Parametric EQ

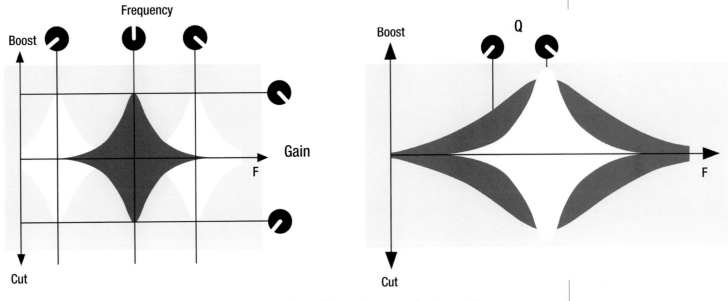

In the left diagram, in addition to cut and boost knob positions, frequency knob positions are shown and in response to these, the characteristic bell shape appears to slide up and down the frequency axis. The right diagram indicates the effect of the Q control. The wider the bell shape, the more frequencies to either side of the centre frequency will be affected by any cut or boost.

Each instance of EQ offered by a given device (typically several) is referred to as a band, and so you might see a three-band EQ or a five-band EQ. A greater number of bands offers more flexible tonal shaping, although this might not be necessary in a given situation.

EQ is typically used to three creative ends. It might correct tonal deficiencies in a recording, it might enhance interesting frequencies within a piece of audio, or it might be used to help a track blend into or jump out of a mix. There are an infinite number of permutations of EQ, but we will investigate a few to highlight certain possibilities for drums.

246

THE
DRUM
PROGRAMMING
HANDBOOK

PRODUCTION AND EFFECTS 1

TIP

Always use EQ as an insert effect. When applying parametric EQ, there is a basic approach that usually helps you to discover the frequencies of interest. Start with the Q control at its halfway position. This ensures that you will affect a reasonable range of frequencies so that you can hear what you are doing. If the Q is too wide, it will sound like you are just turning up the volume, and if it is too narrow you will hear a highly synthetic boost of a specific frequency range that makes it hard to judge if you have targeted what you mean to. Next, turn the boost up quite high, since it is easier to hear frequencies that you are boosting than those you are cutting; do this even if it is your intention to subsequently cut. Using the frequency knob, sweep up and down whilst listening and try to zoom in on the frequencies of interest. Then, adjust the gain to a preferable amount of boost or cut, and fine-tune the Q to have the desired effect. In general, it is always better to try to cut rather than boost since this will give a more natural sound. When boosting, use a fairly wide Q, but when cutting make the Q as narrow as possible. Again, this will give the most natural effect.

The EQ curve that was applied in Pattern 09_01.

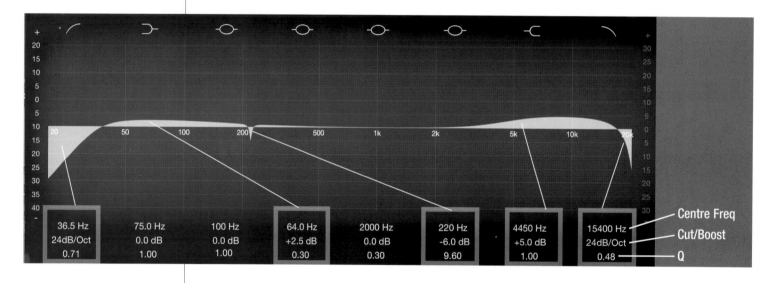

36.5 Hz	75.0 Hz	100 Hz	64.0 Hz	2000 Hz	220 Hz	4450 Hz	15400 Hz
24dB/Oct	0.0 dB	0.0 dB	+2.5 dB	0.0 dB	-6.0 dB	+5.0 dB	24dB/Oct
0.71	1.00	1.00	0.30	0.30	9.60	1.00	0.48

Centre Freq
Cut/Boost
Q

Pattern 09_01

PATTERN 09_01: This is the eight-bar Pattern 05_16 from Chapter Five played firstly as it was (twice through), and then repeated with EQ applied. This is potentially an eight band EQ, although only five are being used here. Each band has a numerical readout for frequency, gain and Q, along the bottom. There is both high pass and low pass filtering, which have the effect of cleaning the audio in spectral terms, a boost centred on 64Hz to fill out the kick drum, a narrow cut at 220Hz, which removes some slight ringing from the snare drum, and a boost at 4450Hz to brighten the cymbals, which combines with the low pass filter to give an asymmetric-looking appearance. You should understand that these numbers are not specific, but have been found by sweeping and listening and are derived only from the effect that they achieved.

CHAPTER 9

PRODUCTION AND EFFECTS 1

THE
DRUM
PROGRAMMING
HANDBOOK

247

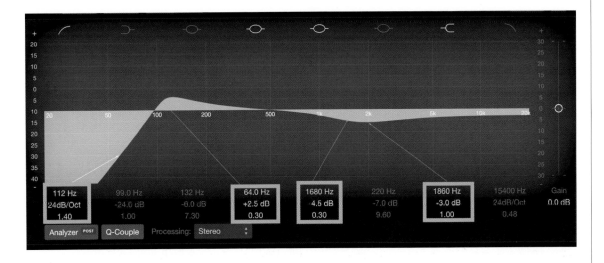

112 Hz	99.0 Hz	132 Hz	64.0 Hz	1680 Hz	220 Hz	1860 Hz	15400 Hz	Gain
24dB/Oct	-24.0 dB	-6.0 dB	+2.5 dB	-4.5 dB	-7.0 dB	-3.0 dB	24dB/Oct	0.0 dB
1.40	1.00	7.30	0.30	0.30	9.60	1.00	0.48	

Analyzer **POST**   Q-Couple   Processing: Stereo

Pattern 09_02: EQ used as a special effect.

Pattern 09_02

PATTERN 09_02: This is the eight-bar Pattern 05_16, played firstly as it was, and then repeated with a different EQ applied. This EQ curve has the effect of giving a muffled and boxy sound. The muffled quality comes from cutting the frequencies above 1kHz and below 100Hz, and the boxiness is from the boost just above 100Hz. The diagram is slightly confusing because this boost is listed as being at 64Hz, but it is the interaction of the high pass filter and the boost that sum to give this effect. Whilst not an EQ that you would wish to use in every song, it does illustrate how the ear yearns for high and low frequencies.

Pattern 09_03: Another special effect EQ.

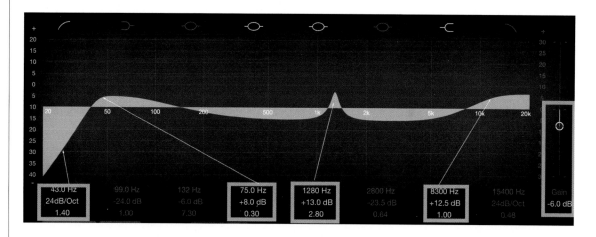

43.0 Hz	99.0 Hz	132 Hz	75.0 Hz	1280 Hz	2800 Hz	8300 Hz	15400 Hz	Gain
24dB/Oct	-24.0 dB	-6.0 dB	+8.0 dB	+13.0 dB	-23.5 dB	+12.5 dB	24dB/Oct	-6.0 dB
1.40	1.00	7.30	0.30	2.80	0.64	1.00	0.48	

PATTERN 09_03: This is the eight-bar Pattern 05_16, played firstly as it was, and then repeated with yet another EQ applied. This curve is in many ways the opposite, with strong boosts to both low frequencies and high frequencies. In addition, there is a sharp peak with a high Q value that gives a resonant quality to the snare drum. Because the high-energy low frequencies were boosted so much, the overall volume of the loop had greatly increased and so to make it the same, a volume drop (as seen on the right) was applied. Graphically, this drop had the effect of making the EQ curve appear to fluctuate around a central point.

Exercise One: Pick one of your audio loops and apply shelving EQ to try both boost and cut to both high and low frequencies in order to gauge the effect of each operation. Try different cut-off frequencies as you do this.

Exercise Two: Using a single-band parametric EQ with a fairly strong boost and a medium Q value, sweep up and down the full range of the EQ until you find something that sounds unpleasant. Change the boost to a cut to see if you can improve the sound by removing just those frequencies, and remember to adjust the Q so that it is as narrow as you can get away with so as not to compromise the greater sound too much. If you found a number of unpleasant frequencies, use further bands to deal with these too. You very possibly found some frequencies that you would like to enhance too, and so now apply further bands with boosts and broad Q to these, in addition to the previous cuts. You have now gone through a complete EQ cycle. Perhaps trying repeating it to different effect.

Exercise Three: Use the EQ to attempt to isolate individual drums, for instance the kick or the cymbals. It is not possible to achieve perfect separation, but practising this helps you learn about the typical frequency content of individual sounds. Working in this way can be a very useful technique when mixing.

CHAPTER 9

PRODUCTION AND EFFECTS 1

THE
DRUM
PROGRAMMING
HANDBOOK

249

COMPRESSORS

A compressor is a device designed to reduce the dynamic range of a signal. It usually needs to be inserted into a channel. Compressors are essential in modern music production; they help you to consistently hear all the various instruments in a mix, or can add punch and change the tone of whatever they are applied to. They can also create special effects.

The most common kind of compressor will detect when the audio is above a certain level and reduce the gain of the audio whilst it remains above this level. Thus, the difference between the loudest part of the audio and the (unchanged) quietest has been reduced; in other words the dynamic range has been compressed. There will typically be a parameter to set a level above which the compressor responds, and this level is called the threshold. The amount that the gain is reduced is described in terms of ratio.

In addition, you will often see controls called attack and release. The attack defines how long the compressor waits after the signal exceeds the threshold before starting to reduce the gain, and the release how long it continues to reduce the gain after the signal has fallen below the threshold. You will usually also see a meter that indicates when the gain is being reduced, and by how much, measured in decibels. Because the act of compression tends to reduce the overall output level, there will be a parameter called make-up gain that can restore the overall level after compression. It is very important to use this to match the loudness of your audio before and after, since psychoacoustically, louder will always seem better, regardless of the effect of the compression.

A graph of output against input for a compressor, ignoring attack and release.

On the right the scale is in decibels, and you can see a line that rises at 45°, where for each decibel that the input increases, the output also increases by a single decibel. In other words, this line represents a signal that is not changing – we could think of this as having a ratio of 1:1. If this same signal were to pass through a compressor with its threshold arbitrarily set to –3 dB, with the ratio at 4:1, then once above the threshold, for each 4 dB that the input increased, the output would only increase by 1 dB. This means that in the 8 dB change in the input from the threshold to the right-hand side of the graph, the output could only increase by 2 dB.

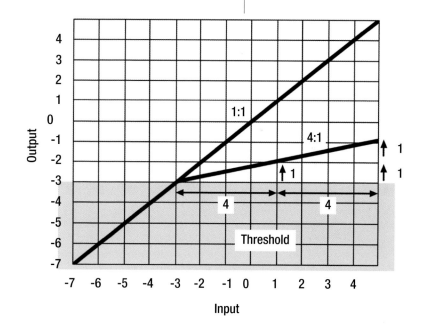

250

THE
DRUM
PROGRAMMING
HANDBOOK

PRODUCTION AND EFFECTS 1

*The main compressor
parameters.*

On the left you can see the fundamental controls for a typical compressor. The meter shows the amount of gain reduction in decibels, but it is common to see meters for the input and output levels as well.

Pattern 09_04

■ **CHECK OUT**
Legendary mix-engineer Michael Brauer, who has mixed tracks for bands from Coldplay and The Kooks to The Rolling Stones and Paul McCartney. He is famous for his use of multiple compressors to shape the sound.

Pattern 09_05

Pattern 09_06

PATTERN 09_04: This is a modified Pattern 04_23 from Chapter Four. It now has a 16D quantise, and a couple of cymbals and toms have been added. Originally this excerpt had a small amount of processing, but here it is 'raw' from BFD3, playing over just two channels. Twice through the eight bar sequence at 120bpm.

We will first consider the effects of compression by applying it to a stereo loop: Pattern 09_04. The compressor is applying between 2–4 dB of gain reduction with a 4:1 ratio, with a fast attack and automatic release time. The effect is of a 'fatter' sounding beat, in which the ghost notes seem more present and the ambience of the kick is more noticeable; the quieter sounds seem louder. The backbeats were played with level differences of up to 4 or 5 dB, and the compressor has now evened these out. Remember that a compressor such as this actually makes the louder sounds quieter, so it is the subsequent application of make-up gain that causes this effect. It can take a little experience to really understand what is happening here, so if you are new to compression, then listen very carefully to Pattern 09_05, tuning in to different details of the sound until you form a clear picture of the effect.

PATTERN 09_05: This is a single eight-bar loop of Pattern 09_04 once through as was, then once with compression applied, repeating the cycle once.

PATTERN 09_06: This is Pattern 09_04 with a lower threshold to give a much more aggressive compression: 6–12 dB of gain reduction, yet after make-up gain, the peaks of the audio remain about the same. It is now massively 'louder', although you will also hear distortion. This is an inevitable side effect, but is not always bad, depending on the musical context. This example uses a basic compressor that ships with a DAW.

PRODUCTION AND EFFECTS 1

THE
DRUM
PROGRAMMING
HANDBOOK

251

PATTERN 09_07: Using a different model of compressor, this is Pattern 09_05 again, with a lower threshold, a gentler ratio of 2.5:1, but with an attack time of around 20ms, and a very fast release.

Pattern 09_07

The 20ms allows the attack of the drum through the unit without being compressed before the gain reduction kicks in, and thus exaggerates the 'B of the bang'. The fast release means that the compressor tends not to work on notes (or even portions of notes) after it is triggered, allowing them to only be boosted by the make-up gain. Again, this approach offers a different sonic texture.

PATTERN 09_08: Using yet another model of compressor, one that this time emulates the buss of a classic SSL mixing desk from the 1980s: a revered and expensive thing. This is Pattern 09_05 again, with a ratio of 4:1, an attack time of around 1ms, and an automatic release, giving a different flavour of full-on squashing and distortion.

Pattern 09_08

Although we have demonstrated only a very small number of the possible parameter combinations, you can hear that there is huge potential for using compressors to sculpt your sound, not least by using different makes and models. It is commonly accepted amongst professionals that, at the point of writing, hardware still sounds better.

Exercise One: Choose an audio loop that you have programmed, select a compressor and insert on the channel. With the attack and release fixed at medium speeds, apply different combinations of ratio and threshold to your loop, being careful to monitor your meters and compensate for any gain differences. Study the resulting sound, switching the compressor to bypass frequently so that you can A/B its effect. Take a note of the parameters of any interesting combinations that appeal to you, or even bounce them as audio, embedding the parameters in the filename so that you understand what you are hearing later on.

Exercise Two: Using a fixed combination of ratio and threshold that worked for you, experiment now with different values of attack and release, again compensating with the make-up gain if required. Make sure that you are able to enhance the transients using the attack to various degrees. Use the tempo to guide your choice of release time; try to make it fit with the flow of the groove. Again, take note of your favourites or bounce. Once you have a feel for the attack and release times, adjust the threshold and make-up gain and experiment further.

Exercise Three: Remove the compressor that you have used above and replace it with a different one, preferably one that you know should behave in a slightly different way due to its design. Replicate a number of your settings from above and compare the sound to the earlier unit.

> **TIP**
> There are many different designs of compressor in the world of hardware electronics, and these are often modelled in software form. They all have slightly different behaviours with characteristic sonic signatures. You will encounter styles such as VCA, FET, and opto, not to mention many bespoke software varieties and emulations of specific items of classic studio equipment. You should spend some time experimenting with all the designs at your disposal and get a feeling for their particular sound. Taking notes or even keeping a dedicated DAW project that showcases different effects will help you remember which unit is best suited to a particular task.

CHAPTER 9

252

THE
DRUM
PROGRAMMING
HANDBOOK

PRODUCTION AND EFFECTS 1

MIXING THE KIT

Although we can take a stereo file of a full kit, apply overall compression, and use EQ to operate on the frequency extremes quite successfully, such an approach is limited since all the drums are embedded together. Since their individual frequency content and dynamic peaks often overlap to some degree, adjusting one element of the kit might have a detrimental impact on another. For this reason, when mixing a track it is generally better to have the drums on separate mixer channels where EQ and compression can be applied to different parts of the kit.

We will now process each part of the kit individually, and will approach this by using a plug-in that is capable of multichannel output into the DAW mixer. Even if you do not have a plug-in with multiple output capability, you could solo each part of the kit in turn and bounce these down to multiple audio channels and process each separately.

Start by inserting a multichannel instance of your preferred plug-in into a channel in your DAW. You will have to consult its manual to understand how to route the individual components of the drum kit to buss channels in your mixer. We are going to use BFD3 here, but it really does not matter what you use. Now create a number of DAW mixer buss channels, and inside your plug-in route all of the various elements of the kit to their own mixer channels. You will need to take some care with mono and stereo signals.

Illustration opposite, BFD3 is inserted on an instrument channel called Ambients. There are a number of individual outputs from the instrument. You can see a number of stereo channels for the tom toms, the cymbals and the ambient channel, which includes both overheads and room mics, hence its name. There are also mono channels for the kick, the snare and the hi-hat. The unusual naming of the inputs to these individual channels is just a function of the DAW.

Stereo channels carry forward their own stereo image from the instrument, and so panning is assigned within it and no further adjustment is necessary. Mono channels on the other hand need to be panned in the DAW mixer. It is normal to pan the kick and snare to the centre, but we have panned the hi-hat to locate it as someone facing the drum kit might hear it. In fact, this pan position was derived by listening to the ambient mics and adjusting the mono channel to match that stereo image; this approach maintains the clearest sound and stereo image overall. Name all the channels in your mixer, and the busses too if you can. This will save confusion later.

Now create another stereo buss channel and route the outputs of each of the the individual drum channels to its input via a buss. This means that the volume of the entire drum kit can be controlled from a single fader, whilst setting the balance between its components on the individual channels.

PRODUCTION AND EFFECTS 1

THE
DRUM
PROGRAMMING
HANDBOOK

253

The basic mixer configuration for playing back Pattern 09_04 in multichannel format.

There are many schools of thought about the workflow of applying EQ and compression to the individual drums. Many people suggest that you work on one drum at a time, however others say turn up all the faders to get a groove going and then fine tune individual elements as required. You should experiment in order to find your own preference. Purely in order to separate out the topics, let's apply EQ and then compress the results.

Work through each part of the kit in turn and experiment with the EQ. It can be a good idea to start off with each kit piece soloed, but never commit to any adjustments without listening in context – an experienced engineer might not use the solo function at all. There are many reasons why things will sound different once everything is playing. It is impossible to

254

THE
DRUM
PROGRAMMING
HANDBOOK

PRODUCTION AND EFFECTS 1

give precise instructions here, since such decisions are subjective and highly dependent on the greater musical context, but you will find many recommended approaches on the internet if you wish more specific guidance. What follows is a description of an EQ approach on the various channels just to get you started. Use your ears and do it your way.

The EQ applied to the kick drum.

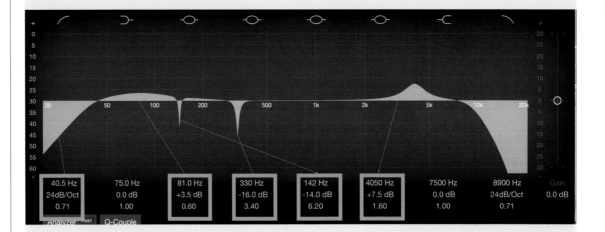

As well as some high and low pass filtering, there is a low-end boost, and another at around 4kHz – this brings out a bit of slap of the beater hitting the head, which helps the kick cut through a mix, especially on small speakers. The lower of the two cuts is reducing a natural resonance of the drum to give it a drier sound, and the upper is twice this frequency to remove some of the next harmonic of this resonance to reinforce this operation. The boost in natural low frequencies has resulted in a volume increase, which we have not compensated for at present.

PRODUCTION AND EFFECTS 1

THE
DRUM
PROGRAMMING
HANDBOOK

255

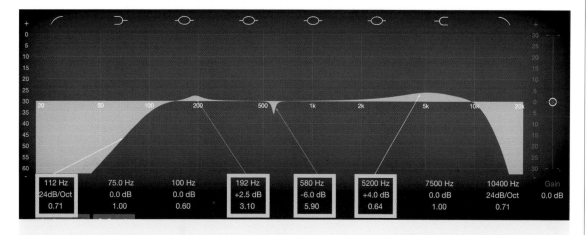

112 Hz	75.0 Hz	100 Hz	192 Hz	580 Hz	5200 Hz	7500 Hz	10400 Hz	Gain
24dB/Oct	0.0 dB	0.0 dB	+2.5 dB	-6.0 dB	+4.0 dB	0.0 dB	24dB/Oct	0.0 dB
0.71	1.00	0.60	3.10	5.90	0.64	1.00	0.71	

The EQ applied to the snare drum.

We now have a more aggressive high pass filter to remove some boom that was present in the snare in order to give that frequency space entirely to the kick – A classic mixing technique – in general, the only things that should be generating low frequencies are the kick and the bass (guitar). The lower of the two boosts brings out some of the resonance of the shell of the drum, and the upper one gives it a little more rattle. The cut is reducing another resonant tone.

450 Hz	75.0 Hz	100 Hz	250 Hz	970 Hz	8800 Hz	3600 Hz	17000 Hz	Gain
24dB/Oct	0.0 dB	0.0 dB	0.0 dB	+2.0 dB	+3.0 dB	0.0 dB	24dB/Oct	-1.0 dB
0.71	1.00	0.60	0.30	0.30	2.80	1.00	0.71	

The EQ applied to the hi-hat.

Even more low frequencies are filtered out here, and two small boosts enhance aspects of the tone. Hi-hats can often take quite a lot of EQ boost at the top and or of the upper middle, depending on what effect you are after, but when in a mix with numerous pitched instruments you might have to compensate for this presence by reducing the volume.

256

THE
DRUM
PROGRAMMING
HANDBOOK

PRODUCTION AND EFFECTS 1

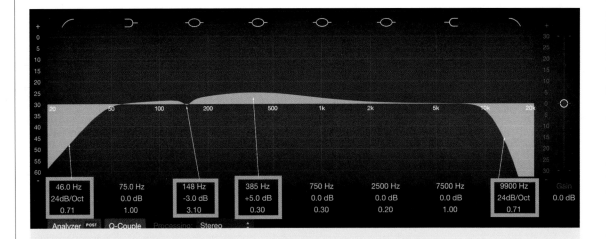

The EQ applied to the tom toms.

The boosted frequencies give the tones a fatter and slightly punchier sound. Again, filtering has been applied. The high pass filter is particularly important for tom toms, again to keep things out of the way of the kick drum.

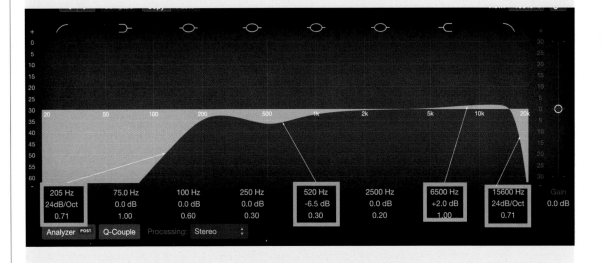

The EQ applied to the cymbals.

Again, all possible low frequencies have been removed, and there is a cut around 500Hz to reduce the knocking quality of the cymbals, as well as some high frequency boosting to brighten them.

PRODUCTION AND EFFECTS 1

THE
DRUM
PROGRAMMING
HANDBOOK

257

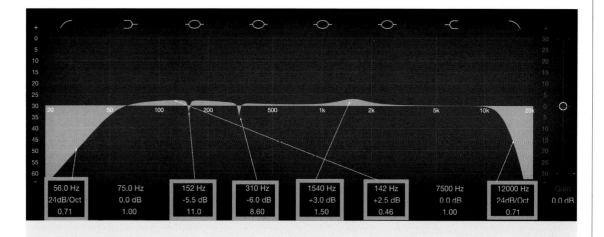

56.0 Hz	75.0 Hz	152 Hz	310 Hz	1540 Hz	142 Hz	7500 Hz	12000 Hz	Gain
24dB/Oct	0.0 dB	-5.5 dB	-6.0 dB	+3.0 dB	+2.5 dB	0.0 dB	24dB/Oct	0.0 dB
0.71	1.00	11.0	8.60	1.50	0.46	1.00	0.71	

The EQ to the ambient signals.

Again we have applied cuts to the resonant frequencies of the kick, which carries through on this audio too. The boosts just bring out pleasing elements of the room ambience. Interesting effects can be generated by quite extreme EQ of the ambience, but only if you do not mind moving away from a perception of authenticity in the recording.

PATTERN 09_09: This is the eight-bar Pattern 09.04 once through as was, then once with multichannel EQ applied, repeating the cycle once. The above EQ process is quite subtle; it just adds a professional sparkle to your programmed parts. Do not underestimate the effect of that. Typically, you will need to EQ the kick drum and the bass guitar to complement each other without their fighting for the same frequencies, and similarly with the snare drum and the electric guitar, etc. EQ can be used to create a variety of special effects, however, and can completely change the tonality of everything to which it is applied.

Pattern 09_09

Pattern 09_10

■ CHECK OUT

Mixing engineer, Dave Pensado
(Michael Jackson and many
more), who has an incredible
number of tutorials on many
aspects of compression and
EQ, not to mention all other
aspects of mixing.
http://www.pensadosplace.tv

PATTERN 09_10: Here, the EQ has been applied to various channels to give a deliberately synthetic, rather lo-fi quality. There are a number of narrow boosts that give a resonant almost howling sound, the cymbals have been deliberately dulled, and the tom toms thinned. Both kick and snare have been processed differently. Twice through the eight-bar pattern with the new EQ.

Now for the compression. Insert a compressor after the EQ on each of the tom toms, the cymbals, the kick and the snare channels.

For the kick drum compressor, start with a ratio of 4:1 and a fairly high threshold that gives perhaps three decibels of gain reduction to start with, although do play with this parameter. Then try an attack time of about 20ms – this will allow a strong initial transient to come through before the compressor starts to act. If the release time is too long, then the body of the drum will disappear as the compressor continues to act after the initial and loudest part of the note, so shorten the release until the drum feels as if it lasts for the right amount of time, and this of course will be a function of tempo. Although the kick was quite loud after the EQ stage, compression is your chance to rectify this by choosing an appropriate amount of make-up gain.

You could take a similar approach with the snare drum, but for now, instead try a much more gentle ratio of about 1.5:1 (this means a bit less than 2:1). This does not do much with a high threshold, but if you lower the threshold considerably it will have a dramatic effect. Try to set the threshold so that the ghost notes are not triggering the compressor, since we want to keep them fairly quiet, and adjust the attack time to get your preferred amount of bite on the backbeat. Set the release time and make up gain as before.

For the tom toms, using a similar range of settings to those used for the kick can work quite well, and simply adjusting the threshold should get you started. If you make the release very fast then the natural sustain of the tom tom will immediately be allowed to benefit from the make-up gain and you will get the effect, should you wish it, of a drum that rings for a long time.

For the cymbals, set the ratio to 3:1 to start with, and with about 20ms of attack you will maintain the immediate impact of the cymbals. Adjust the threshold and the make-up gain to get a controlled amount of sustain, and experiment with the release. You need to be slightly careful with a cymbal as the compressor lets go after its release time – listen to make sure that the overall sound stays smooth.

Lastly, insert a compressor on the buss that is summing the other channels. If you have a plug-in that is recommended as a buss compressor, then you might wish to use that. Set the threshold quite high so that only the loudest notes trigger the unit, and with a ratio of perhaps 4:1 you get a gain reduction on those notes of perhaps two or three decibels. Again, choose

PRODUCTION AND EFFECTS 1

THE
DRUM
PROGRAMMING
HANDBOOK

259

an attack time that sounds appropriate to you, and it can be good to set the release to automatic if you have that facility. If not, again think of the tempo. Be careful with the make-up gain, since if you inadvertently boost the volume you will always think that the compressed version is better. Make sure that you can hear the compressor switched in and out without it affecting the overall volume to really hear the effect of buss compression. The idea is that it 'glues' the drum kit together and gives a more coherent sound without making it obviously different. Be more gentle with the threshold and the ratio if required.

PATTERN 09_11: This is the eight-bar Pattern 09_04, once through as was, then once with both EQ and compression applied, repeating the cycle once. You could compress the ambient channel if you wish (although we have not done this in the audio excerpt). This is sometimes done to get a 'bigger' sound, but you have to be careful of overall clarity since the sound can easily get quite mushy. Compressing the hi-hat must also be done with care, especially if you have microphone spillage from other parts of the kit, which will tend to be boosted in volume.

Exercise One: Bounce down whatever you have created in the workshop, then repeat the workshop from scratch with deliberately different settings. Bounce the result and then compare with your first version.

Exercise Two: For each of your kick and snare channels, copy across to each other, and mute the originals. Listened to the alternative effect of each, and fine tune the parameters to make it interesting. Adjust the EQ if necessary.

Exercise Three: Un-mute the original compressors so that you now have a chain of two levels of compression on each channel. Again, tweak the parameters and try the compressors both ways round.

Things to experiment with

- Try rebalancing the volume of the kit using only EQ.
- Use an extreme amount of compression on the ambient channel and mix it in with the others at very low volume.
- Reverse the order of the EQ and the compressors in the channel strip and listen to the result – some parameter changes might be necessary.
- Try EQ both before and after the compressor. Substitute different models of compressor and EQ in each of your scenarios and compare the effect on the sound.

TIP
Remember not to compress things just because you can, but only when you think that this will be beneficial to the overall effect.

CONCLUSION

We have now considered basic DAW mixer architecture. We have also been introduced to two essential aspects of modern mixing: EQ and compression. We have investigated their key parameters and explored them individually, and in combination; you should continue to listen to music that you enjoy and consider how these have been applied in that context. In the next chapter, we will develop our understanding of production by considering further delay-based effects and the automation of parameters.

Check that you:
- Are comfortable with the layout of your mixer and its signal flow.
- Understand how and when to use busses, insert and send effects.
- Understand how to apply EQ to a number of creative and corrective ends.
- Can apply compression in different ways on both loops and individual drums.
- Can use EQ and compression in combination to enhance and control your sounds.

PRODUCTION AND EFFECTS 2

CHAPTER 10

This chapter will examine more DAW production processes that can enhance your programming. Such processes include automation and time-based effects such as reverberation and delay. We will consider automation as both a mix tool and a sound design tool, and also investigate some classic applications of a number of effects.

AUTOMATION

Virtually every parameter in a DAW Channel can be automated; that is to say its movements can be recorded relative to the timeline of a song. Although such movements can be performed with a mouse, it is much more tactile, and generally more musical, to use a dedicated controller knob on a keyboard, control surface, or a software interface on a tablet. As well as editing such recordings, you can also use the mouse to input such data graphically, and in doing so influence any given parameter, just as if you had recorded parameter movements. This approach offers the greatest precision. The graphical representations of the movements of each parameter are called lanes, and these tend to be grouped by track.

Automation typically has a number of modes such as Touch and Read. When Touch is activated, it record-enables every parameter on a channel strip and any plug-ins therein, so as playback is running any adjustments that you make are recorded. Technically, this is not the same as actually recording MIDI or audio information, which originates outside the DAW. In Read, existing automation is played, but any real-time adjustments that you make will not be recorded. You might also encounter a mode such as Write, which would completely replace all automation of a given parameter for the duration of the timeline, and as such, must be used with care.

Automation is an incredibly powerful feature. It has more obvious applications such as generating repeatable volume fades and panning, but these extend to detailed sound design and performance shaping. Every DAW has a similar approach to implementing automation, although the names of functions and the mouse tools sometimes vary. As ever, you will have to read your manual.

In order to explore some uses of automation, we will use some of the audio layers from the workshop in Chapter Six. Some of these have been bounced from verse one into 12-bar regions at 84 bpm for use here and renamed as follows:

PATTERN 10_01 is the same as Pattern 04_16

PATTERN 10_02 is the same as Pattern 06_22

TIP
A disadvantage of using the mouse to record automation is that only a single parameter can be adjusted at once. Using a control surface overcomes this, offering more flexibility and often more controlled results.

Pattern 10_01

Pattern 10_02

PRODUCTION AND EFFECTS – 2

THE
DRUM
PROGRAMMING
HANDBOOK

263

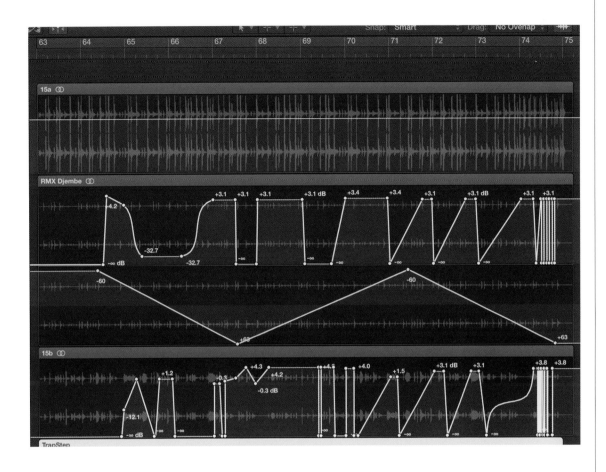

*Here you can see a
number of track-
automation lanes.*

The top lane is Pattern 10_01 volume. Since this drum kit part will be our principal groove element and will simply be required to play continuously, there is no actual automation of its volume. You can see a horizontal line that indicates a constant volume over the duration of the region.

We are also using Pattern RMX Djembe, the volume of which can be seen in the next lane down. This is a percussion part, and whereas it originally played consistently for the duration, now we are using automation to bring it in and out, and thus form something of a musical arrangement. You can see the horizontal line at the left – at the bottom of the lane, which indicates that the track is at minimum volume until it rises sharply, partway through the second bar. The following curved line reduces the volume, but it stays relatively high until suddenly dropping sharply, but slowing towards its destination volume. This destination is very quiet, just to give a texture underneath the beat of Pattern 10_01.

There are then a succession of volume rises and dips, which basically bring the percussion part

264

THE
DRUM
PROGRAMMING
HANDBOOK

PRODUCTION AND EFFECTS – 2

in and out of play. The breakpoints (where a new line segment starts and ends) are generally timed to align with the grid. Three bars from the end, there are a number of similarly shaped changes that repeat several times. This is an example of where the volume envelope shape has been copied and pasted in order to repeat a particular effect, in this case fade-ins that lead onto playback at normal volume in the last beat of each bar (the last one was changed slightly to align with the musical phrasing). In the last bar there are a number of rapid rises and falls to give a staccato sound that appears to chop some of notes to give what is often termed a gated effect – at the speed of 16th-notes.

Magnification of the last two bars.

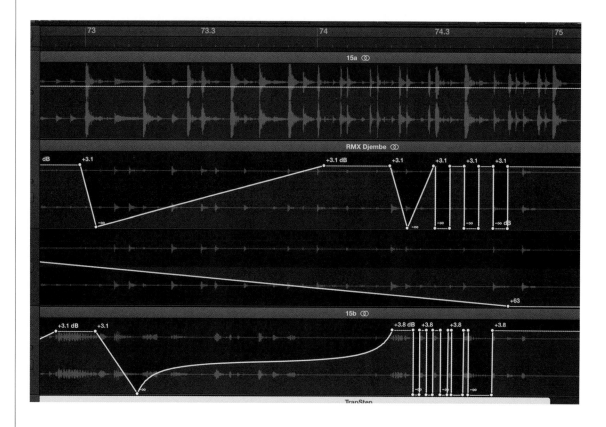

This is a magnification of the four lanes for the last two bars only; the staccato sections are easily discernible. Notice the different timings. In the second lane down the volume steps are metric, but in the bottom lane the steps have been aligned to specific notes, simply because this sounded appropriate.

The third lane down also refers to the Pattern RMX Djembe track; this is a second layer of automation, this time affecting the pan position. When panning a mono track, the track is routed in

CHAPTER 10

PRODUCTION AND EFFECTS – 2

THE
DRUM
PROGRAMMING
HANDBOOK

265

varying proportions to the left and right channels of the output buss. The source here is already stereo, and so when panning (say) left, the left channel maintains its volume, but invisibly the right is reduced, or vice versa. In fact, since this track does not have radically different left and right signals, the effect of such panning is simply to push the sound of the percussion left or right.

The effect of these triangular automation shapes over the duration of the region is to move the position slowly between the left and right channels. Because the percussion can only really be heard in short bursts due to its volume automation, these flurries of notes simply appear in different parts of the stereo image at different times. Because the pan automation takes several bars to move from left to right, which is relatively slow compared to the length of phrases, the sound does not appear to be radically moving, although there is a subtle dynamic effect. Of course, much more specific and precise panning instructions could be implemented instead.

The bottom lane is volume automation of Pattern 10_02. This is similar in spirit to the volume automation of the second lane, the function being to strategically place occasional phrases from the continual background source audio. There are a few sloping lines which act as fades on the longer sounds in this region; these are aligned with some specific sustained noises and thus shape them in the fashion of an ADSR envelope. There is a considered relationship between the volumes here and in the second lane, where sometimes the two regions play simultaneously, and at other times are closer to either/or.

Exercise One: Select a number of your own beats that you might like to use as layers, and after tempo-matching them, apply volume automation to produce some phrasing interaction between them, using steep curves to switch between the beats.

Exercise Two: Working on either this version or a copy, extend this idea to work with relatively slow complementary fades; in other words, as one part is fading in another is fading out.

Exercise Three: Using either one of the above exercises, or with another that you compile, set up some auto-panning – this is when panning moves from left to right with a rhythmic cycle. Start with single bar phrases, and experiment with both fast and slow fades. It might be useful to copy and paste panning automation between two lanes and then invert the stereo image of one whilst maintaining positional information.

TIME DELAY EFFECTS

The most common type of studio effects are based upon time delays, where a portion of a signal is delayed by anything from a few milliseconds to several seconds and recombined with the original signal at a controlled volume. These effects are generally inserted on a buss channel that is fed by a send from the channel of the audio that you wish to affect, and as such are also available to all other channels simultaneously. It is remarkable how many different sounds can be created by this simple concept. Here, we will consider just a small number of the possibilities.

> **TIP**
> When you want regions to instantaneously play or mute in response to an automation curve, it is often a good idea to use steep slopes on such envelopes rather than verticals, since a vertical line can often give a slight click.

CHAPTER 10

266

THE
DRUM
PROGRAMMING
HANDBOOK

PRODUCTION AND EFFECTS – 2

DELAY

A so-called delay effect will capture any audio being fed to it and repeat it one or a number of times at prescribed intervals in the fashion of an echo. A delay effect will typically have a parameter that controls the length of these intervals, either in milliseconds or note values that slave to the tempo of the DAW. It will also have a feedback control that governs the number of times that the echoes repeat. Stereo delay effects can have different settings for the left and right channels. There will also be a mix control that determines the blend of the dry and echo-effected signal. When correctly implemented as a send effect, this control should be set to 100% effect, with the level of the send control determining the blend with the audio from the source channel strip.

The choice of delay times is crucial, as is the nature of the source material. If the source material has rather loose timing, then any notes that do not align with the grid will have this discrepancy exaggerated by the fact that they are repeated, and further, these repeats might align with subsequent notes that have different timing again, giving a flamming effect. It will be for you to judge whether this is acceptable in a specific context. You must also be mindful when working with triplet-based patterns. Problems can arise here with an over-emphasis on the middle note of the triplet, caused by the delay landing here, when in fact this does not sit comfortably with the groove of the song. There can also be problems when using one of the shuffle grooves that were described in Chapter Seven, because the mathematical nature of delays can easily conflict with any such groove.

With drums and percussion, precise delay times generally work better and so setting the delay times to specific note values will often yield the best results. This is also essential if using a tempo map. You still have to be careful and take the timing of the source material into consideration. If, for instance, you have a sequence that is based on eighth-notes (quavers) and you apply an eighth-note delay, then all the repeats will land on subsequent notes, which will give a lumpy sound. In such a case, choosing a value of a single 16th-note (semiquaver) with a low level of feedback to give only a single dominant echo before each subsequent eighth-note will avoid this.

Perhaps even better would be to use a dotted eighth-note delay. This is equivalent to three 16th-notes, which means that the first repeat will fall in between two eighth-notes, although the next will possibly align with a played eighth-note, and this relationship will repeat as determined by the feedback setting. Although there is some overlaying of sounds in this case, the fact that we are working with odd numbers (three) makes this approach quite forgiving. This principle also applies with different predominant note values in the source material – choose a delay that tends to keep out of the way. It is unlikely that you would want to use a dotted 16th-note delay on the 16th-note material since that would end up generating 32nd-notes (demisemiquavers), and this unusual feel might upset the groove. Of course, these suggestions are not a hard and fast rule, so experiment, and if you like it then go with it.

PRODUCTION AND EFFECTS – 2

THE
DRUM
PROGRAMMING
HANDBOOK

267

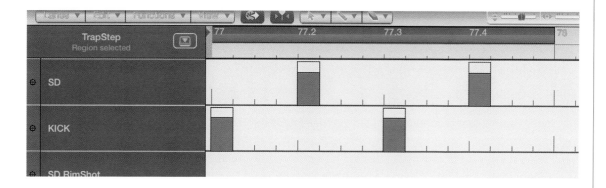

The basic MIDI pattern of Pattern 10_03.

PATTERN 10_03: A simple kick and snare pattern with a delay applied after the first beat of bar two, with another four bars also effected. The tempo is 84 bpm. The first bar is dry (no effect), but the delay send comes in before the second bar. Because the length of the echo cycle is nearly a whole bar (as determined by the feedback), when the delay first starts the overall effect is relatively spacious, but once all the echoes build up the effect is continuous. The output of the delay effect can be heard on its own after the fifth bar where the MIDI notes have ceased. This particular delay is called a ping-pong delay because it features different delay times in each channel of the stereo image; here, one has an eighth-note delay time, and the other a dotted eighth-note. The output of the delay effect is low pass filtered (a native function of this particular effect unit) so that each successive echo has less high-frequency content than the previous one. Not only does this give a pleasing effect, but it helps the delay sit in a mix without the source audio getting too cluttered.

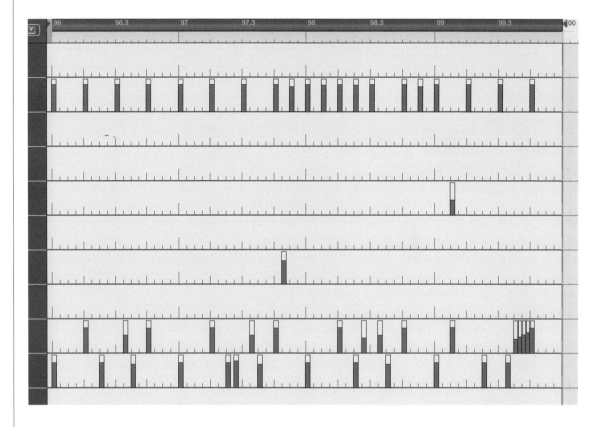

The basic MIDI pattern of Pattern 10_03. There are a number of different (synthetic) snare and hi-hat sounds, which for clarity are indicated on the same lane.

PATTERN 10_04: A four-bar beat with a ping-pong delay applied throughout. Repeated once at 126bpm. This pattern is fairly spacious with a largely quarter-note (crotchet) hi-hat pattern and an eighth-note based kick feel. It has the same delay as above applied to the whole kit. It is the delay that fills this pattern out and gives it a 16th-note feel overall, and the low pass filter make the hi-hat echoes feel more like ghost notes on the snare. The 32nd-note roll at the end gives a pleasing flutter as it is repeated by the delay.

REVERB

Reverberation (to give it its full name) is a naturally occurring phenomenon whereby sound is reflected from surrounding surfaces, causing it to linger. Think of the sound if you were to clap your hands in a large hall. Because the sound travels in all directions at once, it is reflected from every surface it encounters – to different degrees – an infinite number of times, and all these reflections have to travel a different distance and so take a different amount of time to reach your ear. Because there are an infinite number, it is not possible to hear the reflections as separate echoes,

CHAPTER 10

PRODUCTION AND EFFECTS – 2

THE
DRUM
PROGRAMMING
HANDBOOK

269

as with a delay unit, but rather they take the form of what is often called a reverb tail – a smooth decay away to silence.

Although the example of a hall is a rather obvious reverb, every acoustic space has its own unique sonic fingerprint. In music production, capturing the sound of the room when recording is a crucially important aspect of authenticity, but when programming we are also able to add artificially generated reverb to a number of important ends, be that simulating a particular room for a whole kit, or just a particular drum, or adding special effects of an ambient nature.

When working with a reverb plug-in, the most important parameters are the type (eg, hall, room etc), which governs the nature of the sound, and the reverb time, which indicates how long the tail lasts. In addition, you will encounter other parameters such as pre-delay, which is a very short amount of time before the tail commences; a representation of the real world when there is a large space relative to the distance between a sound source and the listener, hence a noticeable difference between the direct sound and the arrival of the reflections. You will also often find a degree of control over the so-called early reflections, which are a number of loud echoes very soon after the source sound. These are very close together, but can sometimes be discerned as individual sounds. They are important to our psychoacoustic impression of a space.

■ **CHECK OUT**
An Internet video called the Wikidrummer. This video shows a drum kit being played in many different spaces, all edited together; it gives you a good impression of the typical sounds of such spaces.

The various routes in a room that sound might take to travel from a source to a listener.

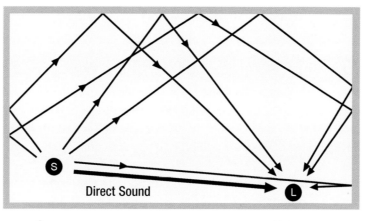

Source   Listener

You can see in the diagram that the direct sound always has the shortest path. All the other reflections have different path lengths and therefore arrive different amounts of time later. In this diagram, there is an early reflection travelling parallel to the direct sound, but bouncing off the wall on the right.

270

THE
DRUM
PROGRAMMING
HANDBOOK

PRODUCTION AND EFFECTS – 2

All of the acoustic drum kit audio examples in the earlier chapters have in fact included room microphones that captured the reverb of the room alongside some direct sound from the kit; the room component is very important in order for the overall kit to sound natural. In BFD3, these microphones can be muted, so all that is heard is the sound of the close microphones. These are placed so close to individual drums that they hardly capture any reverb, although this gives them a rather unnatural quality. The function of close microphones is to give precise control over the volume, EQ, and compression of individual drums.

PATTERN 10_05: An eighth-note-based pattern generated by BFD3. Two bars at 115bpm with room microphones as normal, then repeated once without. The effect is dramatic.

There are two principal approaches to create synthetic reverb: modelling and convolution. The modelling approach is very like a delay effect, but with an enormous number of controlled echoes. Convolution mixes your audio with a recording from a real space and can give very authentic sounding results that are close to the sound of particular rooms. When adding synthetic reverb with a plug-in, the plug-in should generally be configured as a send effect. The main reason is that if you want to blend the various instruments in a track, then using multiple sends to the same shared virtual space will provide the most coherence. Conversely, inserting reverbs on audio or instrument channels can soon use up all your CPU power. It can be useful for special effects, though.

Choice of reverb unit and setting makes an enormous difference to your sound. Once you are comfortable with the range of preset sounds on a given unit you should explore the effect of adjusting the various parameters, and doing this will give you real control of your productions. The following examples demonstrate a tiny fraction of typical possibilities.

PATTERN 10_06: Pattern 10_05 without its own room microphones, sent to a convolution reverb representing a particular 10m x 15m wooden hall with a reverb time of two seconds.

PATTERN 10_07: Pattern 10_05 without its own room microphones, sent to a convolution reverb representing a 5m x 5m room in a famous UK recording studio, with a reverb time of one second.

PATTERN 10_08: Pattern 10_05 without its own room microphones, sent to a convolution reverb representing a 14m x 73m cathedral in France. The reverb time is 12 seconds.

PATTERN 10_09: Pattern 10_05 without its own room microphones, sent to a modelling reverb with a reverb time of under one second.

PRODUCTION AND EFFECTS – 2

THE
DRUM
PROGRAMMING
HANDBOOK

271

 Pattern 10_10

PATTERN 10_10: Pattern 10_05 without its own room microphones, sent to a modelling reverb with a reverb time of 0.4 seconds. The pre-delay and early reflections are such that an effect known as slapback is generated, and this appears as rhythmic pulses between all the eighth-notes.

 Pattern 10_11

PATTERN 10_11: Pattern 10_05 without its own room microphones, sent to a modelling reverb designed to emulate a small room with a reverb time of 0.5 second.

There are numerous other effects based on the concept of time delays. Such things include auto-pan, chorus, flanger and more. Such things are beyond the scope of this chapter, but do investigate them and their application to drum programming and beyond.

Exercise One: Choose a stereo pattern that you have programmed: one with a straightforward and fairly simple feel (a busy pattern can quickly get messy with long reverbs), and preferably without much reverb in the source sounds. Set up a send to the reverb plug-in of your choice. Turn up this send to about half way, and audition all the presets with your pattern. Try to learn how to identify categories by their characteristic similarities.

Exercise Two: Change the reverb plug-in for a different one and repeat the exercise. This time, focus on identifying the different sonic qualities between sounds that might be categorised similarly in the two plug-ins. Repeat this exercise for other plug-ins that you have.

Exercise Three: Using one particular plug-in that you enjoyed, consult its manual and experiment with different combinations of parameter. If you create any sounds that you particularly like, save them as user presets. Obviously, such an exercise can be repeated many times.

TIP
Increasing the pre-delay on a reverb can allow drums to punch through before being smeared by the tail, thus increasing clarity while still allowing a 'big' sound.

PRODUCING A DRUM TRACK

In Chapter Nine, we looked at some approaches to mixing a multichannel kit in order to focus and enhance its sound. Leaving this to the side for the moment, we will now extend our concept of production by developing three layers from the earlier automation section of this chapter. We will augment them with some further textures that exploit a number of production techniques. As with so many things, there are an infinite number of possibilities that might be applied here, but this workshop will serve to showcase just a few in order to get you thinking.

Firstly, if you have not already done so, create a version of the audio tracks and beats from the automation section of this chapter. It does not have to be exactly the same, but something along those lines will be a good starting point. If you did the exercises, then you can use the results from there instead: it is the process and principles that count.

272

THE
DRUM
PROGRAMMING
HANDBOOK

PRODUCTION AND EFFECTS – 2

In order to add some different textures to the three layers previously assembled, program another layer of MIDI one-shots. The idea here is not to lay down yet another groove, but to add occasional hits that function as production sparkle, almost as fills without being fills. If you can find sounds such as synthetic snare drums, claps and electronic noises, they might prove useful.

PATTERN 10_12: This is a layer of MIDI one-shots from PlugInGuru Mega Macho Drums, just playing back on a stereo channel. This is a 12-bar sequence, played with a click.

As a starting point, try adding a clap or synthetic snare on beat 4 every second bar. Also place a few short-sounding notes – hi-hat-type sounds or short electronic snares would be good – fairly quietly, on 16th-note offbeats at places where you can help the groove to skip along. You can also use these types of sound to produce short flurries of notes that function as fills, based either on 16th-notes or 32nd-notes. In Pattern 10_12, we have a 32nd-note roll in bar eight, and a 16th-note flourish in bar 12. An occasional electronic kick would be good too. Do not insert too many, otherwise it will have the effect of functioning as part of the groove except in a rather haphazard fashion; the kicks should only punctuate the greater piece. You might also want to place the occasional crash, or crash-like sound.

We will now spice up this one-shot sequence with some MIDI-based manipulation. First of all, let's use pitch bend to manipulate some of the sounds. On your chosen sound source, set the pitch bend range to be large: one or two octaves will be good. The idea here is that sweeping the pitch will produce radically different sounds, quite divorced from their original form. This approach will not work well if you are using anything with an inbuilt timing content, such as a triggered loop (it will go out of time), but one-shots are ideal.

Now choose a target passage from what you have programmed above, set up a cycle of a bar or two, and practise performing with the pitch bend lever. Remember to have the appropriate channel selected in order to direct your MIDI information to the instrument. If you find that you are generating interesting results, drop your DAW into record and record the movements. If upon listening you are not satisfied, press undo and re-record. Further, you can always edit the pitch bend information later to fine-tune it.

TIP
Try to find a kit that has some interesting sounds that can punctuate what you have already, preferably from a source with some sonic-manipulation facility such as pitch bend and filters. Sounds generated by a sampler will have useful flexibility.

CHAPTER 10

PRODUCTION AND EFFECTS – 2

THE
DRUM
PROGRAMMING
HANDBOOK

273

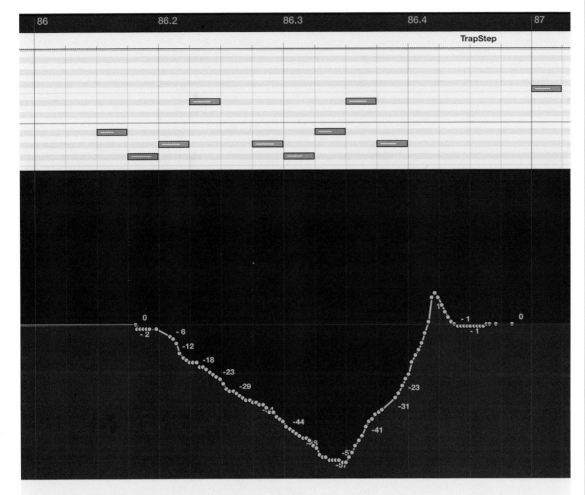

*Pitch bend information
that was recorded in bar
12 (hence the many nodes)
in real time.*

The notes in the piano roll are hi-hat-like sounds, but a two-octave pitch dive changes them into a more clangorous industrial sounding thing, rather reminiscent of DJ scratching.

PATTERN 10_13: The last two bars with pitch bend, repeated once.

PATTERN 10_14: Bars six and seven, demonstrating the pitch bend on the cymbal, repeated once.

Sometimes it is better to add pitch bend information with the mouse to get absolute precision.

 Pattern 10_13

 Pattern 10_14

CHAPTER 10

Pitch bend information that was manually inserted into bar seven.

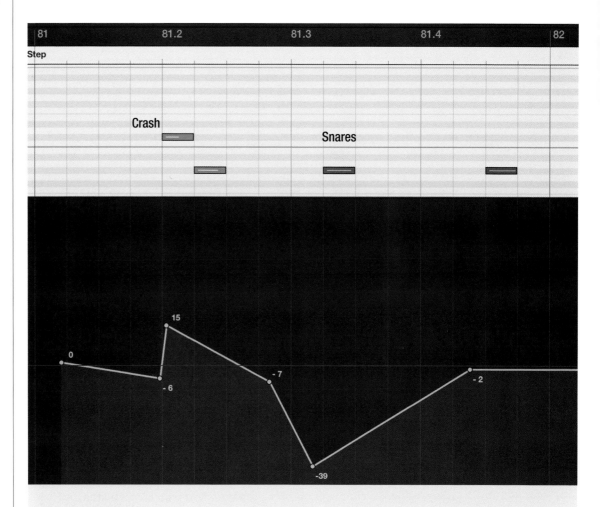

The principal function of this curve is to make the crash descend in pitch. Because its sustain overlaps a number of snare drums, these are also affected by the pitch bend; however, we have just allowed this. This diagram also illustrates a potential problem; on the right you will notice that the pitch bend has been inadvertently reset to a value of –2 whereas it should have been zero (the numerical value has little meaning here since it does not have a tangible relationship to the pitch bend range). If you have the pitch bend range set to a very large value, even the value –2 could be noticeable and affect the continuity of the sound past this point. Of course, this kind of thing is a considerable problem if it occurs when dealing with pitched material. If this happens, just edit it back to zero.

PRODUCTION AND EFFECTS – 2

THE
DRUM
PROGRAMMING
HANDBOOK

275

Whereas automation is a proprietary DAW-based control system, MIDI controller information is much more generic and compatible. If you have any movable controls that can output MIDI controllers, on your keyboard, control surface, or tablet, then setting them up to control parameters on your DAW can prove very useful. Whichever system you have, configure it so that it can send at least one MIDI control change number (CC#) into your DAW. Ensure that you know which CC# you are sending – your DAW will usually be able to report this to you. Consult your manual if necessary, and map the CC# to control a useful parameter on your sound source; filter cut-off frequency is always a fun choice. Once you have done this, adjusting your external controller will change the value of the cut-off with tactile hands-on control.

USING CC# DATA TO CONTROL AUTOMATION

It is easy to get confused between automation control data and MIDI controller data, not least because they often have overlapping functionality and look similar when you are editing them. CC# data must be recorded like any other MIDI information, and as such resides in regions, just like notes. It will often have a similar effect on each of a range of hardware and software synthesizers, depending on where you direct it. DAWs can however receive CC# data and convert it into proprietary automation information for any given parameter that you might specify. This is then captured like any other automation using the Touch mode, etc. The data can reside either in individual regions, or on a track. So, you can be generating and sending CC# data, but using it to create DAW-specific automation. The point is that despite the apparent complexity, this conversion system allows a large range of external controllers to work with many different DAW systems to give you incredibly flexible control. The benefits of learning to work this way are enormous, so invest a little time in getting it together.

Now work through your sequence and perform with your assigned controller. You might wish to adjust the resonance (perhaps just with the mouse) in order to get a more pronounced filter-sweep effect. In the audio example, the filter has been swept in bar eight over the 32nd-note roll.

276

THE
DRUM
PROGRAMMING
HANDBOOK

PRODUCTION AND EFFECTS – 2

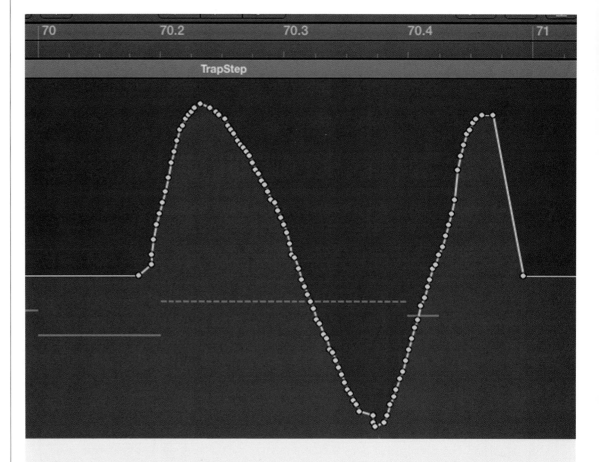

The filter sweep in bar eight that was performed with a MIDI controller.

Note that you have to be careful lest you inadvertently leave the filter cut-off in the wrong position for the remainder of the sequence. Record and edit some moves that you like. You do not have to fill the whole sequence with these manipulations; just the occasional section will have a powerful effect.

 Pattern 10_15

PATTERN 10_15: Bars seven and eight – the second bar features the 32nd-note filter-swept roll.

We will now use automation to provide further textures. Previously, we have only automated major parameters such as volume and pan over substantial periods of time, but now we will work at a much more detailed level, down to individual notes.

CHAPTER 10

PRODUCTION AND EFFECTS – 2

THE
DRUM
PROGRAMMING
HANDBOOK

277

If you have not already done so, first set up sends for each of two buss channels for reverb and delay, using a tempo-synced delay and a fairly long reverb. Next, on your new MIDI one-shot track, turn up the send to the delay. Listen to the effect that it has, not least to where it overly clutters everything. Identify either individual notes or brief phrases that work, and experiment with different levels of send for them. You now have a choice. Either put the track into Touch mode and manually 'play' the automation as the transport is running (remember that you could, of course, assign the send to an external MIDI controller), or simply draw in the required shape with the mouse.

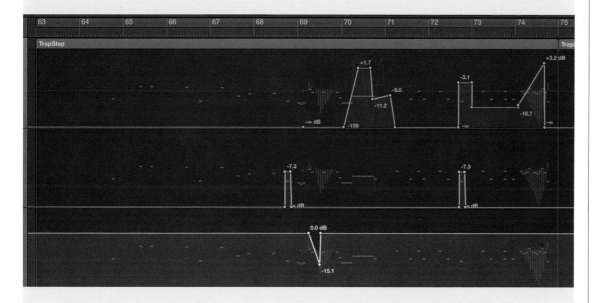

Automation sends for the MIDI one-shot track.

The upper lane is the delay send, the middle is the reverb send, and the bottom lane is volume, where a small amount of correction was required to counter the effect of the pitch bend treatment.

You can see in the diagram that there are roughly three levels of delay send used here: none, some or lots, but this is purely arbitrary. What is more specific is that where the shape is squarer, individual notes are being abruptly given to the send, which then gets sharply out of the way to avoid sending the following note. This approach is good for echoing individual notes. You will also notice ramps, and these give a rather more ambient phrasing with the delay fading in or out over groups of notes.

TIP
If your DAW does not immediately display the appropriate lane before you have actually written any automation (some behave in this fashion), them simply put the track into touch mode, enter a couple of movements and you should then be able to see the lane and edit out these unwanted movements, after which you will be able to manually input as required.

Identify the claps that you inserted earlier, and for one or a number of them draw automation for the reverb send. Adjust the send level for the clap reverb; the outcome should be a wet/dry-balanced reverb tail only on those particular notes. Notice that in the audio example, this first occurs in bar six, where a pause has been edited into the main groove. The reverb tail is allowed to carry through the space, accompanied by some percussion and a burst of synthetic kick drum. You may or may not enjoy the delay send acting simultaneously on the same note(s), but naturally edit until you are happy.

PATTERN 10_16: Pattern 10_12 with all the various processing applied.

Now for another special effect. Firstly, create a new track and import the 160bpm Pattern 05_16. Since we are currently working at 84bpm clearly this pattern will be out of time. Half of 160 is 80, and so only a small amount of time stretching can change this pattern to 84bpm. The key with this four-bar phrase is to identify where beat 1 of the fifth bar would be. If you slice the pattern at this point, locking to the transient if possible and discard the portion of the fifth bar, then it should be easy to stretch the remaining four bars of 160bpm (using your preferred algorithm) to fit into two bars of our 84bpm sequence here. Obviously, this busy double-time pattern rather takes over, and so we need a strategy to accommodate it.

First of all, apply an aggressive EQ to the pattern in order to remove all but a narrow band of frequencies in the mid-range. The pattern will now sound very thin and squeaky if played on its own. You might even exaggerate this further with a boost around 2kHz. Such EQ settings stop it from interfering with the kick and hi-hats in the main pattern and allow just a hi-mid-range texture to sit 'above' the main snare drum.

PRODUCTION AND EFFECTS – 2

THE
DRUM
PROGRAMMING
HANDBOOK

279

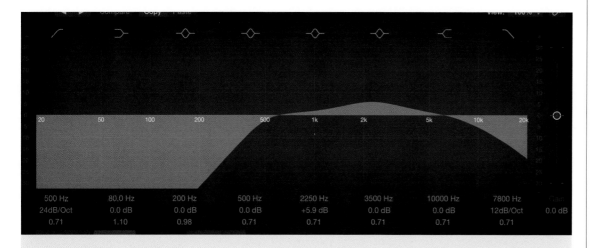

500 Hz	80.0 Hz	200 Hz	500 Hz	2250 Hz	3500 Hz	10000 Hz	7800 Hz	
24dB/Oct	0.0 dB	0.0 dB	0.0 dB	+5.9 dB	0.0 dB	0.0 dB	12dB/Oct	0.0 dB
0.71	1.10	0.98	0.71	0.71	0.71	0.71	0.71	

The EQ acting as a band pass filter – only allowing middle frequencies through.

Applying this to a human voice and tweaking the frequencies (even more aggressively) can make it sound like the voice is coming through a telephone. In order to help it cut through further, you should now apply harsh compression to it, perhaps with a 4:1 ratio to give at least 6 dB of gain reduction, and if you are feeling brave, even as much a rather extreme 12 dB. This will completely squash and distort the pattern, but allow us to switch it 'on and off' with more control at whatever volume, although perhaps testing the artistic merits of controlled distortion!

Now that you have a texture that works, use automation to bring the loop in wherever you see fit. Again, you can do this with an assigned controller or use mouse precision, as you prefer. Experiment with different degrees of fades in and out.

280

THE
DRUM
PROGRAMMING
HANDBOOK

PRODUCTION AND EFFECTS – 2

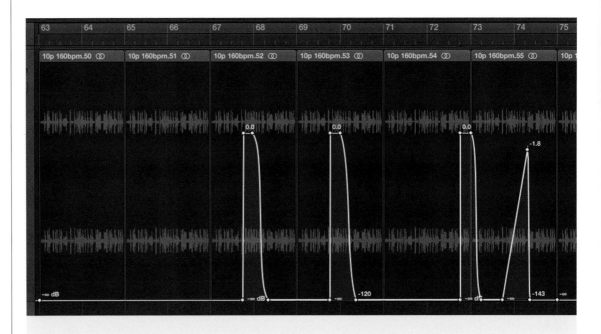

The automation that fades the time-stretched Pattern 05_16 in and out.

Finally, you might wish to buss all the various drum parts together, and apply some compression to glue them together, and perhaps even apply some overall EQ.

PATTERN 10_17: The 12-bar phrase of all the various layers with their automation and processing. They are played twice.

PATTERN 10_18: Pattern 10_16 with a bassline. The upright bass sound here is coming from Spectrasonics Trilian, which allows for a wide range of performance subtleties to be replicated for considerable realism. Hearing a rhythm section in this way gives more context to our creation – listen to how the production effects interact with the bassline.

 Pattern 10_17

 Pattern 10_18

Exercise One: Substitute Pattern 10_01 with an equivalent MIDI pattern and a multichannel-capable instrument. Using the multichannel mixing techniques of Chapter Nine, apply EQ and compression as appropriate to individual drums to get an even better controlled and balanced overall effect.

Exercise Two: Apply some reverb and delay via sends to this pattern; the kick and the snare are obvious candidates. You will likely end up with something that is far too dense and frenetic, so use

PRODUCTION AND EFFECTS – 2

THE
DRUM
PROGRAMMING
HANDBOOK

281

automation to pare them back except for the occasional chosen notes, eg, applying reverb to the snare drum on beat 2 every second bar, or catching one particular note on the kick with a delay.

Exercise Three: Assign an external controller to one or a number of parameters on your multichannel instrument, and record a performance of those parameters. Edit the performance to your satisfaction.

Things to experiment with

- Copy a section of automation from one lane to another.
- Try both EQing and compressing the output of each of the reverb and delay plug-ins.
- If using the MIDI one-shot kit overdub technique, bounce its output to audio (with its effects) and change the kit for any repeated section in your track.
- Set up an interesting automation curve for a send over a bar or two, then repeat this cycle.
- On successive repeats of a passage with automation fades, move the fades around by an exact number of bars to trigger the audio at different places.
- If you have them, assign multiple controllers to different sends and instrument parameters and learn to perform a dub mix, and record it when you feel confident.
- Explore chains of insert effects on the send channels.

CONCLUSION

We have now considered automation both for obvious mixing techniques like volume and for more intricate production effects when applied to specific parameters, and further, developed a hands-on approach to real-time performance of these parameters. We have investigated two of the most common time delay effects, reverb and delay, and considered some of their applications. We have also pulled many production techniques into a single demonstration scenario to set up a model approach that you can adapt to your own music. In the next chapter, we will revisit the sampler and develop its potential by both sampling our own sounds and considering aspects of synthesis and automation in this context.

Check that you can:

- Create and edit automation with the mouse.
- Assign an external controller to input automation in real time.
- Understand both delay and reverb effects and their associated parameters.
- Apply effects and automation creatively to multichannel productions.
- Link the principles of the preceding chapter with those of this one.

MORE SAMPLERS AND SAMPLING

CHAPTER 11

MORE SAMPLERS AND SAMPLING

THE
DRUM
PROGRAMMING
HANDBOOK

283

We have already seen a number of uses for the sampler, but there are many applications of this powerful tool that we have yet to explore. In this chapter, we will consider a number of other, more sophisticated techniques that draw from areas such as synthesis and production. We will also record our own samples, process them, and build an instrument from them.

BUILDING A MULTI-SAMPLE INSTRUMENT

Strictly speaking, a multi-sample instrument is any sampler instrument that features multiple samples. We created such instruments in Chapter Five. Having said that, the term is more commonly employed when we have more than one sample on a single key. Whichever sample is triggered might be dependent on velocity, for instance. This approach is very common when creating sampler instruments that emulate acoustic ones, since many acoustic instruments sound different depending on whether they are played loudly or quietly. Triggering the relevant sample relative to performance velocity gives considerable added realism. The acoustic sounding kits used in the audio examples earlier in this book exploit this approach with many 'velocity layers'.

Creating such sampler instruments requires detailed recording and performance of the sources and considerable diligence in assembling all the appropriate samples and zones. What we will do is to apply the same principle to building a synthetic kit with some interesting performance capability. We will initially assign a number of different kicks, snares, and hi-hats to each of only three MIDI notes that will trigger different drum sounds depending on velocity. We will also use this as an opportunity to explore some subtle sonic variations that can provide changing texture over an extended timeline.

We need to select three or four sound sources for each role and edit the audio to ensure well trimmed one-shots. Previously, when assigning samples to zones we assumed that the entire velocity range would trigger the given sample, with velocity controlling its volume. We will now create multiple zones on each of our chosen MIDI notes. Each zone will be designated to respond to a fixed range of velocities. However, these velocities do not necessarily dictate the playback volume, since the zone will have a parameter to trim this independently. We must decide which sample will respond to the loudest, the middle, and the quietest velocities.

A three-note drum kit.

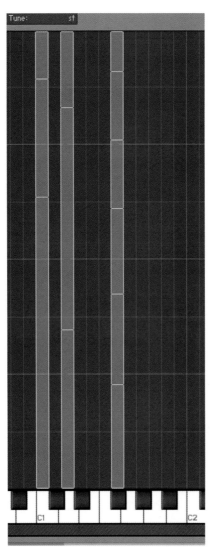

TIP

When you want to take sounds from an existing MIDI instrument, a good way is to program a MIDI sequence that has notes playing each sound in turn, making sure that each has time to decay naturally. Bounce this sequence to a new audio file. Open this new audio file in a system that can detect transients and export slices, such as Propellerhead ReCycle, or, if you have one, the inbuilt system in your DAW. You can then detect the transients of each note and export the individual slices, each of which will contain a single drum sample. It would be a good idea to trim the air from the end of each sample, since playing these samples back in one-shot mode could silently increase polyphony and make your sampler work harder unnecessarily.

Although there are only three notes in this GM-mapped kit, you can see that each note has a number of zones stacked vertically. The kick and the snare have three each, but the hi-hat has six, containing both open and closed sounds. The precise crossover points do not align between notes, but this was determined purely out of how the keys felt when pressed, and is therefore subjective. When setting up the zones in this way, we could define areas of vertical overlap where a given velocity triggers samples from each zone simultaneously, but this has not been done here. The sounds have been taken from a couple of kits from PlugInGuru Mega Macho Drums.

Zones typically have a number of parameters that can be changed for each of them. There will be a mode to make all zones change simultaneously, for instance tuning or volume, but there will be another mode whereby you can make adjustments to a given zone independently of all others, or indeed adjust a selection of several. In this kit, we have set up the different hi-hat zones to pan to different parts of the image, to add life to playback. We have also reduced the volume of the snare drum in the quietest zone, since otherwise the notes might tend to play back at the same volume regardless of velocity. Although interesting timbrally, this will always give a rather leaden performance dynamically. You might also be able to choose the amount that velocity maps to volume for each zone; and there could be additional parameters that adjust other things, such as filter settings.

MORE SAMPLERS AND SAMPLING

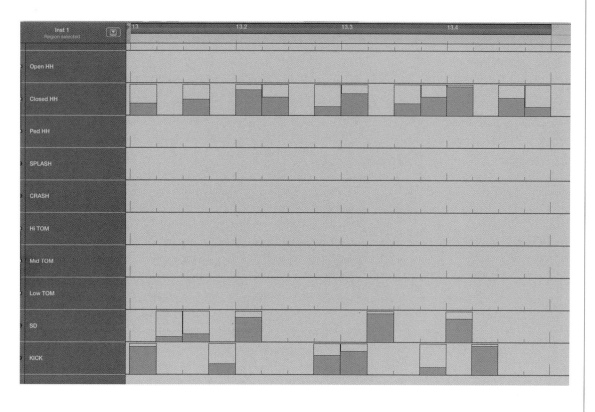

A simple-looking pattern that masks its sample-driven sonic complexity.

You can see the graphic simplicity of a pattern that only uses three pitches despite there being numerous sounds playing back. We have inputted notes to establish the basic feel that we want, and then adjusted the velocities to trigger specific zones. In practice, this often means revisiting the zone parameters and adjusting them to ensure controlled and intuitive playback. Although the snare on beat 3e has the highest velocity, the relative volumes of the snare zones were arranged to make it quieter than the sound on the backbeat.

PATTERN 11_01: A simple one-bar pattern that could work in a hip-hop track, and demonstrates a range of timbres from only three MIDI notes. The first two bars are just the hi-hats, and the next two with the full kit, at 104bpm.

Pattern 11_01

Many samplers also have a facility known as 'groups'. Groups can have one or a number of zones assigned to them and certain operations can be applied to a group, in other words simultaneously to a set of zones. Such operations include assignment to a particular output in a multichannel instrument, application of an effect internal to the sampler, response to an external control signal

such as a CC#, or becoming subject to an internal (synthesizer-type) modulation as we explored in Chapter Eight. Consult the manual for your sampler to find out how to assign zones to groups and also what can then be done.

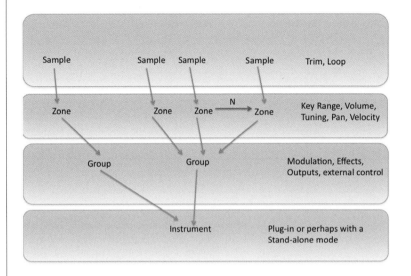

Relationship between samples, zones and groups.

This diagram shows the relationship between samples, zones and groups. Each zone contains only a single sample. On the left is a group containing a single zone, but on the right, up to N zones can be assigned to a single group.

In Pattern 11_01, there is a kick-drum zone that is triggered by a particular velocity, which happens only on beat 4e. We have firstly created a group to hold this zone and then applied an ADSR envelope to the group. This particular sound has an analogue drum machine type of sustain to it that did not come through when it was simply dropped into its zone, since the MIDI note that triggers it only lasts for a 16th-note (semiquaver) by default. On the ADSR, increasing the sustain and the release beyond their default values can allow the natural sustain of the sample to be heard. Working in this way allows the envelope of an individual drum to be controlled independently of note length or the other drums. Alternatively, samplers typically have a one-shot mode that could be used. This mode triggers a sample and plays it all the way through to its end.

An EQ insert effect was also placed on this group (which acts as an insert effect only on this sound) in order to boost some low frequencies; the other kick drum sounds were unaffected by this. To add further life to this pattern, a sine-wave LFO has been set up to modulate the centre frequency

MORE SAMPLERS AND SAMPLING

THE
DRUM
PROGRAMMING
HANDBOOK

287

of the EQ, which causes a wah-wah effect. The speed of the LFO is unrelated to the tempo, and so effectively the LFO runs out of phase with the bars making the sound slightly different every time. In the audio example it is set to 1.1Hz, which is an arbitrary number that gave a pleasing effect.

PATTERN 11_02: Pattern 11_01 with a LFO on the beat 4e kick-drum EQ. Repeated six times. Focus your listening just on this note: it is subtly different each bar.

Pattern 11_02

Another group was defined that included all five hi-hat sounds, and this group allows processes to be applied to all of its constituent zones. A low pass filter was inserted on this group, and with the resonance set to a modest amount, another LFO was assigned to modulate its cut-off frequency. This LFO had a triangle shape and a frequency of 0.25Hz. Again, the fact that this frequency is unrelated to the tempo creates a filter sweep that does not appear to repeat exactly for a long time, thus creating a subtly moving texture. The fact that these hi-hat sounds only contain a narrow range of high frequencies means that the filter tends to let the sounds through or block them, as opposed to giving an obvious sweep sound through a broader range of frequencies. You can still hear a characteristic sweep at the beginning and end of the phrases. Also, a distortion effect was inserted on the group that holds the snare drum that plays on the backbeat, a technique that gives a more aggressive sound and is typical of this style.

PATTERN 11_03: Pattern 06_02 with a LFO on the cut-off frequency of a filter on the hi-hat group. Repeated eight times. The hi-hat appears to slide in and out at different points in each bar purely through its varying frequency content.

Pattern 11_03

A mechanism commonly employed in many commercial sampler instruments is called 'round robin'. What this means is that rather than re-trigger the same sample each time a note is played, a different sample from a designated set is triggered. An acoustic instrument will always sounded slightly different every time it is played. Imagine if you had recorded an acoustic snare drum being hit twice and made two different samples from it. If you then programmed a roll using each of these samples alternately, it might sound as if a drummer were playing RLRLRL... with a subtle difference between the strokes of each hand, thus adding realism and preventing an unrealistic machine-gun effect. Although it would be quite possible to achieve this using two different MIDI notes, it is much more convenient if the two snare drums are implemented in a round robin arrangement so that when a roll is programmed on a single note, they alternate automatically. There is also a system known as key-switching that allows a silent MIDI note to be pressed that will select a particular sound or set of sounds from the round robin pool of audio.

Instead of using round robin to enhance authenticity, here we will apply it to create an exotic synthetic effect. The idea is to use a single MIDI note to create complex flurries of different sounds.

> **TIP**
> Modulating a parameter by a very small amount with an LFO running at a low frequency can produce excellent effects. It is worth trying to set the LFO in so subtle a way that you hardly notice it unless you are listening for it. Doing so can just add a professional sound and keep things interesting. Of course, there will be many times when it is better to run an LFO in sync with tempo instead.

We have selected a number (in this case seven, for no particular reason) of tom tom hits from the same drum kits as above, trimmed them, and imported them into the sampler, each on a new zone on single MIDI notes. The round robin system generally works at a group level, so we now assign each of our new zones to its own new group. We have tuned each tom tom up a bit (although by different pleasing amounts) to make a thinner, more percussive sound, and locked the tuning so that it does not change if we move the placement of the zone. The reason for the latter is that we then dragged all the zones to a specific single MIDI note of our choice; the GM-map mid tom tom is appropriate, but not essential.

If we were to press that key now, we would hear every tom tom sounding simultaneously. Instead, we have activated round robin mode in the group parameters and assigned a successive round robin number to each group. Read the manual for your sampler if you do not know how to do that. Each time we press the MIDI key now, we hear a different single tom tom. We can now program in a string of notes on this MIDI pitch, paying attention to the general phrasing and velocities, and a complex sequence will result. This sequence will repeat every seven notes, and that means if the number of hits in our sequence is not a multiple of seven, then once again the effect will be different in every bar. There are 13 notes per bar in the audio example. We have avoided placing notes simultaneously with the principal kick drums to avoid a cluttered sound.

PATTERN 11_04: The tom tom sequence over eight bars with a click. The effect is of something that is almost the same yet is subtly moving and changing. To make things even more interesting for this percussion sequence we can apply a couple of modulators. We have set up one sine-wave LFO that is routed to pan position. It runs at a speed of about 0.5Hz, which once again moves out of phase with the natural progression of the bars, but keeps the percussion dancing between the speakers. We also have yet another sine-wave LFO routed to pitch of all these tom-toms. It can sweep the pitch by up to an octave, and runs at a speed of 1Hz. This gives yet another variable that changes against the bar lines. Because such a dynamic sound could easily take over and make things messy, the tom tom sequence has been mixed quite low to act just as background percussion.

With so many parameters changing at different speeds it would be easy for things to get out of control, but subtlety is the key. Taking this approach allows us to use the repetitive beat that many genres require, yet add dynamic interest and give quality to our programming beyond just firing a static sample loop.

MORE SAMPLERS AND SAMPLING

THE
DRUM
PROGRAMMING
HANDBOOK

289

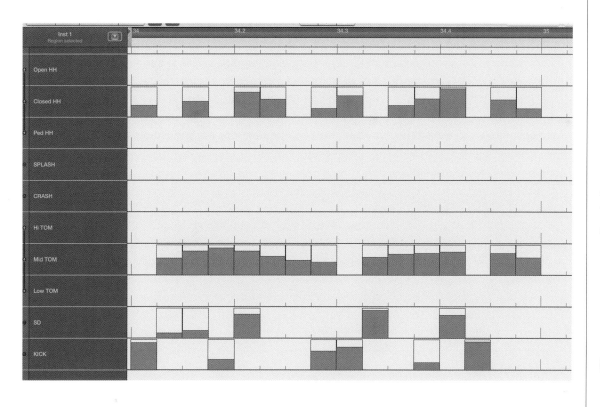

*Pattern 11_04: The beat
with a one-note tom tom
part added.*

PATTERN 11_05: Pattern 11_02 with additional modulation and the tom tom part. The tom toms are quite hard to discern, but also help to keep the pattern feeling alive, even though on a casual listen it feels very repetitive.

Exercise One: Create a basic multi-sample instrument with a number of contrasting sounds on a small number of MIDI notes. Experiment with the velocity responses by tapping the relevant key on your piano keyboard. Once you have something that is playable, program a beat with the sounds and refine the velocity zones if necessary.

Exercise Two: Use the zone parameters to further edit the kit, and also try out overlapping velocity layers; audition the sound as you adjust things.

Exercise Three: Assign your zones to a number of groups and apply various manipulations to these groups, including modulations and effects. Be sure to explore working with both a single-zone group and a multi-zone group.

■ **CHECK OUT**
On the Internet, look up movie composer Tom Holkenborg (also known as Junkie XL) who is known for his extensive custom-sample instruments.

290

THE
DRUM
PROGRAMMING
HANDBOOK

MORE SAMPLERS AND SAMPLING

CREATING A SAMPLED DRUM KIT FROM ORIGINAL SOUNDS

We will now build a sampled drum kit from our own recordings. This is a fun and creative way to develop a unique palette of sounds. After we have recorded a few noises from the kitchen, we will process them using the modulation techniques typically available in a sampler, to enhance them further. This is rather like the subtractive synthesis of Chapter Eight, but simply replaces the basic waveforms with samples. Synthesis in this context is sometimes referred to as 'sample-based synthesis'. The noises that we might choose and employ in this process are often called 'found sounds'.

ABOUT RECORDING

Recording is a highly specialised topic and as such is beyond the scope of this book, but there are many excellent resources that deal with this, both in books and online. We will offer some basic pointers that are relevant to capturing sounds in order to build a sampled drum kit.

Although phones, tablets, and computers have inbuilt microphones, they will not be capable of recording good quality audio. It is better to use an external microphone. The differences between these devices are vast, as are their prices. Depending on how much recording you do, you might wish to invest more or less in your microphone. There are a number of types: dynamic microphones tend to be more robust although slightly less sensitive when capturing quiet and high-frequency sounds; capacitor microphones are more sensitive but slightly more susceptible to damage when handled roughly. As with most things, the more you pay the better they will be, up to a point; do some research online in order to inform your decision. You should not need to pay a vast sum of money for professional-type equipment in order to capture some drum sounds with reasonable quality.

Microphones are analogue devices and typically use a cable known as an XLR. In order for your computer to record this signal, you will need to use an audio interface, into which you can plug your XLR cable. The interface will convert the analogue signal into a digital one that can be sent to your computer via USB or Thunderbolt. If you use a capacitor microphone, then it will need to be supplied with phantom power, and this is something that most interfaces can provide with the press of a button. Always mute your speakers before you press it though, since there could be a loud pop. It is also possible to get microphones with an inbuilt interface; these feature a USB cable that can plug directly into your computer. This is a convenience, but does not affect audio quality.

Ensure that your DAW is set to record at 24-bit resolution. This gives noticeably better audio quality, especially with subsequent manipulations in the sampler. Take care when setting

MORE SAMPLERS AND SAMPLING

THE
DRUM
PROGRAMMING
HANDBOOK

291

levels – the quality of your final result is massively dependent on this. Your source sounds can have a potentially large dynamic range. You need to set the input gain on your interface to capture the loudest possible sound without overloading either it or your DAW, so test things by playing the loudest possible sound and check the meters on both.

Having said this, if you are trying to record very quiet sounds, then you might need to increase the gain on the interface, but be careful because this will also increase the noise floor. It is worth reading more on the subject of gain structure. Do not be tempted to set a gain that pushes your DAW meters within 10 dB of their maximum just because that looks a nice amount on the GUI. 24-bit recording has a dynamic range of around 144 dB. Everything will sound fine if the signal peaks at around –20 dBFS (dB Full Scale: this is 20 below the absolute maximum shown on the meter. Things will distort horribly if this is exceeded).

Microphones can either be directional and principally respond to sound coming from a specific angle relative to themselves, or omnidirectional where they capture sound from all angles in a space. For our purposes, directional will generally be better since the sound of a room might not be desirable in the final drum kit that we build. If you place a directional microphone very close to a sound source there will be a natural exaggeration of low frequencies, which can be usefully exploited if that is what you are after. A microphone stand can be very useful since handling a microphone whilst recording percussives is awkward and can generate additional noise. You need to wear headphones whilst recording, otherwise the sound from your speakers will also be captured by the microphone and you will get feedback.

The sound sources chosen for the kitchen drum kit.

SAMPLING

Now to get on with the fun. Go to your kitchen and tap, rattle, scrape, and roll everything that you can think of; remember that each of these can usually be done in a number of different ways. You are looking for interesting sounds that might represent parts of a drum kit, with a little encouragement. Try to get a balanced palette of metal to non-metal sounds, and do not stick to utensils: remember food too! You need to make a choice of whether to record in your kitchen or transport your chosen sources to your usual music-making environment. Consider background noise as well as carrying things.

Record-enable a single mono audio track in your DAW, name it according to your first sound source, eg, spoons, and record whatever you are doing with that source. Listen to the

292

THE
DRUM
PROGRAMMING
HANDBOOK

MORE SAMPLERS AND SAMPLING

recording and check for quality and levels. Delete and repeat if necessary. When satisfied, change the name of your track to the next source, eg, rice, and record further along the time line and check it. Renaming in this way will carry forward to the audio files that you record and make subsequent file management easier. You will have your own sound sources, but the raw recordings here are as follows:

- Tapping the side of a plastic bottle, with the microphone by the open neck. TWO HITS.
- Dropping four metal dessertspoons into the palm of the hand. TWO HITS.
- Tapping the handle of one dessertspoon against another, whilst suspending it from its end. ONE HIT.
- Running a chef's knife across a sharpening steel. ONE HIT.
- Repeatedly sharpening the knife. ONE EXCERPT.
- Hitting the steel with the knife. ONE HIT.
- Hitting the knife with the steel whilst holding the knife from its tip. TWO HITS.
- Sharply turning a plastic packet of wheat biscuit breakfast cereal. TWO HITS.
- Tapping the base of a plastic measuring jug with a drumstick. THREE HITS.
- Rattling the stick around the interior of the plastic measuring jug. ONE EXCERPT.
- Running a drumstick over a wire roasting tray from an oven. TWO HITS.
- Suspending the roasting tray and tapping the edge with a metal dessert spoon. ONE HIT.
- Running the bowl of a metal dessert spoon over the wire roasting tray. ONE HIT.
- Shaking a bag of couscous. ONE EXCERPT.
- Tilting a metal frying pan with dried chickpeas on the base. TWO EXCERPTS.

PATTERN 11_06: The raw audio recordings from the kitchen.

BUILDING THE KIT

You now need to do some editing. You will likely have many recordings, several of which might be quite similar. You need to decide on the takes that will make it through to your final kit. Edit the regions to leave only what you wish to finally use, but be mindful that round robin or multiple velocity layers might require more than one take of a given sound. In this regard, it is useful to be planning ahead at this stage. You need to decide on whether to accurately trim the regions to represent samples now or once they are in your sampler. Even small differences in workflow could save you a lot of time here, since you will likely be preparing a considerable number of samples. With a multichannel version of your sampler on a new instrument track, import all the samples onto individual zones in a new instrument in your

CHAPTER 11

MORE SAMPLERS AND SAMPLING

THE
DRUM
PROGRAMMING
HANDBOOK

293

sampler, and check that the trimmed samples play back accurately and correctly. Remember to save your instrument at this point, and also regularly through its subsequent build. Use incremental filenames, eg, v1, v2, v3, etc.

Now, put the sampler into an 'edit all' mode whereby any changes affect everything, and set the zones to retain their pitch if placed on a different key, and start moving them around to form the layout of playable drum kit. It is useful to conform to the GM map here, at least to some degree – this will give transferability and intuitiveness to your kit. If you have multiple instances of the same sound, leave them at the high end of the keyboard for the moment. It could be useful to assign every zone to its own group at this stage, since you can always create a few groups of multiple zones later. If your sampler does not automatically assign velocity response to groups, then probably best to do that now whilst in a global mode. Then change the mode to allow individual and specific editing of groups and zones.

You will now need to apply a range of manipulations, including further grouping, tuning, panning, trimming (adjusting the volume), assigning individual outputs, applying modulation, and inserting effects on individual groups if your sampler allows this. To illustrate all this, we will work through the manipulations in our demonstration scenario. Since your sounds will be quite different, you should not attempt to follow the instructions verbatim, but rather trying to absorb the greater approach and then try out your own interpretations of the specific processes.

KICK DRUM

Hopefully, you have a sound that was recorded with the kick in mind; ours is the bottle. This has a naturally deep sound and is quite resonant. The zone has been placed on key C1. In order to accentuate the bottom end, the sound has been de-tuned by 18 half-steps (semitones), and it is panned to the centre. The trade-off here was that detuning lost its resonance and it became rather flappy, but inserting a quite aggressive compressor on the group restored this, and a slow attack time enhanced the transient. EQ boosts at about 70Hz and 4kHz gave some boom and click to the sound. It now resembles a Roland 808 kick drum sound. There are numerous other ways that this bottle could have been processed simply to different effect.

SNARE DRUM

Our starting sounds here are the cereal biscuits. Twisting the packet gave a burst of noise from the plastic wrapping with quite convincing attack and noise components. We have used two different twists in order to give the snare some variation between beats 2 and 4, once sequenced. We have layered these (by arranging the zones) with the pop sound created by hitting the plastic jug with the drumstick and also the suspended knife being struck with the sharpening steel. The pop sound contributes something of a click to the snare (only on notes with a velocity greater than 50), and the knife some shell resonance.

Pattern 11_07

PATTERN 11_07: The four raw components of the snare drum in succession: wheat biscuit one, wheat biscuit two, jug pop, and knife hit.

In order to accentuate the difference between the two wheat sounds, we have transposed one by two half-steps. The pop did not give a convincing click on its own, but after transposing up by 33 half-steps, it did so. In order to make the resonance appear to swell and then die away, a volume envelope was applied to the knife hit with an attack of about 50ms and a decay of around 100ms.

Pattern 11_08

PATTERN 11_08: The four components of the snare drum, playing in succession with transpositions and a volume envelope on the knife click.

The volume envelope applied to the knife hit.

TIP
Samplers always feature a function called 'loop'. This defines the start and end points of a loop within the waveform such that when the triggering key is held down, the note continues to play whilst cycling around the looped portion of the waveform. This feature is generally used to create artificial sustain, for instance with string sounds. It can also be used for special effects with short percussion sounds.

Upon listening to the four sounds layered together it felt like there was not enough rattle coming from the snare. In order to generate a synthetic rattle, setting a loop that was longer than the duration of the actual click and triggering the click several times in quick succession from a single MIDI note gave a degree of this effect. We have also inserted a distortion effect on the wheat sounds in order to make them a little more aggressive and set up a round robin to alternate between the two hits.

MORE SAMPLERS AND SAMPLING

THE
DRUM
PROGRAMMING
HANDBOOK

295

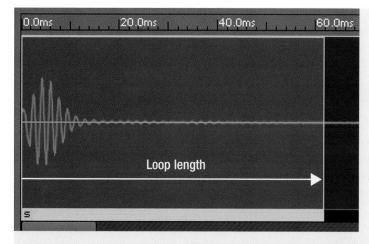

The relatively short duration of the pot hit with a longer loop. It is the length of the loop that determines how rapidly the pot repeats.

PATTERN 11_09: The four components of the snare drum in succession now with the distortion effect on the snare. It also has the looped click – although it sounds quite comical on its own.

Pattern 11_09

PATTERN 11_10: The four components layered together, played in succession. The round-robin alternation is quite apparent, although the click and the resonance are subtle. They really do help with the overall shape of this snare drum though.

Pattern 11_10

HI-HAT

In order to create a closed hi-hat sound on F♯1, we have used two overlapping velocity layers. The lower one uses the muted metallic tone of the steel being struck by the knife, and the upper one uses the spoons in the palm. Whereas the steel sounded nice when tuned down by a half-step, the spoons needed to be pitched up by 18 half-steps. The velocity zones have been allowed to overlap between values of about 70 and 90. In this area, both sounds can be heard at once. Whilst not being terribly realistic, this combination produces an interesting and playable kit piece.

PATTERN 11_11: A number of closed hi-hat notes of increasing velocity. You can hear how the sound changes between the zones.

Pattern 11_11

The pedal hi-hat sound on G♯1 only has a single velocity zone, and also uses the spoons-in-the-palm sound source. This time however, the sound has been tuned up by 14 half-steps.

CHAPTER 11

296

THE
DRUM
PROGRAMMING
HANDBOOK

MORE SAMPLERS AND SAMPLING

Pattern 11_12

Pattern 11_13

Pattern 11_14

Pattern 11_15

TIP

Tuning tom toms in intervals of a fourth helps when playing in different keys. Sometimes it can also be effective to tune the tom toms (and indeed the kick) to be in in the key of a specific song to give a melodic quality.

PATTERN 11_12: A number of pedal hi-hat notes of increasing velocity.

To make an open hi-hat sound on A♯1 we have used the chickpeas in the frying pan. These have been pitched up by four half-steps. In order to control the sustain, an ADSR envelope has been added to modulate the volume of this sound. This approach allows the duration of the MIDI note to control the sustain. In some samplers, it is possible to assign groups to interrupt each other so that a closed or pedal hi-hat would cut short an open one. In such a case, the envelope would not be necessary and the open sound should play for its duration, set as a one-shot unless cut short. All of the hi-hat zones from all three keys were then selected simultaneously and panning applied to move them to the same place in the right of the stereo image.

The volume envelope applied to the chickpeas in the pan.

PATTERN 11_13: A number of open hi-hat notes of the same velocity, but increasing duration.

TOM TOMS

The tom toms were created using a bottle hit, just like the kick. The low tom tom was up by eight half-steps, the middle tom tom up by a further five, and the high tom tom up by a further five again. In order to give the tom toms a more interesting sound, an ADSR envelope was set to modulate pitch with an attack of around 20ms and a release of around 150ms; the bend range was half-steps. The three tom toms were panned left, centre, and right.

PATTERN 11_14: The three tom toms played in sequence with only tuning and panning applied.

The pitch-bend envelope applied to the toms.

PATTERN 11_15: Pattern 11_14 with pitch modulation.

MORE SAMPLERS AND SAMPLING

THE
DRUM
PROGRAMMING
HANDBOOK

297

CYMBALS AND PERCUSSION

As well as the previous core elements of the kit, we have added a number of other one-shots to act as percussion instruments and cymbal-type textures.

We created a crash-like sound by scraping the roasting rack with a drumstick. We recorded two different hits. They each had a slightly different sound, and we had earlier assigned each to its own zone. In order to accentuate the difference between the two we have detuned them by one half-step; this also changes the speed of the scrape, which adds to the density when they are played both at once. These zones were panned hard left and right and placed on the same key, C#2. The zones were then assigned to a single group so that subsequent processing could be applied to both simultaneously. The group's volume is controlled by an ADSR envelope, which allows more control of the release of the sound than just triggering it by a one-shot. The release is set to about five seconds.

PATTERN 11_16: The two rack scrapes, first solo and panned to each side and then both playing together.

 Pattern 11_16

The next stage was to insert a high pass filter on this group and tune the cut-off frequency to around 1kHz; this removed the 'boom' that the original sound had. A compressor was then inserted after the filter and adjusted to reduce most of the loud initial stick hit, and therefore to increase the relative volume of the tail of the sound. The attack was set to around 100ms in order to preserve the sense of a transient.

PATTERN 11_17: Pattern 11_16, now filtered and compressed.

 Pattern 11_17

CHAPTER 11

298

THE
DRUM
PROGRAMMING
HANDBOOK

MORE SAMPLERS AND SAMPLING

Lastly, in order to make the sound rather more exotic, we have modulated the pitch of the group with a second ADSR envelope. The modulation range is set to 12 half-steps, and an attack of about 20ms towards a steady sustain at maximum modulation gives a rapid pitch rise. Setting the release to around 70ms (this is just a pleasing number obtained by experimentation) gives an interesting option. If the triggering note is depressed for the duration of the sound, only the attack sweep will be heard and the remainder of the sound will play raised by an octave. If however, the note is released before the sound has finished, the release phase of this envelope will drop the pitch down even though it is continuing to sound as determined by the volume envelope.

The volume envelope with the longer release at the top, and the pitch envelope with the shorter release below it.

PATTERN 11_18: Three instances of the crash sound. The first is a very short MIDI note, the second is a little longer and the third is with the note held down for the duration of the sound.

On D2 is the sound of the single sweep of the knife being sharpened. This has been detuned by six half-steps and set to play in reverse which gives a crescendo feeling. An LFO has been set to modulate the pan position rapidly; a triangle wave at about 4Hz. This is free running – not synchronised to the onset of the note – which means that each time the sound is played it pans slightly differently.

PATTERN 11_19: Four instances of the reverse sound: each has a subtly different dynamic pan.

For a ride-bell-type sound on F2 we have used the knife striking the steel. This sound has been assigned to three different zones on the same key, one at natural pitch, one de-tuned by 16 cents, and another tuned up by 35 cents. These zones each cover a different velocity range, but overlap by design with a range of velocities between around 80 and 100 where all three are triggered simultaneously. The effect of hearing two or more de-tuned sounds is a

MORE SAMPLERS AND SAMPLING

THE
DRUM
PROGRAMMING
HANDBOOK

299

thickening of the timbre, which provides an interesting variation of tone as notes of different velocities sound.

PATTERN 11_20: A number of hits of ride-bell-type sound with increasing velocity. Although the volume does not increase evenly, different velocities allow playback of a range of subtly varying textures.

 Pattern 11_20

The three taps on the base of the plastic jug were used in three non-overlapping velocity zones on F#2. Each tap naturally had a slightly different tone and pitch, and performing with a mixture of the three gives an authentic acoustic feel, reminiscent of the variations that a human would create whilst playing. The sounds were compressed (via setting up a common group) with an attack time of about 25ms in order to enhance their transients, and EQ boosts at around 60Hz and 4kHz improved their tone. All three zones were panned left, but by slightly different amounts to offer even further liveliness to their ultimate performance.

PATTERN 11_21: A sequence of the jug hits with increasing velocity.

 Pattern 11_21

On G#2 is a percussive noise derived from the sound of hitting the knife with the steel. The sound is then passed through a low pass filter with about 50 percent resonance and a cut-off frequency of around 440Hz. The result of this is quite a muffled sound, but these values were chosen so that when the cut-off is modulated upwards it has some space to sweep through an interesting range of frequencies that are also accentuated by the resonance.

PATTERN 11_22: The knife being hit with the steel passing through a low pass filter: no modulation. We seem to have made a bell.

 Pattern 11_22

We have now set up an ADSR envelope to modulate the cut-off. This has a fast attack and decay – around 50ms, along the lines of the filtration that we used on the kick drum in Chapter Eight. We have also used even further modulation here – modulating a modulator! The decay of the filter envelope is modulated by velocity, which gives a slower sweep downwards on louder notes. Further, in order to produce a shorter sound, the volume has been modulated with another envelope. This was tweaked relative to that of the filter until a pleasing sound was achieved.

PATTERN 11_23: The sound of Pattern 11.22 with increasing velocities, passing through the filter and envelopes.

 Pattern 11_23

CHAPTER 11

300

THE
DRUM
PROGRAMMING
HANDBOOK

MORE SAMPLERS AND SAMPLING

The sound of the roasting rack being struck once was assigned to A#2. A band pass filter was applied, with its cut-off controlled by an envelope that swept downwards, synchronously with each hit; this had the effect of thinning the sound and adding a timbral movement. The resonance of the filter was influenced by a slow LFO, sweeping at about 0.1Hz, which gave further variations in the sound by contributing a metallic whistling quality. Sometimes the varying resonance setting gave an overly aggressive attack to the notes, so another envelope was added to modulate volume with a 7ms attack segment to soften this. The pan position was modulated by a random LFO running at about 6Hz.

 Pattern 11_24

PATTERN 11_24: Two hits of the processed roasting rack hit.

For special effects beyond any GM mapping, a wind-chime-like effect was created with the spoon bowl scraping the roasting rack. A MIDI note was placed in a region and the DAW run at a desired tempo. The zone was tuned until, purely time-wise, the sound made a nice fit landing on the subsequent beat. An ADSR envelope was assigned to modulate the pan, synchronously, so that every hit moved between the speakers.

 Pattern 11_25

PATTERN 11_25: Two hits of the scraped roasting rack.

Another sound with its own rhythmic content was generated from the drumstick rattling inside the plastic jug. This was tuned up by 24 half-steps, which made the pattern sound very rapid. The sample was then looped so that it would continue to sound for as long as the note was held. A high pass filter was then placed in the group, and with a small amount of resonance, the cut-off frequency was assigned to a MIDI control change #1 – the modulation wheel, for convenience. This enables us to 'play' filter changes over pre-sequenced notes, or of course offers various options for real-time recording.

PATTERN 11_26: A single note of the rattling jug. You can hear the loop if you listen to the changes in timbre, although the MIDI control change that sweeps the filter rather masks this.

MORE SAMPLERS AND SAMPLING

THE
DRUM
PROGRAMMING
HANDBOOK

301

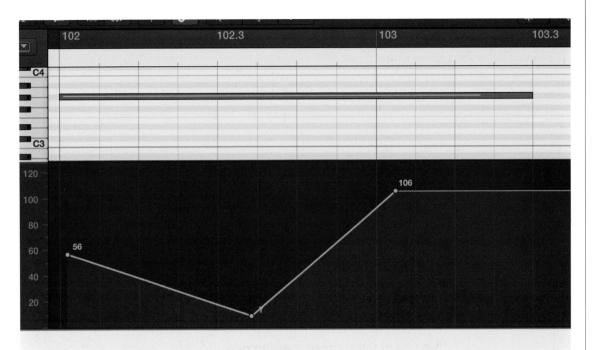

The rattling jug trigger-note, also showing the control change #1 data that sweeps the filter.

Pattern 11_26

Shaking the packet of couscous provided quite an authentic shaker sound. All that it really needed was to be tuned in order to play in time with our desired tempo. Its success is rather dependent on the performance, and either you need to shake accurately as you record, or perhaps quantise and bounce the audio before importing into the sampler. It is not a good idea to try to loop such sounds in order to achieve sustain from a single MIDI note. It is almost impossible to get the loop accurate enough to stay in time for long. Re-trigger a note that plays a shorter and rhythmically accurate section.

PATTERN 11_27: Four notes playing the shaken couscous.

Pattern 11_27

The last rhythmic sample in this kit is the knife being sharpened. An excerpt of a few strokes was selected and again the sample was simply tuned to play at the desired tempo.

PATTERN 11_28: Four notes playing the knife being sharpened. The timing is inexact, but it had quite a pleasing lilt.

Pattern 11_28

302

THE
DRUM
PROGRAMMING
HANDBOOK

MORE SAMPLERS AND SAMPLING

That completes the construction of our drum kit. What you need to do now is program a sequence that uses every single sound with typical velocities, and then tweak the relevant volumes of your groups and zones in order to balance the overall levels. It is also highly likely that as you listen to the sequence, you will revisit various parameters and change them in order to make the whole thing more coherent and ensure that the sounds complement each other.

PATTERN 11_29: A 13-bar pattern that demonstrates all of the sounds in this drum kit, twice through at 90bpm. There is a little reverb and delay on some of the kit.

Pattern 11_29

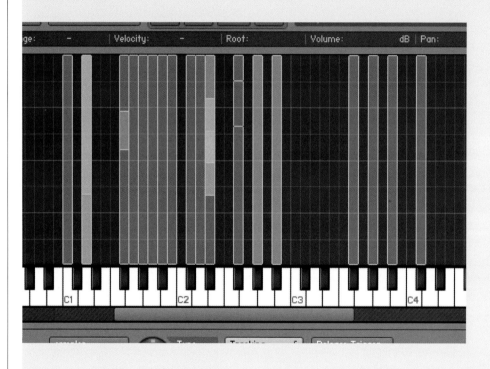

The final key map of all the zones. You can see the change in tint where zones overlap.

MORE SAMPLERS AND SAMPLING

THE
DRUM
PROGRAMMING
HANDBOOK

303

Exercise One: Take specific techniques that were applied to the various groups and zones in the workshop and apply them to different components of the kit.
Exercise Two: Try to build a functioning drum kit from a minimum number of sound sources, focusing on stretching your understanding of modulation and sample manipulation.
Exercise Three: Set yourself a fun discipline to work with, for instance using only vegetables or noises from a car. Build a kit from this, or even both merged together.

Things to experiment with

- Study ready-built multi-sample instruments that you might already own (they might for instance have shipped with your DAW) and translate techniques that you find into your own instruments.
- Try some radical round-robin techniques to add dramatic variations to relatively minimal MIDI programming.
- Apply the advanced modulation techniques presented here to your work from the earlier sampler chapter.
- Copy and paste zones and groups from a number of existing instruments into your own hybrid super-instrument.
- Create an instrument of performed rhythmic loops using found sounds.
- Research the Internet for tutorials on sample manipulation and apply these to your own home built instruments.

CONCLUSION

We have now developed a much more intimate and advanced understanding of the sampler, including the recording of bespoke sounds in order to build custom instruments. We have manipulated the sounds in numerous ways, although we have not dwelt on using subtractive synthesis techniques in order to maintain the integrity of the original recordings in a novel fashion. The possibilities of working like this are endless, and the creative potential is huge. Whilst it can be great fun to create such instruments, when time is against you, there are many that someone else has built – available to buy. In the next chapter, we will mix many of the techniques from this book together and program a number of case studies in different genres.

■ **CHECK OUT**
The album *Foley Room* by Amon Tobin. The concept of the album was to construct it from found sounds. It also ships with a DVD that covers the making of the album. 'Foley' is the cinematic term for the performance and recording of the everyday sounds that you hear as the actors move about in movies.

Check that you can:
- Understand and control the architecture of your sampler: zones, groups, modulation, round robin, etc.
- Record individual sounds to reasonable quality, and import them into your sampler.
- Manipulate the sounds in your sampled instrument using bespoke modulation features available to you.

PROGRAMMING IN STYLES

Metal

Reggae

Drum & Bass

Glitch

CHAPTER 12

PROGRAMMING IN STYLES

We are now going to combine and extend many of the techniques from this book into a number of case studies in genres of music that have not yet been covered. The genres we will consider here are metal, reggae, drum & bass, and glitch. It really does not matter whether you like any of these, since they will simply serve to demonstrate techniques. If you like a given genre, then you should enjoy working within it; but even if you do not, ask yourself what you can learn from it and apply in your own world. The possibilities are endless. But this final chapter should not be the end of your study of drum programming; instead it should broaden your perspective so that you can really develop your own music in the future.

METAL

Despite live appearances that suggest the contrary, many contemporary metal albums have drums that are programmed rather than actually played, or at least, recorded with triggers that convert the acoustic drum hits into MIDI, which will often then be edited. You do see some musicians credited with programming, for instance Misha Mansoor, guitarist with Periphery. There are many subgenres of metal that imply different inflections of beat, and to identify and classify them all is beyond the scope of this book; but if you want to sound like American metal legend Gene Hoglan, this will get you started.

A couple of stylistic features are very common, and we will investigate these here. The first is the use of double kick drum patterns. An acoustic drum kit might have only a single kick drum, but a double pedal that allows both feet to play this drum. Use of this can provide rapid-fire kick drum phrases, but every hit will have the same timbre. Alternatively, a drum kit might have two actual kick drums, quite possibly of different sizes, and these will typically have different sounds. In this case, fast phrases will typically have two alternating tones.

Another common characteristic is contrasting sections of a song that appear to be fast and slow. This is often a single tempo, sometimes in the order of 250bpm or more; but the backbeat may only be on beat 3, beats 2 and 4, all the &s, or even on every 16th-note (semiquaver). Each of these will give a very different impression of tempo and, regardless of the backbeat feeling, the kick drum might play rapid flurries or ostinato 16th-notes.

306
THE
DRUM
PROGRAMMING
HANDBOOK

PROGRAMMING IN STYLES

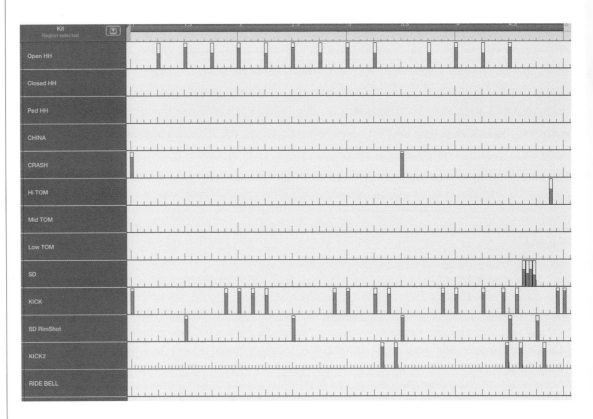

Pattern 12_01: The first four bars with the half-time feel.

Pattern 12_01

PATTERN 12_01: A 20-bar metal pattern at 175bpm, with sounds from FXpansion BFD3. We have programmed a metal-style sequence at 175bpm to illustrate some of these stylistic features and how they might weave together. The first eight bars have a backbeat on beat 3 (sometimes called a half-time feel) and use a quarter-note (crotchet) hi-hat, with a natural accent on the downbeats. Whereas in most styles it is relatively unusual to hear more than two rapid kick drums in succession, in metal it is common to hear longer groups. When playing faster, these groups will typically be spread between the feet. Such phrasing can be heard on beat 2 of bar three and into beat 3 of bar four, the latter of which runs into some 32nd-notes (demisemiquavers) that play a five-stroke roll on the snare drum. The pattern develops with further double kick flourishes, including a 16th-note example that doubles with two different cymbals. Then there's another phrase on beat 2 of bar eight that uses triplet 16th-notes (triplet semiquavers), followed by another 32nd-note phrase that has tom toms superimposed on the kick, from beat 3 into beat 4.

PROGRAMMING IN STYLES

THE
DRUM
PROGRAMMING
HANDBOOK

307

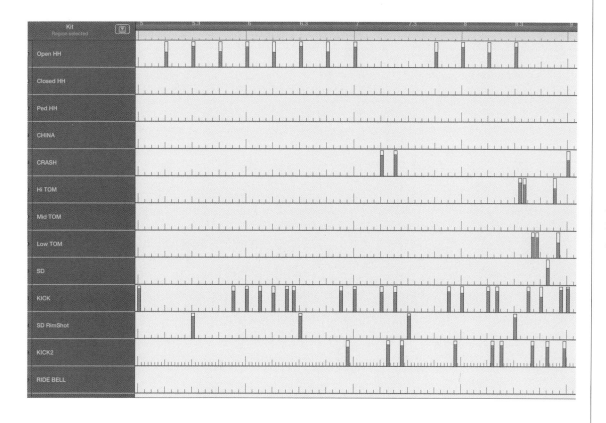

Pattern 12_01: The second four bars, continuing the half-time feel.

The next four bars change gear with a largely quarter-note kick pattern, and the snare on all the &s. Curiously (backbeat apart), this rhythmic construction is similar to house, disco, and ska – all of which are related rhythmically to the European polka folk-dance. What is very different, however, is that the hi-hat pattern is played between the crash and a China cymbal. There is a 32nd-note fill in bar 12, with a double-kick roll on the last quarter-note driving into the next section.

308

THE
DRUM
PROGRAMMING
HANDBOOK

PROGRAMMING IN STYLES

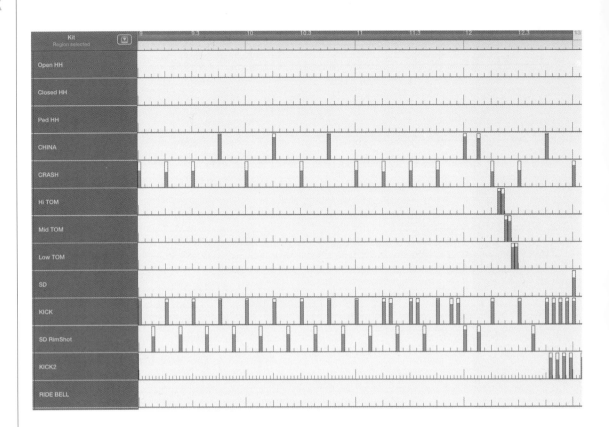

Pattern 12_01: Bars nine to 12 with the snare on the &s.

PROGRAMMING IN STYLES

The last eight bars are in the style known as blast beat, where there is an ostinato 16th-note double-kick part. Here it is tightly quantized, which is common in the genre; at the frenetic pace of metal, things need to be tight to stop the band sounding messy. There is a slower counter rhythm with the cymbals, in this case the crash and the china. The snare drum plays 16th-notes, which a proficient human would do with a single hand. Again we have a fill at the end of the first four bars of this section, after which the cymbal part becomes a ride bell, followed by another fill into the downbeat of the following section.

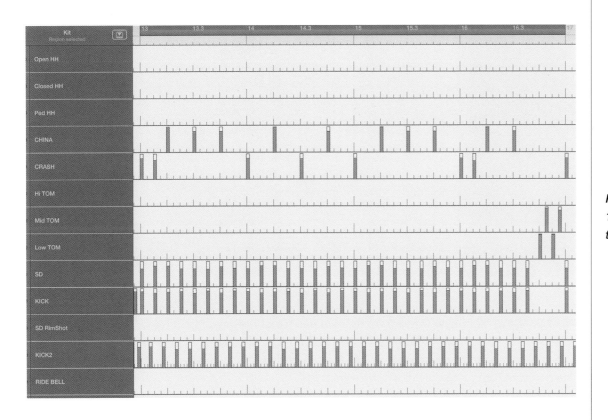

Pattern 12_01: Bars 13 to 17. The first four bars of the blast beat section.

310

THE
DRUM
PROGRAMMING
HANDBOOK

PROGRAMMING IN STYLES

■ **CHECK OUT**

Search the Internet for videos of George Kollias, who can often be found playing his blast beats slowly to demonstrate, before speeding them up to a quite staggering degree.

Pattern 12_01: Bars 17 to 21. The last four bars of the blast beat section.

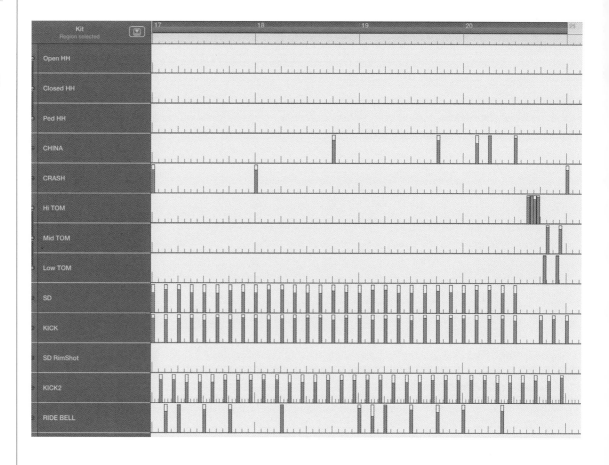

PATTERN 12_02: Using Pattern 12_01 as a palette of phrases, the pattern has now been edited to run for longer in order to fit with real guitars and bass. The fills have been adjusted so as not to repeat exactly, and there are small variations to the repeating sections of the grooves. The drum sounds are slightly more processed.

PATTERN 12_03: The drums from Pattern 12_02, soloed.

PATTERN 12_04: Just the guitars and bass from Pattern 12_02, in case you want to try to program your own sequence along with them.

PROGRAMMING IN STYLES

THE
DRUM
PROGRAMMING
HANDBOOK

311

REGGAE

Although reggae drumming has a rich heritage and many distinctive approaches, a band will sound closer to this genre if short chord stabs are played on the upbeats (a motif known as the skank) almost regardless of the drum part. Having said this, there are certain stylistic features of the drums that are well worth highlighting.

Perhaps the most distinctive reggae beat is known as the 'one drop'. This features a kick drum on beat 3 that functions as the backbeat, and there is often a cross-stick played simultaneously but no regular snare on beats 2 and 4. The hi-hat does often accentuate these beats, and it is these that align with the skank. This basic structure might be played with either a straight eighth-note (quaver) or a shuffled feel, and it is worth noting that despite the spacious feel of these grooves, the tempo might typically be at around 160bpm; but sometimes you will see the tempo being described as something like half of that, with a 16th-note feel instead.

The cross-stick might play syncopated patterns against the above, and the hi-hat can also vary along with this. The quarter-note triplet (crotchet triplet) is a common rhythmic building block and you can hear drummer Carlton Barrett delivering endless subtle variations of it on Bob Marley's 'Running Away'. Although the snare drum part is often based around the cross-stick, the full (ie, normally struck) snare might occasionally play surprise accents on beats 4, 4&, 4a (or the last note of the triplet if the groove is shuffled) or perhaps even on beat 1. Sometimes the crash will be played in unison with this.

Fills in pop and rock music tend to end on beat 1 with a unison crash and kick drum. In reggae, however, they might finish like this on beat 1, but it is also common for them to finish on beat 3. Fills can also end on beats 4, 4& or 4a, often with a snare or snare and crash in unison. It is also common for the drummer to play a fill before the main groove starts at the beginning of a song. These fills can often be surprisingly busy, and sometimes quite long.

We have programmed a one-drop-based sequence in a shuffle style at 160bpm, and included a few fills and a change of feel. It is not tightly quantised. It was originally, but the positions of every note have been randomised by a tiny amount to give a looser feel; this was done with a global DAW function. The sequence is quite long and is used as a vehicle to showcase a number of rhythmic variations. We will first highlight a number of these from within the greater sequence and offer short commentaries on each. The emphasis on beat 3 can feel rather strange when heard on its own (the ear can be drawn to perceiving it as being beat 1), but when we later add other instruments, the phrasing will be properly contextualised.

A common feature in reggae is rhythmic tension created by playing straight eighth-notes against a general shuffle feel. The opening snare fill in Pattern 12_05 does exactly that, with a crash on beat 4. You will notice the hi-hat accents on beats 2 and beat 4 of the groove. If you listen carefully to the hi-hat, you will hear that it is not simply repeated but is subtly changing using different articulations (not visible in the diagrams) and velocities.

■ **CHECK OUT**
The legendary Sly Dunbar, one half of the rhythm section Sly & Robbie, along with bassist Robbie Shakespeare. It is said that together they have played on 200,000 tracks. Whilst nice to believe, that number is probably a bit high; but the reality is still a lot of tunes.

Pattern 12_05: The fill that leads into the start of the groove, and one bar of the basic one drop beat with the kick and cross-stick on beat 3.

Pattern 12_05

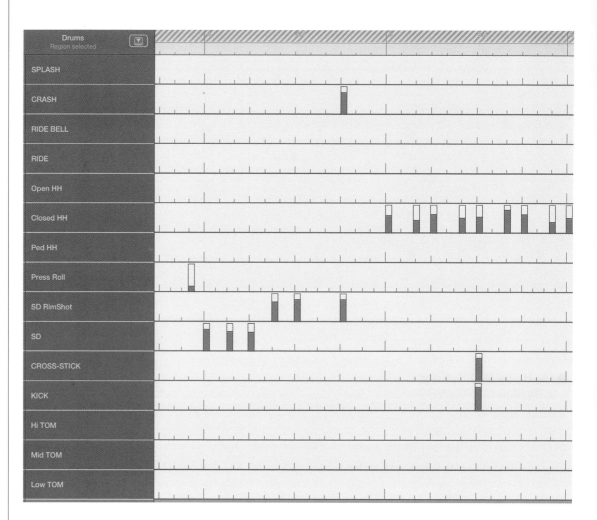

PATTERN 12_05: The opening fill followed by three bars of the basic groove.

CHAPTER 12

PROGRAMMING IN STYLES

THE
DRUM
PROGRAMMING
HANDBOOK

313

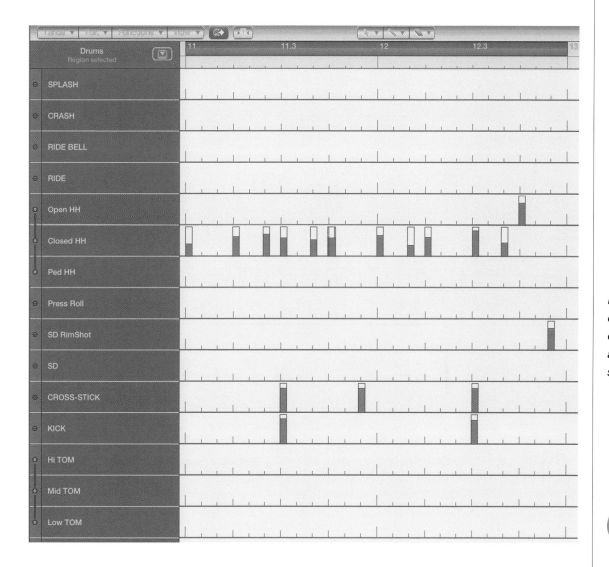

Pattern 12_06: The characteristic syncopated cross-stick in the first bar, and snare drum in the second.

Pattern 12_06

PATTERN 12_06: It is common to put a syncopated accent at the end of a bar without landing on the following downbeat.

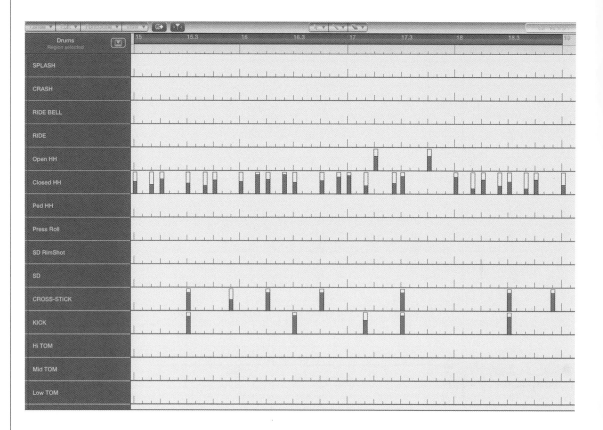

Pattern 12_07: Some cross-stick syncopations.

PATTERN 12_07: The cross-stick can play on beat 2 and beat 4, and occasionally the kick drum and open hi-hat might also join to form a three-way interplay.

PROGRAMMING IN STYLES

THE
DRUM
PROGRAMMING
HANDBOOK

315

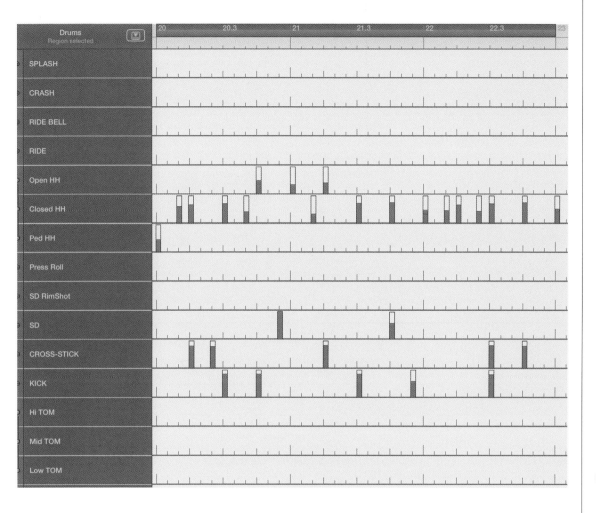

Pattern 12_08: Further syncopation, now incorporating the kick drum and full snare hits.

Pattern 12_08

PATTERN 12_08: Further textures can be added by incorporating the full snare and different articulations of the hi-hat.

CHAPTER 12

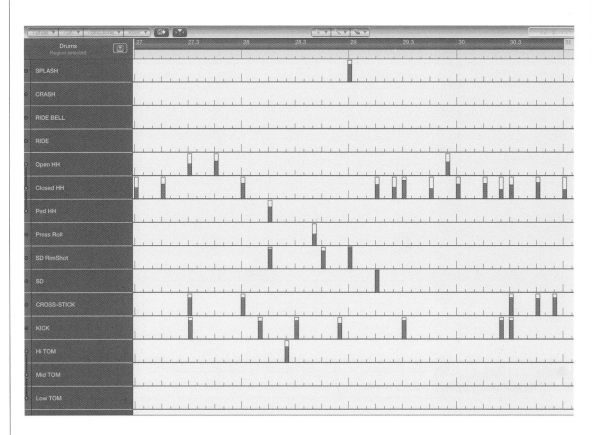

Pattern 12_09: A four-bar phrase that includes a fill.

PATTERN 12_09: This is a fill that lands on beat 1 on the snare. You will also hear a short buzz on the snare drum that leads into the hit on beat 4 in the second bar. This is a common stylistic feature, sometimes referred to as a ruff or a press-roll. Such a sound can be played with a cluster of fast and quiet individually programmed notes, but many drum kits come with a dedicated press-roll sample on a single key, which is what has been used here (you may also have noticed one in Pattern 12_05). You will hear some variations after the fill, too, and this is a commonly used rhythmic device to create a less abrupt final crash and melt back towards the steady groove.

PROGRAMMING IN STYLES

THE
DRUM
PROGRAMMING
HANDBOOK

317

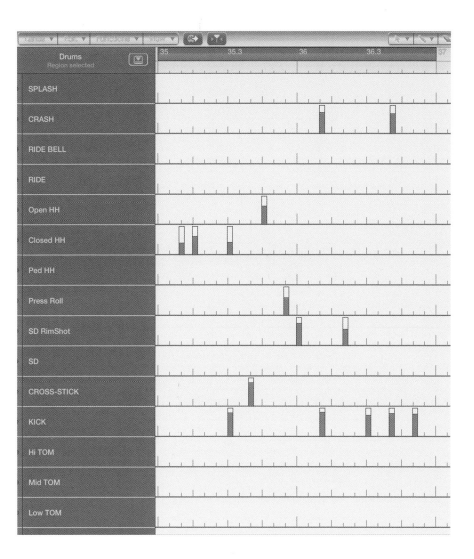

Pattern 12_10: The tutti accents.

Pattern 12_10

PATTERN 12_10: A two-bar phrase, the second bar of which are quarter-note triplet accents. The first beat of that bar is a snare ruff, after which kick and cymbals take over. If the whole band plays such accents in unison, this approach might be called tutti, meaning together.

CHAPTER 12

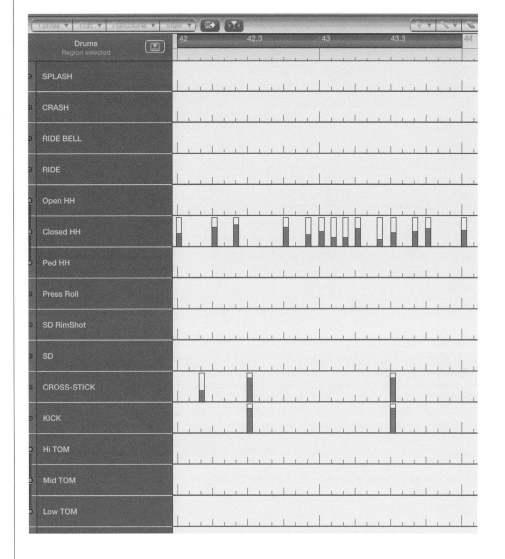

Pattern 12_11: Eighth-note triplets on the hi-hat.

PATTERN 12_11: The general shuffle feel might be decorated with eighth-note triplets (quaver triplets). The second bar has one such phrase on the hi-hat.

PROGRAMMING IN STYLES

THE
DRUM
PROGRAMMING
HANDBOOK

319

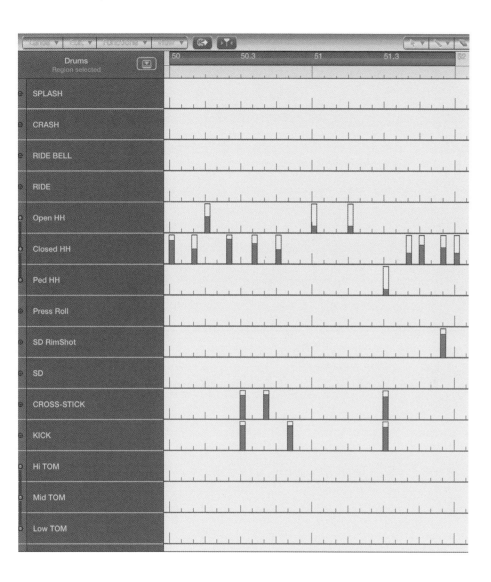

Pattern 12_12: A syncopated triplet-based phrase.

PATTERN 12_12: The quarter-note triplet is a common device in reggae. If a drummer's hands were to play eighth-note triplets from hand to hand, each hand would actually be stating quarter-note triplets. You can hear such interplay between the hi-hat and the cross-stick, landing on the kick at the end of the first bar of this two-bar phrase.

Pattern 12_12

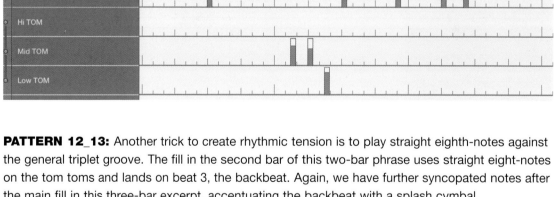

Pattern 12_13: A straight eighth-note fill – you can see that the notes do not align with the triplet grid.

Pattern 12_13

PATTERN 12_13: Another trick to create rhythmic tension is to play straight eighth-notes against the general triplet groove. The fill in the second bar of this two-bar phrase uses straight eight-notes on the tom toms and lands on beat 3, the backbeat. Again, we have further syncopated notes after the main fill in this three-bar excerpt, accentuating the backbeat with a splash cymbal.

PROGRAMMING IN STYLES

THE
DRUM
PROGRAMMING
HANDBOOK

321

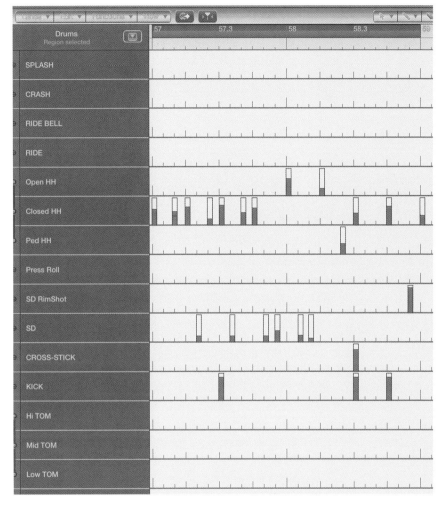

Pattern 12_14: A reference to the Purdie shuffle.

PATTERN 12_14: The Purdie shuffle. In the 1970s, legendary session drummer Bernard Purdie popularised an interpretation of the shuffle that used ghost notes on the middle note of every eighth-note triplet cluster. When playing a backbeat on the snare on beat 3, this formed a groove called the half-time shuffle; Bernard liked to call it the Purdie shuffle. In this excerpt, such a technique forms a rhythmic flourish. Notice that the hi-hat breaks its shuffled feel on beat 4, but an extra ghost note on the snare keeps the momentum going, and this continues until beat 2 of the following bar.

Pattern 12_14

Pattern 12_15: A different and rather more funky and contemporary feel that does not feel like reggae in isolation, but could when played in the right context.

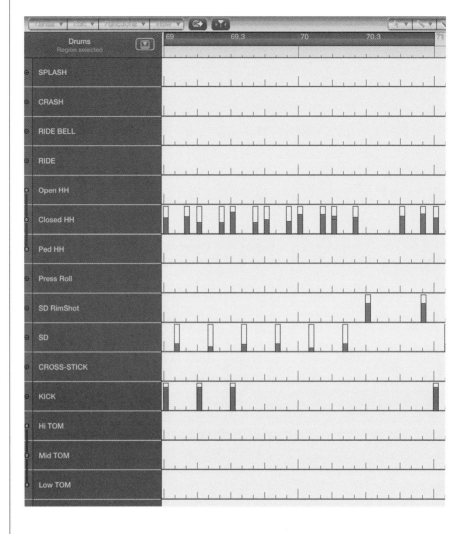

PATTERN 12_15: A more contemporary feel. The influence of reggae has crossed into many other genres and the beats have often mutated somewhat, combining with styles such as funk and rock. Sting is one artist who has long embraced reggae, most especially in his early days with The Police, and also used it in a variety of contexts in his solo career. Pattern 12_15 represents something of a gear change, moving away from the one drop and at first implying quarter-notes on the kick (in reggae, a quarter-note groove is referred to as a stepper), but actually then breaking up the pattern with a full snare backbeat on beat 3 of the second bar. Ghost notes in the style of the Purdie shuffle drive the beat along and fill the space with a rather funk-like quality.

CHAPTER 12

PROGRAMMING IN STYLES

THE
DRUM
PROGRAMMING
HANDBOOK

323

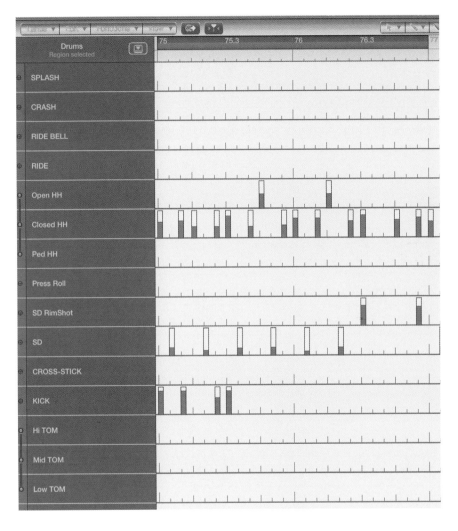

Pattern 12_16: One of the kick and snare variations.

■ **CHECK OUT**
Drummer Manu Katché brought some innovative reggae-influenced phrasing to songs by artists such as Sting and Robbie Robertson. Listen to Sting's track 'History Will Teach Us Nothing'.

PATTERN 12_16: Building on Pattern 12_15, there are a number of kick and snare variations, this being one of several. The general phrasing allows the kick drum to lead on the first bar of each two-bar phrase, and the snare backbeat to resolve things on the second. The second bar is sometimes decorated with additional snare hits and other variations. Each bar of this section is slightly different.

 Pattern 12_16

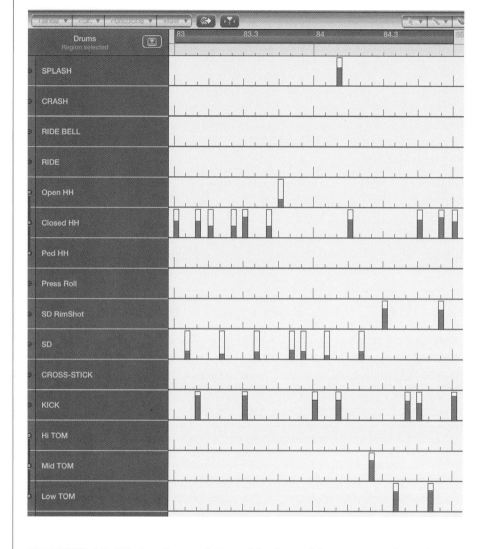

Pattern 12_17: A tom tom fill.

PATTERN 12_17: Another variation, this time with a tom tom-based fill that maintains the rolling triplet-feel of the groove.

PROGRAMMING IN STYLES

PATTERN 12.18: This is the full sequence using BFD3 sounds. All of the above phrases are in here, but these are only part of the whole. The various concepts listed above are often applied in slightly different ways.

Pattern 12_18

PATTERN 12_19: Pattern 12_18 is the drum part in this band version. Hearing it like this helps to contextualise the phrasing. There is also percussion coming from Spectrasonics Stylus RMX and a MIDI bass from Spectrasonics Trilian. The guitars are real.

Pattern 12_19

PATTERN 12_20: The band accompaniment without any drums, in case you would like to program your own along with it.

Pattern 12_20

DRUM & BASS

Drum & bass grew out of the style known as jungle in the 1990s club scene. The drums in jungle were all about slicing samples into short rhythmic chunks and then reordering the samples into long and often complex phrases, layered with deep basslines and punctuated with vocal and effects samples. Gradually, MIDI one-shots became more popular and the beats generally became more repetitive as the emphasis moved away from the purely rhythmic, and greater emphasis was placed on melody and harmony. This made drum & bass more radio-friendly, as demonstrated by British groups Sigma, with the track 'Nobody to Love', and Rudimental, with 'Feel The Love'.

By the 2000s, the style was firmly rooted in the DAW, and naturally the feature sets began to guide the genre. Tempo-flexible audio meant that loops could be easily dragged and dropped, and the MIDI beats started to form what are sometimes referred to as skeletons. A skeleton is a basic framework of a groove – perhaps just kick and snare – that then has a number of loop-layers superimposed on it for texture and variation. Drawing from the DJ tradition, it was common to apply aggressive EQ to make space in the mix for the various layers. It is also common to hear different degrees of swing (or just accuracy of timing) layered together, which gives a very dense, but slightly floppy, overall effect. The skeleton would typically emphasise eighth-notes, but even at the typical tempi of 150–180bpm, overlaid 16th-note hi-hat and ride grooves are the norm.

Drum fills can be either MIDI or audio-based. MIDI fills might be rhythmic variations, substitution of sounds, more traditional clusters of notes, or machine-gun rolls. Audio fills include the introduction of a different loop for just (say) a single bar, or perhaps some editing or stuttering of existing loops to alter the phrasing. Sometimes, effects might be automated to produce the feeling of a fill. This automation might range from increasing a send level to a delay or reverb-type effect to the introduction of a filter and the automation of its cut-off frequency. It can often be the case that rather than actually implementing a drum fill, a special effect sample is introduced instead. Such samples may or may not have pitched content.

Mixing and layering loops can be a bit subjective, and so we will build an arrangement and

326

THE
DRUM
PROGRAMMING
HANDBOOK

PROGRAMMING IN STYLES

include some pitched elements – synthesizers and samples. It is very common in drum & bass for the organisation of the drum loops to define the musical arrangement itself. Again, we will highlight a number of combinations and transitions and offer short commentaries on each.

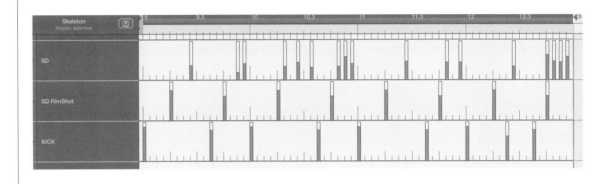

Pattern 12_21: The skeleton rhythm using one-shot sounds from PlugInGuru Mega Macho Drums.

PATTERN 12_21: The skeleton rhythm between kick and snare at 170bpm. This is a four-bar phrase, although the basic kick and backbeat pattern is the same except for the kick drum on 3& in the fourth bar. There are ghost-note-like decorations on a different snare drum that vary throughout the four-part phrase. Played twice through.

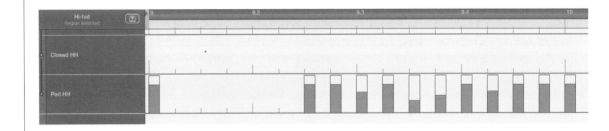

Pattern 12_22: The hi-hat part.

PATTERN 12_22: A 16th-note processed hi-hat part that can layer against the skeleton rhythm of Pattern 12_21, again made with one-shots. One-bar, repeated four times.

PATTERN 12_23: Pattern 12_21 and Pattern 12_22 played together. Twice through the four bar phrase. Together these could make the basis of a signature beat for a track, and a drum & bass programmer will often be mindful of this when forming this groove near the beginning of the creative process.

PROGRAMMING IN STYLES

THE
DRUM
PROGRAMMING
HANDBOOK

327

PATTERN 12_24: **Pattern 12_23 has been layered with a two-bar loop from Stylus RMX.** This loop has been processed by high-pass filtering at around 500 Hz, compressed and then passed through a distortion effect. Together, these effects give the loop a lo-fi sound and allow the skeleton beat to remain dominant, simply adding a texture to it.

 Pattern 12_24

PATTERN 12_25: **Another four-bar loop from Stylus RMX has been layered on top of Pattern 12_24.** This beat has a syncopated interplay between cymbals and snare, and again has been aggressively EQ'ed to keep it in the background. Building up layers in this way is characteristic of drum & bass – the effect of individual layers is quite subtle, but adding together several little things ends up making a lot of difference. An eight-bar sequence.

 Pattern 12_25

ROMPLERS

There is a category of instrument known as the ROMpler: a contraction of ROM (Read Only Memory) and sampler. These devices cannot perform actual sampling, but typically have audio waveforms embedded in their ROM that they can use for sample-based synthesis. The term is slightly anachronistic in our software-dominated world, but we still find instruments largely populated by manufacturer-supplied samples being referred to as ROMplers. Most of the instruments employed for the audio examples in this book fall into this category.

Key-switching is not just used in samplers for round robin effects, but also for changing performance nuances, as we have heard in Trilian. Key-switching has also been used in several ROMplers to select which one of a number of internal MIDI loops plays a set of sounds. Such switching can seamlessly change loops part way through their duration, thus allowing complex hybrid patterns to be constructed from a simple sequence of MIDI notes.

BFD3 has this functionality (its groove palette), but another such instrument is iZotope BreakTweaker. This device is optimised for electronic music. It features its own internal step sequencer, and the unique feature of being able to specify a note length in its sequence. Within that it can perform microedits, dynamic chopping and stuttering of a number of parameters to produce exotic and detailed sounding parts with minimal effort. Strictly speaking, BreakTweaker is not just a ROMpler, since it is also capable of generating its own sounds from its synthesizer and sample engines.

328

**THE
DRUM
PROGRAMMING
HANDBOOK**

PROGRAMMING IN STYLES

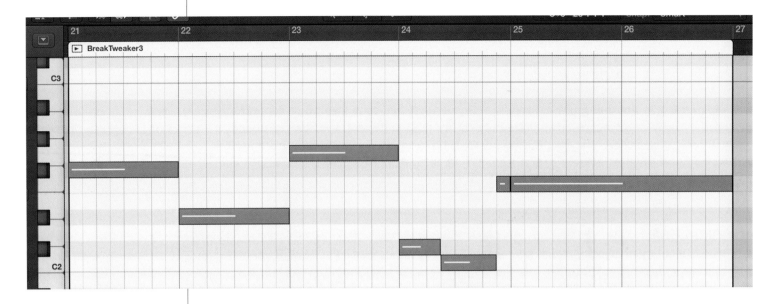

*Pattern 12_26: The MIDI
notes that trigger the
BreakTweaker patterns.*

**PATTERN 12_26: A six-bar loop from BreakTweaker, with a click for reference. This loop
has a highly synthetic feel and features the characteristic stuttering microedits associated
with that software.** Each MIDI note here is a keyswitch that triggers a particular combination of
notes in BreakTweaker's internal step sequencer. Each pitch represents a different sequence, and
the duration of the notes defines the time that a given sequence plays for.

PROGRAMMING IN STYLES

THE
DRUM
PROGRAMMING
HANDBOOK

329

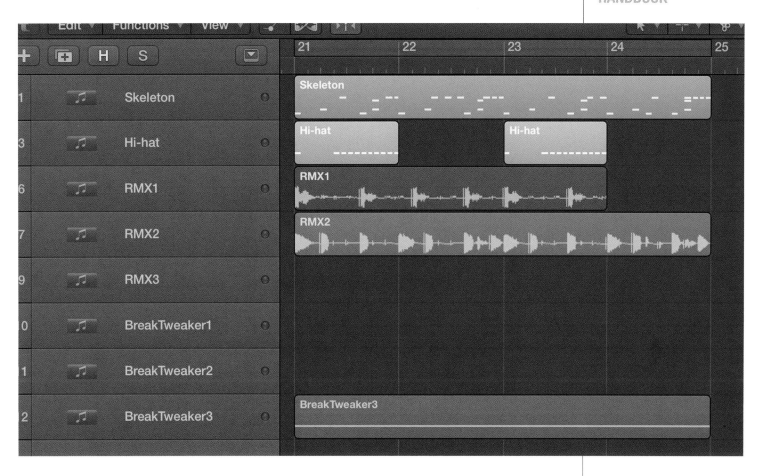

PATTERN 12_27: Here is a four-bar excerpt that adds another Stylus RMX layer, with the one-shot hi-hat loop now only playing in alternate bars. To stop things becoming too busy, the cymbal-based RMX loop has been dropped out; and the original RMX loop is not playing in the last bar, which creates a feeling of space emerging towards the breakdown that will follow.

The layering of Pattern 12_27.

Pattern 12_27

330

THE
DRUM
PROGRAMMING
HANDBOOK

PROGRAMMING IN STYLES

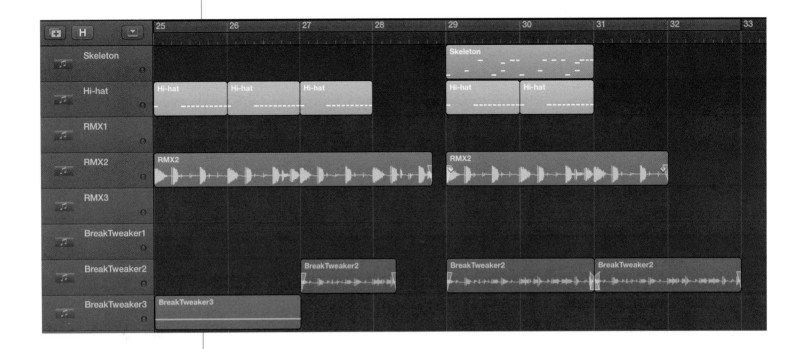

The layering of Pattern 12_28: notice the gap at the end of bar four.

PATTERN 12_28: An eight bar section of breakdown with a less relentless beat. The skeleton rhythm has dropped out for the first four bars and one of the RMX loops is carrying the groove. It is only now that it is in relative isolation that you can be hear how this loop anticipates the backbeat on beat 4, instead playing its accent on beat 3&. A new and light-sounding loop from BreakTweaker (bounced to audio) is also introduced. There is a short silence at the end of the fourth bar, which introduces a momentary tension that feels as if everything has stopped. And the eighth bar features only the new BreakTweaker loop, which appears to tinkle away in the background.

PROGRAMMING IN STYLES

THE
DRUM
PROGRAMMING
HANDBOOK

331

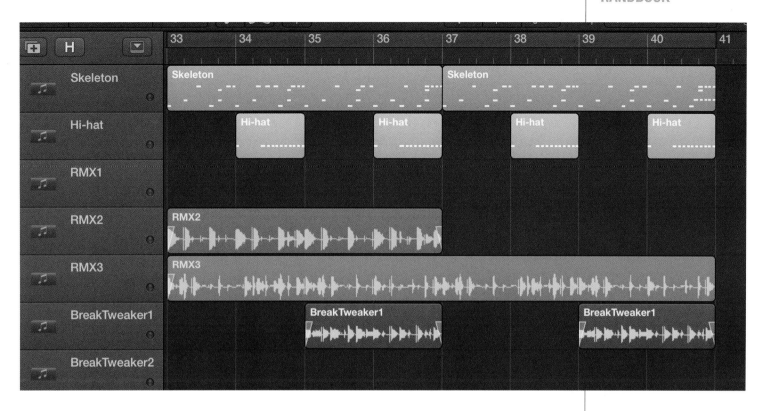

PATTERN 12_29: The next eight bars again use different combinations of loop, and introduce a new two-bar loop featuring some further stutters, bounced from BreakTweaker. The skeleton rhythm sequence has a 16th-note fill at the end of the eighth bar.

Pattern 12_29: Further combinations of loop layers.

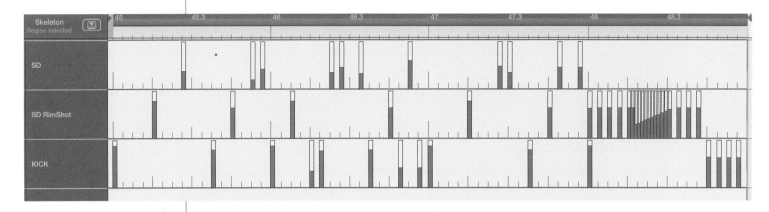

Pattern 12_30: The two one-shot fills in the skeleton rhythm.

 Pattern 12_30

 Pattern 12_31

TIP
If you wish a filter to be inactive for part of your song, then be sure to find a place in the arrangement where you can automate its bypass when there is no music playing on its channel. Switching plug-ins in and out whilst they are processing audio will cause unwanted glitches.

PATTERN 12_30: This excerpt is four bars long and repeated once. Here, the skeleton rhythm has two fills. The first is a rhythmic groove-based turnaround, where the backbeat first happens an eighth-note early and the kick drum plays some 16th-note double hits. The second fill is a machine-gun roll that uses a burst of 48th-notes (triplet demisemiquavers) with 16th-notes both before and after.

PATTERN 12_31: A 14-bar excerpt with filter sweeps on a number of tracks. When you want a filter to affect a number of different tracks simultaneously, there are a couple of strategies. Either you need to have a filter inserted on each channel, and automate each one separately, or you will need to buss the channels together and have a single automated filter on that buss.

The advantage of the former method is that not only can you have different types of filter on different channels, but you can control not just the cut-off, but also the resonance of each independently, thus preventing too much howling at certain frequencies. The advantage of the latter approach is that it is much easier to implement with less automation spread over a number of channels; it can be tricky to automate multiple channels and make them sound unified. At the beginning of this excerpt you will notice the unfiltered hi-hat while the filtered loop has its cut-off increased. In the fourth bar, there is a machine-gun roll to reintroduce the skeleton groove. There is then a highly resonant filtered descent on a different loop.

As the groove completely melts down to the point of being indistinguishable, the loop changes in the background, and as the filter opens up again, a different loop emerges. At all times, the resonance was controlled relative to the filter sweep to contour the sound in a controlled fashion.

CHAPTER 12

PROGRAMMING IN STYLES

THE
DRUM
PROGRAMMING
HANDBOOK

333

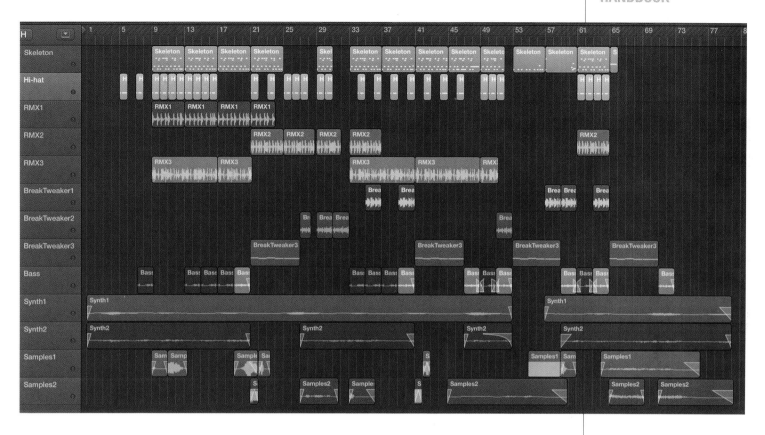

PATTERN 12_32: The entire drum & bass sequence.

PATTERN 12_33: Pattern 12_32 with some ambient synthesizer lines and samples.

PATTERN 12_34: Just the ambient synthesizer lines and samples at 170bpm, in case you want to program your own drums along with them.

The arrangement that plays Pattern 12_32.

 Pattern 12_32

 Pattern 12_33

 Pattern 12_34

CHAPTER 12

334

THE
DRUM
PROGRAMMING
HANDBOOK

PROGRAMMING IN STYLES

GLITCH

When the genre of glitch first started, it employed such things as malfunctioning equipment, distortion, and damaged CDs to create its textures. Software programming and sampling were always key components in the construction of glitch. Thanks to those, the genre has now crept into many styles of music, bringing its attitude and inflections. There is no longer the need to sit and listen to a damaged CD on its own. It is worth investigating some approaches in this context. As was the case in the workshop in Chapter 11, you should not attempt to replicate this exercise step-by-step, but rather follow the processes and the approach. Consider how you might apply the techniques and tools in your own music. Listen to how Squarepusher draws from his glitch heritage in a fresh context in the second half of his track 'Exjag Nives'.

Glitch is often characterised by highly synthetic sonic textures and ultra-fast rolls and stutters. What we are going to do is first of all record some very shabby beat boxing, then process it using time-stretching to develop the sounds. Then we will slice and load it into a multichannel sampler and route the groups out of separate outputs into their own audio channels. Next we will apply some intricate editing in the MIDI domain, apply some effects, and automate some key parameters of the sampler. Lastly, we will combine it with another audio layer from BreakTweaker and create something reminiscent of the UK duo Autechre.

First, we will record some vocal sounds to use as a starting point in the process. We will

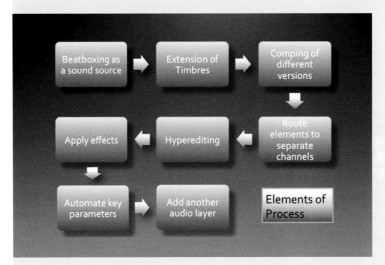

The process.

CHAPTER 12

PROGRAMMING IN STYLES

THE
DRUM
PROGRAMMING
HANDBOOK

335

take little care over the performance or the recording and deliberately allow plosives (bursts of air hitting the microphone). While all this would normally be regarded as very bad practice, doing it in this context merely shows that almost any sound source will do, and maybe even gives you the confidence to try it yourself.

PATTERN 12_35: 12 bars of beat boxing at 120bpm, recorded to a click.

Pattern 12_35

We next need to detect all the transients and apply audio quantisation to drag all the sounds notionally into time. Depending on your time-stretch algorithm, you will likely incur various artefacts at this point. This is by no means a bad thing in this context, and as was the case in Chapter Six, we will exploit these as a mechanism for sound design. In fact, it would be a good idea to deliberately drag some of the transients quite some way by hand in order to exaggerate the artefacts. You might find it useful to put a dynamic range compressor on the audio signal before doing this in order to control possible pops, etc.

PATTERN 12_36: The beat boxing with time stretching, using a speed algorithm that changes pitch depending on the amount of stretch or compression. There are still a number of unwanted noises here, but these will be addressed later.

Pattern 12_36

Bounce this audio to a new file to remove all the stretching information. Then on the region you have just processed, change the stretch algorithm to one of the others that your DAW has. Possibly adjusting stretch parameters, tweak the transient timing so that it sounds interesting and bounce it to audio as well. Repeat this process two or three times with different algorithms to create a palette of different-sounding rhythmic material. Line up each of these on its own audio track, and then comp together your favourite bits to create a hybrid of the various time-stretch artefacts. When you are satisfied with your editing bounce the result to a single new audio file once more.

PATTERN 12_37: The comped-together and bounced audio file.

Pattern 12_37

We now want to increase the tempo to 160bpm. Assuming that your edits are accurately in time, the simplest way would be to change the tempo in the DAW, and place Pattern 12–37 on a new audio track and time-compress it to a length of exactly 12 bars. The entire audio file will be subjected to another layer of artefacts, so audition the result and if it is unsatisfactory change the algorithm and try again.

CHAPTER 12

Pattern 12_38

PATTERN 12_38: Pattern 12_37 at 160bpm.

The audio file that we now have is certainly more interesting and also less human. It would be nice if we could treat it as a drum kit and process individual sounds as we might a kick or a snare etc. In order to do this, once again you must define all the transients in this audio (you have one more chance to tighten the timing if necessary) and slice it, then place the slices on separate zones in your sampler, and create a MIDI region that triggers them, as you did in Chapter Five. Most keys should now play only a single sound in the fashion of a one-shot instrument, but when placing the transients, allow little rolls here and there on some keys. We could think of these as fills.

> **TIP**
> Another approach to changing the tempo would be to do this before bouncing the individual algorithms. Another way still would be to time stretch the individual bounces to 160bpm and comp at that tempo. These approaches will each yield different types of artefact.

The second four bars (which carry more information than the first four) of the MIDI region that triggers the slices. Note a small amount of corrective editing that breaks the regularity of the shape.

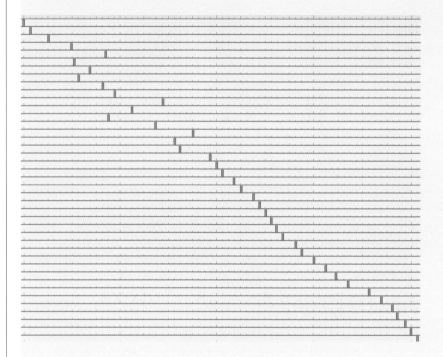

 Pattern 12_39

PATTERN 12_39: The second four bars with a click.

We must now set up a number of audio outputs from the sampler into individual channels in your DAW. One stereo and a number of mono channels would be good. Name the mono ones: kick, snare and hi-hat (pan this one). Name the stereo one: fills. We now assign all

PROGRAMMING IN STYLES

THE
DRUM
PROGRAMMING
HANDBOOK

337

Pattern 12_40

TIP
If you can, assign a key command to switch the grid between the desired note values. This will greatly speed up your workflow when drawing in rolls. Also, if you have one, inserting a de-clicking plug-in can help control any clicks that are induced whilst editing.

zones in the sampler to their own individual groups, and then, while working through each key one at a time, decide which channel we would like to send that sound to, and route it accordingly. Try to anticipate the type of processing that you will likely apply to each channel.

If we now play the triggering MIDI region, it should still sound identical to the un-sliced file, but you will see all the individual hits coming through on their allocated channels. Repeat the region three times and merge the regions together into a single longer one. We can now edit in a number of machine-gun rolls on individual slices. In a glitch style, choosing note values of 32nd-notes, 48th-notes, 64th-notes (hemidemisemiquavers) and 96th-notes (triplet hemidemisemiquavers) will give a good variety of stuttering and buzzing effects. You can also move slices around, either by transposing the pitch or juxtaposing them on the timeline, but be careful of clicks, since many of the slices will be of different lengths. Although we have repeated the basic sequence, different edits throughout the greater duration will keep it lively and interesting, and produce different textures.

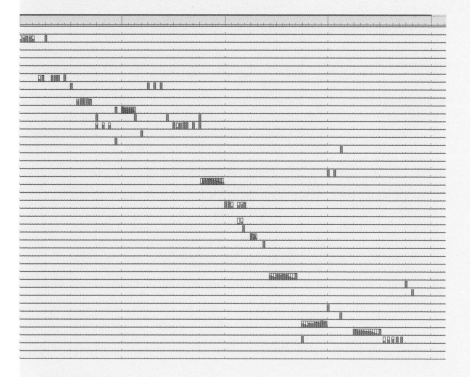

The second four bars of the MIDI region after some editing.

PATTERN 12_40: The second four bars after some editing, with a click.

338

THE
DRUM
PROGRAMMING
HANDBOOK

PROGRAMMING IN STYLES

The effect chains are purely subjective, but they are as follows:
- kick: amp simulator > compression > sub-bass enhancement
- snare: high pass filter (300 Hz) > compressor > transient enhancer > limiter
- hi-hat: high pass filter (5 kHz) > bit crusher (set to seven bits) > EQ (cut below 2 kHz) > limiter
- fills: high pass filter (200 Hz) > EQ (low and high boosts) > compressor > bit crusher (seven bit)

PATTERN 12_41: Solo kick with effects; the second four bars with a click.

PATTERN 12_42: Solo snare with effects; the second four bars with a click.

PATTERN 12_43: Solo hi-hat with effects; the second four bars with a click.

PATTERN 12_44: Solo fills with effects; the second four bars with a click.

The penultimate stage involves automation. Three sampler parameters were set to be automated: the low pass filter cut-off, the filter resonance, and the amplitude sustain parameter. Whilst we have discussed cut-off and resonance previously, it is worth noting that when we reduce the sustain level to zero, the envelope generator on this particular sampler plays only the attack portion of the envelope, effectively just a click sound that is very suitable for a glitch.

We can of course create suitable automation curves with the mouse, but real-time performance from one or a number of hardware controls can give great results and can be a lot of fun to perform. The pan control of the rolls channel was also automated in slow asynchronous LFO-like sweeps, simply to give a dynamic image to the whole. We will also use pitch bend as an effect. With the pitch bend range set to ±12 half-steps on the sampler we have recorded a live performance of the pitch bend lever.

PROGRAMMING IN STYLES

THE
DRUM
PROGRAMMING
HANDBOOK

339

The top lane shows the real-time pitch-bend performance, the next one down is the cut-off, which was performed and then tidied by editing, the next one down again is resonance, which was input solely by mouse. At the bottom is sustain level automation, another real-time performance.

Pattern 12_45: The automation.

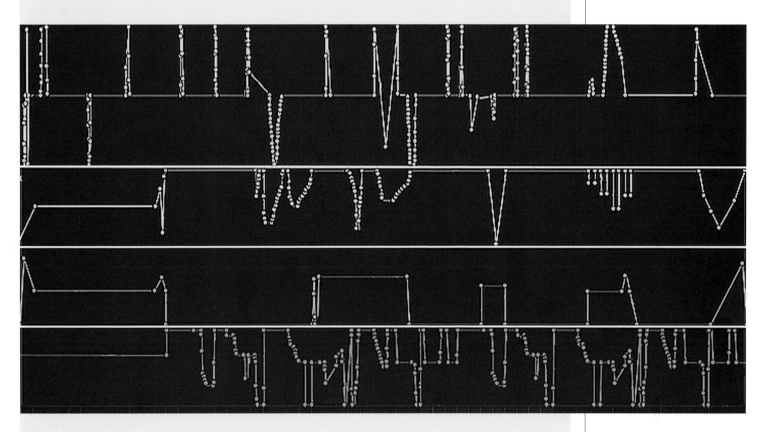

PATTERN 12_45: The 48 bars of the sequence, now with pitch bend and automation.

 Pattern 12_45

CHAPTER 12

340

THE
DRUM
PROGRAMMING
HANDBOOK

PROGRAMMING IN STYLES

*Pattern 12_46: The MIDI
notes that drive
BreakTweaker.*

For the last stage in this workshop we will now add another two different layers from BreakTweaker. It is certainly not essential to complete a useful workflow here, but it does further demonstrate key-switch-driven pattern changing as well as slaved step-sequencing (when a step sequencer is driven by the DAW's clock). The first layer contains many pitched sounds, although they do not really have a solid key centre. Many of the pitches are stuttered by the microedit system, which can create pitch sweeps as well as the accelerating machine-gun rolls on drums.

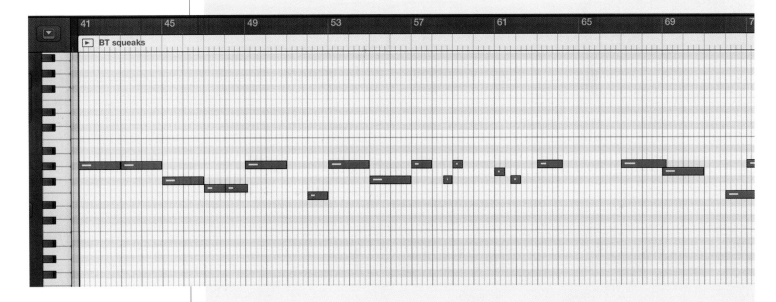

PATTERN 12_46: A layer of pitched and un-pitched step-sequence, with a click.

PROGRAMMING IN STYLES

THE
DRUM
PROGRAMMING
HANDBOOK

341

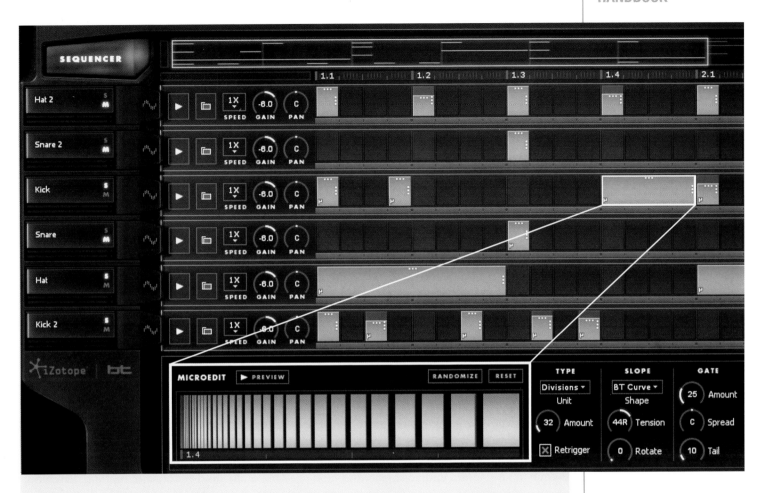

The interface of BreakTweaker showing lanes of its step sequencer with notes placed on them. The highlighted note is one that actually contains microediting instructions, and the inset indicates that this note will start with fast stutters and then slow over its duration.

BreakTweaker Interface

■ **CHECK OUT**
The album *Exai* by Autechre, which will bombard you with two hours of glitch.

Pattern 12_47

Pattern 12_48

Pattern 12_49

Pattern 12_50

PATTERN 12_47: This is the second layer of BreakTweaker and is one of a number of add-on presets that contain both sounds and sequences from PlugInGuru. Here it adds hi-hat textures and other occasional hits, with a click.

PATTERN 12_48: 48 bars of the voice kit and both BreakTweaker layers at 160bpm.

PATTERN 12_49: Pattern 12_48 with added synthesizer drones.

PATTERN 12_50: Just the synthesizer drones in case you want to program your own drums along with them.

Things to experiment with:
- Take specific ideas or concepts from the genres in this chapter and apply them to other genres that you like – try to do this to create both authenticity and crossover fusion.
- Think about the most appropriate techniques for programming in genres not featured here and try them out.
- Try to emulate performances that you admire, be those human or computerised.
- Think about what your tools are designed to do, and then use them to do something interesting that was never intended.
- Try everything …

CONCLUSION

Of course, there are many genres of music that have not been listed either in this chapter or elsewhere in this book. Should you wish to work in any of those genres, then hopefully by now you will have enough technique, options, and understanding to be able to approach them in an authentic and sophisticated fashion. Above all, keep practising, reading, listening, and creating and be sure to link all these activities. Study your tools and push them to their limit. Do not fall into repeated patterns of safe usage; you will become bored and so will your listeners. Learn how to do what you cannot, and become better at what you already can. Keep a positive and supportive attitude when you make music with others. Always try to move forward with your taste, expectations and aspirations. Above all, have fun in your journey through the art of drum programming.

INDEX OF MUSICIANS AND MUSIC

ACKNOWLEDGEMENTS

I want to thank Jo Pearson for her endless patience and support during the writing of this book. She gave up many things to give me the space to do this, and without her love it would not have been possible.

I also want to thank my editor John Morrish, my designer Paul Cooper, and Nigel Osborne and his team at Outline Press Limited.

Big thanks to my go-to session guitarist Brian Miller, who patiently indulges all of my projects. I would also like to thank John Gummery and Sara Raybould, my managers at the university day-job, for being so understanding and supportive in this project – not to mention all the others. Thanks also to Charlie Norton and Russ Hepworth-Sawyer for their encouragement, Jamie Frost for his thoughts, and to my friend Paul Ramshaw for the use of the drum & bass samples from his Tunejet library. Thanks to Daniele De Rossi for generous support for a stranger.

I am also indebted to the industry guys who gave their faith and support, and wish to offer my thanks for their commitment: Angus Hewlett at FXpansion (www.fxpansion.com); John 'Skippy' Lehmkuhl at PlugInGuru (www.pluginguru.com); Melissa Misicka at iZotope (www.izotope.com); and Paul J. de Benedictis and Eric Persing at Spectrasonics (www.spectrasonics.net). They all make great products, and I use them because I love using them.

Credits
Brian Miller: guitar, bass, keyboards.
Justin Paterson: programming, production, keyboards, voice.
All music composed by Justin Paterson, except: Pattern 7.28 – Live in Orpington; Pattern 12.19 – Kingston (Upon Thames); Pattern 12.2 – NCFOM. They were composed by Brian Miller.

Mastered by Russ Hepworth-Sawyer at Mottosound (www.mottosound.co.uk).

Other great books in this series:

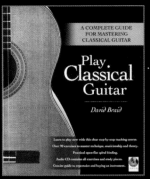

ISBN 978-0-87930-657-1

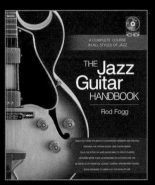

ISBN 978-1-4803-4104-3

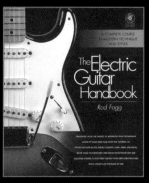

ISBN 978-0-87930-989-3

ISBN 978-0-87930-853-7

ISBN 978-1-61713-011-3

ISBN 978-0-87930-872-8

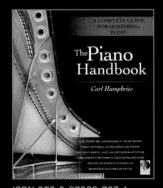

ISBN 978-0-87930-727-1

ISBN 978-0-87930-978-7

ISBN 978-0-87930-958-9